A GLASTONBURY READER

THE Son of God
Thy hill hath trod
And its curse is broken.

Frontispiece: 'Glastonbury Tor' by Horace Knowles

A GLASTONBURY READER

Selections From the Myths,
Legends and Stories of Ancient
Avalon

Selected and edited by
JOHN MATTHEWS

The Aquarian Press
An Imprint of HarperCollins*Publishers*

The Aquarian Press
An Imprint of GraftonBooks
A Division of HarperCollins*Publishers*
77-85 Fulham Palace Road,
Hammersmith, London W6 8JB

Published by The Aquarian Press 1991

© JOHN MATTHEWS 1991

John Matthews asserts the moral right to
be identified as the author of this work

A catalogue record for this book
is available from the British Library

ISBN 0-85030-999-9

Printed in Great Britain by
Mackays of Chatham, Kent
Typeset by Burns & Smith Ltd. Derby

To the Luminaries of Glastonbury

Frederick Bligh Bond (1864–1945)
Dion Fortune (1891–1946)
John Cowper Powys (1872–1963)

AND

For Geoffrey Ashe, in token of all he has done to promote the Matter of Britain, and for many years of friendly support.

Contents

O Glastonbury, Glastonbury: the Threasory of Carcasses of so famous, and so many rare Persons . . .

John Dee, *General & Rare memorials*
Pertaining to the Perfect Art of Navigation

'The Holy Grail . . . What is it?
The phantom of a cup that comes and goes?'

'Nay, monk! what phantom?' answer'd Percivale.

'The cup, the cup, itself, from which our Lord
Drank at the last sad supper with His own.
This, from the blessed land of Aromat —
After the day of darkness, when the dead
Went wandering o'er Moriah — the good saint,
Arimathean Joseph, journeying brought
To Glastonbury, where the winter thorn
Blossoms at Christmas, mindful of our Lord.
And there awhile it bode; and if a man
Could touch or see it, he was heal'd at once,
By faith, of all his ills. But then the times
Grew to such evil that the holy cup
Was caught away to Heaven, and disappear'd.'

To whom the monk: 'From our old books I know
That Joseph came of old to Glastonbury,
And there the heathen Prince, Arviragus,
Gave him an isle of marsh wheron to build;
And there he built with wattles from the marsh
A little lonely church in days of yore,
For so they say, these books of ours, but seem
Mute of this miracle, far as I have read.
But who first saw the holy thing today?'

Tennyson, 'The Holy Grail'

Foreword

I was drawn to Glastonbury like many others by its magnetic atmosphere, its peculiar light, its enchanted landscape and the richness of its history, myths and legends. As a Scot, my sense of majesty in nature was well satisfied by the mystically sculptured landscape of the sacred hills of Avalon, in particular the Tor. As a Christian, Glastonbury was quick to reveal to me its ecclesiastical treasures, its potential for reconciliation and change, its ecumenical purpose and its power for effective prayer and invocation.

To talk of a place as powerful is not a generally accepted idea. Power assumes energy. I do believe that energy exists all around us: it exists as the thoughts and feelings that we project. Energy comes from the earth itself, the land, the trees, the animals, and each place on earth has a different energy which we can learn to sense. This became clear to me while living in Glastonbury for, when one is open, it is a place that gives insight into the nature of life and the mysteries of nature.

Clearly others have had a similar experience according to their own reality. It has been given to some with a literary flair who quest for the meaning of the mystery of Glastonbury to present both historically and from the inner world of the imagination their view of this unique place. Over the centures Glastonbury has attracted an impressive array of chroniclers: historians, poets, mystics and visionaries who have, with passion, brought to light the mysterious beauty and astonishing history of the place. Their love for Glastonbury was their inspiration.

In this volume John Matthews has devotedly gathered together the works of many of these people. They are literary treasures, many out of print. He has carefully and successfully provided us with a unique anthology from the pens of those who, in their own way, have been struck by the magic of this fair Isle of Avalon.

May you enjoy this book as much as I have.

JAMIE GEORGE
Co-Director, *Gothic Image*
Glastonbury, 1991

Introduction

The one word that can never be applied to Glastonbury is 'ordinary'. This small Somersetshire town, with its Tor, topped by the tower of St Michael, stands out from the flat plain traditionally known as Avalon, and it stands out also from the ordinary world. Here, according to tradition, is the remains of a prehistoric (though by no means primitive) zodiac circle, impressed into the very shape of the land; here Christ came as a child, accompanying his uncle, Joseph of Arimathea; and here the mystic vessel, the Holy Grail, was brought by that same Joseph, who established the first Christian church in Britain in the Isle of Avalon. Later still, the bones of King Arthur supposedly found rest here — though to some this is a heresy that is still deeply felt.

Such are the traditions. The reality may be different. Certainly the present editor does not subscribe to all that is told of Glastonbury. What is undoubtedly true is the curious aura of 'oddness' that surrounds the place. It has drawn generations of pilgrims from all over the world, and continues to do so. The reasons for this are perhaps not hard to find: for from the moment one enters Glastonbury one knows one is entering a sacred enclosure. 'Welcome to England's Ancient Avalon' announces the sign as one approaches, showing that even the local authorities recognize the mystery of the place.

Later on, in the nineteenth and early twentieth centuries, antiquarian and mystical interests came together in the works of such people as Frederick Bligh Bond and Katherine Maltwood. Bond discovered, through psychic archaeology, the location of the lost Lady Chapel in Glastonbury's great abbey, while Maltwood claimed a vast terrestrial zodiac impressed into the landscape around the sacred site. Early in this century the esotericist Dion Fortune resided in Glastonbury and found inspiration for much of her magical work there.

The present collection of essays, extracts from books, and texts has been chosen to reflect the diversity of people and ideas that Glastonbury has attracted over the centuries. Some verge on the unlikely, if not the unbelievable; others offer testimony to the enduring traditions of Britain; some are printed here because their authors have an indissoluble link with the place. All bear witness to

the effects that living in, or even visiting, Glastonbury can have upon
the minds and hearts of a wide variety of people. It is hoped that the
collection will encourage others to go in search of the mystery of
Glastonbury, to experience for themselves its peculiar alchemy.

JOHN MATTHEWS
London, 1990

PART I
ENGLAND'S AVALON

England's Avalon

Inevitably, the first aspect of Glastonbury that strikes most of its visitors is the very strong tradition regarding its association with King Arthur. A few miles to the south lies the Iron Age hill-fort of Cadbury, for long held to be the original site of Arthur's Camelot, and the subject of archaeological investigations in the nineteenth century and again in the 1960s. On the occasion of the earlier dig at least one local man was moved to enquire if the antiquaries had 'come to dig up the king?', a sufficient indication of the strength of local tradition. A path across the marshy lowlands is still known as King Arthur's Causeway, and is believed to have been the route by which the great king crossed from his citadel to the holy shores of Glastonbury.

But the associations do not end here. Once almost, if not entirely, islanded by water, tradition records as the oldest known name for Glastonbury 'Ynys Witrin', which may be translated as 'Isle of Glass'. This has lent credence to the idea of a mystical Celtic background, since the Isle of Glass was a distinctive name for the Otherworld. Later associations have recorded the names 'Island of Apples' or 'Avalon' — the last a name that has rung down the ages as the otherworldly island to which Arthur, wounded at the Battle of Camlan, retired to be healed of his wounds. From there, it is said, he will return to the world of men when his country needs him: and there are a number of legends relating to various hills and caves across Britain where he is supposed to be sleeping, along with the twelve greatest knights of the Round Table.

It was probably this belief that lead to a larger-than-normal human skeleton, discovered in the grounds of the Abbey exactly 800 years ago, being identified as the bones of Arthur. A leaden cross, apparently attached to the coffin, declaring that 'Here Lies Buried the Renowned King Arthur in the Isle of Avalon,' has since vanished and remains a mystery, despite claims of its rediscovery in 1988 amid a flurry of media attention.

The discovery of Arthur's bones has since been attributed to the needs of the Abbey, which had been virtually destroyed by fire in 1184, presenting the monks with an urgent need for rebuilding funds. The last resting place of King Arthur clearly required a great religious foundation in which to house them, and this they received. However,

it must be said that archaeological evidence, assembled by Dr Ralegh
Radford after his excavations of the sites in 1962–3, does indicate that
a person of some importance was buried there at about the right date
— though whether it was truly Arthur, who has a more indefinite
destiny, is less easily proved. A plaque marks the place where the
bones were re-interred, beneath a splendid marble altar dedicated by
Edward I, but all other traces were lost in the destruction of the Abbey
during the Reformation.

Nevertheless, the traditions continue to be upheld by the thousands
of pilgrims who visit Glastonbury from all over the world, and the
various themes are taken up in the chapters which make up the first
part of this book. M. L. Hall sets the scene with a concise account of
the Arthurian connections. This is followed by a brief account, taken
from the writings of the fifteenth-century monk John of Glastonbury
concerning the legend of the cross given to Arthur by the Virgin Mary
after he had experienced a vision of the Mass. This story may derive
from an earlier, more elaborate version found in another medieval
text: *Perlesvaus*, sometimes called *The High History of the Holy Grail*,[1]
reputedly written at Glastonbury Abbey in the twelfth century. This is
followed by two more general accounts of the history of the area,
firstly from A. Herne's *History and Antiquities of Glastonbury* originally
published in 1726, and then C. R. Davy Biggs' scholarly account of the
multi-layered historical associations that permeate the area.

---

[1] *The High Book of the Grail: A Translation of the Thirteenth-Century Romance of
Perlesvaus* (Cambridge, D. S. Brewer, 1978).

1

Arthur of the Holy Grail[1]
THE MYTH AS ASSOCIATED WITH AVALON AND GLASTONBURY

M. L. HALL

In the wide world there is but One Truth. All theories, doctrines, revelations, illuminations, experiences, are but aspects of it, approaches to it. Man in his infancy learned to recognize it; and since that far-distant date in no age has it not been re-stated, re-embodied, in tradition, legend, mystic writing. And all these re-embodiments, each of which is, naturally, clothed in a language adapted to, or rather the outcome of, the genius of the race that gave it birth, form in reality a single tradition, traceable from our own day back into the night of time.

Further: not only have we writings, endeavours to enunciate the One Truth, there have also appeared figures, personages so august and of such spiritual stature that their names have been revered through countless generations. How is it they have left so deep a mark — a peculiar mark, different to that of other thinkers, seers, humanitarians — that they not only evoke gratitude and reverence, but are looked upon almost as gods? Did they possess some secret knowledge? Or accomplish some rare feat? Or is it, perhaps, that by *using* rare knowledge rightly they were able to surpass other men in accomplishment; in approach to the Supreme Truth: at-onement; experience of identity of origin with all, through realised union with the Divine. Union of such a nature, such actuality, that love, wisdom and power from the Divine are with him who has attained.

Belonging to our own country, is a person particularly suited to serve as indicating this attainment. Arthur of Britain, Arthur of the Holy Grail: who was he? When did he live? What was his sphere of activity?

Now there can be little doubt for those who see in the legends of the Round Table and the Holy Grail a re-statement, in beautiful and dramatic form, of the ancient tradition referring to man's eternal quest, that King Arthur, reigning in the sixth century AD, is not the rightful hero of these stories. A warrior king, renowned for prowess in battle, rather than for patronage of art and culture; his attention absorbed by physical warfare; how could he have prepared himself for outstanding spiritual achievement? No aspersion is cast upon him; his duty was to fight, and he fulfilled it.

[1] Privately printed pamphlet, (n.d.).

But is there another Arthur? The figure who left an indelible impression on his country. His memory is even perpetuated in Scotland by Arthur's Seat at Edinburgh; and was he not closely associated with the Isle of Avalon?

If one knows Glastonbury, and the sphinx-like Tor, it is easy to accept the suppositions and conjectures surrounding them. The Tor is thought to have been a great religious centre several thousand years before the Christian era; indeed, wise men from the continent of Atlantis may have visited it; for, by founding a seat of religion and learning, they would help to keep the torch of truth alight in this portion of the West. As the cataclysm which finally submerged Atlantis swept away much of Western culture.

Therefore is it not probable that during that long epoch some one lived who attained to the supreme union, and in so doing acquired super-normal powers? Such a man would have the age-old symbolism woven round him; and Arthur is believed to have eluded death. Enoch and Elijah did not die.

And if he lived at Tintagel, he would surely come to Avalon, famed seat of learning. And possibly take part in the wonderful ritual of the Druidic ceremonies; vestiges of which can still be clearly seen in the spiral processional paths encircling the Tor.

At Tintagel, according to the archaeologists, no remains of a castle exist, but there are definite traces of a Celtic monastery. An appropriate ruin to find on the site of the habitation of a pre-eminent teacher; whereas a monastery would hardly be founded in honour of a warrior king.

The very name Arthur is arresting; linking Assyria and Atlantis with British mysticism. In the book *A Guide to Glastonbury's Temple of the Stars* it is connected with the Assyrian god Assur and the Median god Ahura. And it is said: 'The now practically extinct race of the Guanche in the volcanic island of Teneriffe called their most high sun god Ach-Ahura-han; it used to be thought that the Guanche were the last of the Atlanteans; some think that they crossed over to Teneriffe from Spain or Morocco.' Arthur is also allied to 'Archer' and to 'Harper', or Bard. The word, starting as a title, or description of him who adopted it, would gradually become transformed into a personal name, reached us finally as 'Arthur'. In the same way that Buddha means 'Enlightened' and Chrestos 'Anointed'.

The designations of the 'Knights of the Round Table' likewise furnish valuable clues. Had they been actual people, friends of Arthur the King, it would be hard to account for their varying appellations. For in the earlier Grail legends some of them bear totally different names to those used in the stories of later date. But if one sees in these twelve personifications the ancient symbology of the Signs of the Zodiac — twelve followers of a spiritual leader recurring in occult tradition — then one understands how their 'table' must necessarily have been 'round'; for no Sign of the Zodiac is greater or less than another; whilst in the centre is the 'most high sun god Ach-Ahura-han', the Initiate who has conquered matter, shedding light and blessing on all.

At the time of King Arthur, chivalry, in its medieval significance, was unknown in Britain. The word itself — 'chevalerie' — denotes a Norman derivation. And it was not until the coffin containing the remains of the king was disinterred at Glastonbury Abbey in the reign of Henry II that the myth of the Grail began to adhere to his life. During six hundred years they had been unrelated.

Then, the Troubadours, the custodians at that period of the mystic truths, commenced to sing of King Arthur and of his Knights of the Round Table and their great quest. Once again the secret tradition was proclaimed to those 'that had ears to hear'.

But why was confusion created with regard to historical fact? What was the intention of the Troubadours in transferring the exploits belonging to Arthur of Tintagel and Avalon to Arthur the King?

Truth to be assimilated must be adapted to its environment. For if they are incompatible, the environment, becoming antagonistic, is prone to ostracise the truth. Hence the fate of the Gnostics, expelled from the Church; and the care exercised by the original Rosicrucians, successors to them and the Troubadours as custodians of the mysteries, to work anonymously. Therefore the wisdom, in the twelfth century, of substituting as hero a Christian king for a Pagan teacher can hardly be queried. And we owe the Troubadours of the court of Henry much; for had they not taken the opportunity offered by the revival of interest in King Arthur of weaving round him the story of the Grail, it might, in that particular guise, have been lost to us.

Tennyson, again, by employing Christian terminology, reached the public of his day; albeit he knew of two Arthurs, as stated by his son in the latter's biography of his father. Tennyson speaks of 'the Arthur who taught me as a child'.

In the earliest accounts, the Grail appears to have been a precious stone. We hear elsewhere of 'a pearl of great price', and we are counselled not to 'cast our pearls before swine' nor to 'give that which is holy unto the dogs'. Afterwards, it became a vessel; one that moved about in the air, and of the contents of which all could partake without their diminishing; that is to say, all who could gain contact with it. But they were the very few. A Fisher-King guards it; the situation of his castle reminding one of the Isle of Patmos: placed between the sea and the land. And was not he to whom that marvellous occult book *The Apocalypse* is attributed called John *the Divine*?

A lance with drops of blood on it is carried in the Grail processions; and throughout the descriptions, of the ritual connected with the mystery or the adventures of them who sought it, the undying tradition reappears, concerning the search and the goal of man. The question is asked: 'What is the Grail?' But no answer could be given, lest it be heard by the profane, and 'trampled under foot'. Sometimes it is portrayed as one thing, sometimes as another; as in Palestine the 'Kingdom of Heaven' was 'likened to a pearl of great price', or to 'treasure hid in a field', or 'a grain of mustard seed'. Yet the Kingdom was none of these; and the Grail was no material object.

When Joseph of Arimathea came to Avalon, most of the ground occupied by the present town of Glasonbury lay under the sea. For at that date the sea covered much of the level country, reaching many miles inland. So quite probably Joseph disembarked with his companions on what is now Weary-All Hill; an eminence which, with the Tor and the smaller Chalice Hill, must have formed the coast line of that portion of the 'Isle of Avalon'.

Joseph brought a staff: symbol of power. Moses possessed a miraculous staff; we read of the 'rod of Aaron'; and, turning to another culture, we find the trident of Neptune and the caduceus of Mercury.

Joseph's staff was also miraculous. When struck into the earth, it flowered. In Ancient Egypt a similar occurrence is believed to have taken place.

And this great man, this person of power, established his mission under the very slopes of the Tor. There he erected a shrine, that was round, with the altar in the centre, and twelve encompassing cells representing the Signs of the Zodiac. He is reputed to have had eleven companions. Over a millennium later, the site of this shrine was preserved; and an Abbot of the Abbey of Glastonbury constructed a floor on the site declaring it to be a facsimile of the ancient church. In the centre was the altar, and on the periphery of the circle were marked the Zodiacal Signs. The floor was subsequently purposely destroyed. Not long after, the Abbey fell.

Mr Bligh Bond, to whom we are indebted for the information regarding Joseph's circular church, tells us in the most interesting books *The Gate of Remembrance* and *The Company of Avalon* that Glastonbury Abbey embodied in stone a cosmic message. It was evidently the wish of the builders to record, in a manner precluding the possibility of their being 'turned upon and rent', a fragment of the eternal verities. The measurements and design of the Abbey are said to be occultly perfect.

Yet it was this community which countenanced, even if it did not inaugurate, a great deception. When the Troubadours revived the Grail legend in connection with King Arthur, the symbol of the Grail as a vessel became materialized. From a thing of deepest mystery it was transmuted into a tangible object, and one which was the exclusive property of the Christian Church. When the illiterate people inquired: 'What is the San Graal?' they were told: 'It is not San Graal, but Sang Réal; a chalice brought to Britain by Joseph of Arimathea, that contained actual blood of the Christ.' And as Joseph came to Avalon, the vessel was supposed to be at Glastonbury.

But for more than twelve hundred years there had been no reference to the theory. No mention of it can be found earlier than the reign of Henry II.

At the foot of the Tor there is a pre-Christian well called Chalice Well. It is flanked on another side by Chalice Hill. Doubtless the names originate from some ritual cup; such an object being known to have had a part in Druidic ceremonial. Thus it is thought that a sacred cup from the Tor may lie hidden in Chalice Well, or that it may be buried under Chalice Hill.

But the Christian story of the relic brought by Joseph gained firm hold, through its emotional and religious appeal. The significance of the San Graal could not be sensed by the populace; a Sang Réal was more readily understood.

Meanwhile the Abbey of Glastonbury attracted an increasing number of pilgrims. Let us, however, turn from this to a quotation from *The Gate of Remembrance*, purporting to be the outlook of a twelfth century monk.

I, Galfrith, knew in my day. They who came spake in Latin, and not all knew the wisdom hid in the british tongue, nor eke the saxon. Some were wrote again, but the fathers were more sought than the Bards and much was hearsay.

What do ye long after, my son? The memory of man is but as the grass that fadeth, and they who would fain translate the word of the barbarian oft inserted what they desired but would not an they could (? translate truly). The hidden meaning they knew not which looked for the husk which covered it and so much was lost for all tyme. The merlins spoke in what ye call an allegory, but the parable was what these fathers read, not the mystery.

Another quotation from the same book.

Ibericus, who wandered hither bringing strange gifts and treasure. Watch ye, for out of the wish it is created, and out of the myth will come the solid truth. Mystery of Faith and of Matter! Out of a thought all things were created, and out of a thought will old-time things renew their being.

One of the Controllers of Things That Are.

A thought in Being.

Now let us read statements by Augustine, Justin Martyr and Origen.

What is nowadays called the Christian religion existed amongst the ancients, and never did not exist, from the beginning of the world till Christ came in the flesh, at which time the true religion, which had hitherto been in existence, began to be called Christianity. [St Augustine, *The City of God*.]

Christ the first born is Reason, the Word, in Whom the whole of mankind exists. All who have lived in conformity with Reason are Christians, even though they may have been looked upon as Atheists. Such, among the Greeks, are Socrates, Heracleitos [Justin Martyr.]

He who deals candidly with histories, and would wish to keep himself also from being imposed on by them, will exercise his judgement as to what statements he will give his assent to, and what he will accept figuratively, seeking to discover the meaning of the authors of such inventions. And we have said that by way of anticipation respecting the whole history related in the Gospels concerning Jesus. [Origen, *Against Celsus*.]

Are we not reminded of Paul's admonition to the Galatians, in the fourth chapter of his Epistle to them, where he writes: 'Which things are an allegory'?

In the paper *The Theosophical Movement*, the issue for September 1935, there was an article on the Indian epic poems *The Ramayana* and *The Mahabharata*, of which the following is an extract.

Like other stories of the Epics this one about the exile, the obtaining and the using of celestial weapons, etc., has a spiritual significance. Actual historical events have been used to convey to the populace, for whom the epics were prepared, some idea of deep occult truths; these were garbed in symbols and in story form, and while the heart-devotion of the masses was awakened by narration of the stories, the intuitive among them felt that there were more in them than met the eye; some of these were led to study, to ferret out the meaning of the myths and thus learn the hidden truths of Soul-Science. . . .

While it is true that the Mahabharata heroes are historical characters they are also, as H. P. Blavatsky points out, 'highly important personified symbols in esoteric philosophy'.

So we are brought once more to Arthur of the Holy Grail. He attained to Adeptship, becoming 'perfect even as his Father in Heaven is perfect', at a time before 'the true religion which had hitherto been in existence began to be called Christianity', but here is an 'Ancient Prayer found written in an old Roman Breviary'.

Lord of all Powers, Light of all Lights, Source of all Wisdom, shine in the hearts of Thy servants, and restore to Thy Church the knowledge of Thy Hidden Mysteries of Wisdom.

Jesus, Thou Light most Holy: lead us to the ancient and narrow Path, which was, is, and will be evermore. Thou, O Christ, art that Path, and we also by the Power of our Life hidden in Thee are the Way, the Truth, and the Life.

Thou art One, and from Thee the many come forth, rooted in Thee. Thou sustainest Angels and men. Thou art the Father and Mother of all worlds. By the hidden Way of the Cross, to the glory of the Risen Word, lead us, O Lord, that we and all Thy Church may find Peace and Union with the changeless Father of our souls. Amen.

And let us not forget how it has been said that 'every scribe which is instructed unto the kingdom of heaven is like unto a man that is an householder, which bringeth forth out of his treasure things new and old'.

Now the Holy Thing is here again
Among us, brother . . . .
That so perchance the vision may be seen
By thee and those, and all the world be heal'd.

— Tennyson's 'Holy Grail'

It is true today, as it has always been, and ever will be, as the undying
tradition teaches, that the way is open, 'narrow' though it may be, to
the fulfilment of man's destiny: the reaching to the level of
consciousness epitomised in the words: 'I and my Father are one.'

2

The Legend of King Arthur's Cross[1]

JOHN OF GLASTONBURY

There was at that time in Wirral within the island of Avallonia a monastery of holy virgins, dedicated in the name of the Apostle Peter, wherein Arthur oftentimes rested and abode, attracted by the amenity of the place. Now it came to pass at a certain time that the king was staying there and sleeping in his chamber; and there came to him an angel of the Lord and said, 'Arthur, Arthur.' And he awoke and said, 'Who art thou?' The angel answered, 'It is I who speak with thee. At break of day arise and go to the hermitage of St Mary Magdalen of Bekeri in this island: behold and understand what there shall be done.' The king arose in the morning and told the vision to a knight of his named Gawayn. But he suggested to his lord the king that it was of no account. The angel appeared again the second night, and the king determined that if a third summons should come it must be obeyed.

As the shades of night drew on, the king bade his attendant (*simmistam*) to be ready in the morning to set forth with him to the hermitage. (Here something has been omitted.) And he (i.e. the attendant), entering the chapel, beheld there a corpse on a bier, and four candles standing on this side and on that, after the manner of the monks; and on the altar two golden candlesticks. Stirred by avarice he seized one of these and hid it wickedly beneath his cloak — a thing which the issue proves to have been ill done. When he would go forth from the chapel, there met him one who, chiding him withal for sacrilege, smote him in the groin. Grievously wounded he cried aloud even as a madman. The king awoke, and in great fear sought what this might be: he rose up and went forth at once to the bed of his attendant, demanding what had come to him. He told the thing in order to the king, shewed him the candlestick in his cloak and the weapon in his groin, and expired; and he was buried among the nuns in Wirral. In testimony whereof, as it is said, the candlestick and the knife remain in the treasury of the king of England at Westminster unto this day.

The king therefore, perceiving that God would have none enter that

---

[1] Originally appeared in J. Armitage Robinson, *Two Glastonbury Legends* (Cambridge University Press, 1926).

chapel save for his soul's salvation, as soon as it was dawn maketh his way thither alone. And as he drew near the chapel, lo, two hands holding swords on either side of the door, that smote against each other, and struck out fire, as it were lightning, before the king's eyes. Smitten with great fear he bethought him what he should do, since so holy a place he might not enter. Then falling on his knees he besought the Lord to shew him mercy and make him worthy to enter therein. (His prayer was granted.) And seeing that the swords were gone he entered the holy place, which was adorned beyond compare. There met him a venerable old man, clad in black robes, with a long beard and white hair; and he saluted the king. And he, humbly returning the salutation, set himself at one side of the chapel to see the end. He saw all this his servant had related. The old man now began to vest himself in priestly robes; and forthwith there came the glorious Mother of the Lord, bearing her Son in her arms, and began to serve the old man. But when he began the Mass and came as far as to the offertory, Our Lady offered to the priest her Son. The priest set Him on the corporal next the chalice. And when he came to the immolation of the Host, that is, to the Lord's words 'This is My Body,' he elevated the Boy in his hands. King Arthur stood for that Sacrament of the Lord, nay for the Lord Himself, and made suppliant adoration. The old man, after this immolation of the Boy, set Him where He was before. When he came to the reception of the Host, he took and received and ate that Boy, the Son of God, according to the institution of the Lord who said 'Take and eat.' When He had been received and the communion made, He appeared in the same place as before, sitting unharmed and entire, the spotless paschal Lamb. When the whole divine office was

Figure 1: The Blessed Virgin Mary

completed, Our Lady, the glorious Mother, in testimony of all this gave to the king a crystal cross, which to this day, by gift of the same king, is honourably kept and preserved in the treasury of Glastonbury, and year by year in Lent is carried in procession on Wednesdays and Fridays: for on Wednesday was the marvel done, even on Ash Wednesday. Then she took back her Son, and they passed out of sight. [The old man interpreted all this to the king, and explain that the corpse in the chapel was that of a brother hermit from Andredesey, who had come to visit him and had fallen sick and died. The king repented him of his sins and made vows of contrition to Our Lady and her Son our Lord Jesus.] His arms also he changed in their honour. For whereas they were silver, with three lions red, turning their heads to their backs, from the time of the coming of Brutus even until this change of King Arthur; now, in memory of the crystal cross given him by the Blessed Mary, he made them to be green, with a cross of silver; and over the right arm of the cross, in memory of the miracle aforesaid, he set the image of Blessed Mary ever Virgin, holding her Son in her arms. And the king bade farewell to the old man, being confirmed in the faith of the Lord, and went from strength to strength, and was mightily rejoiced.

3

The History and Antiquities of Glastonbury[1]

A. HERNE

Ad majorem Dei gloriam

1. My Curiosity having led me twice to Glastonbury within the two years, and inquiring there into the antiquity, history and rarities of the place, I was told by the inn-keeper, where I set up my horses, who rents a considerable part of the inclosure of the late, dissolved Abbey, 'That St Joseph of Arimathea landed not far from the town, at a place, where there was an oak planted in memory of his landing, called *the Oak of Avalon*: That he and his companions marched thence to a hill, near a mile on the south side of the town, and there being weary rested themselves, which gave the hill the name of *Weary all Hill*: That St Joseph stuck on the hill his staff, being a dry hawthorn stick, which grew and constantly budded and blowed upon Christmas Day, but, in the time of the Civil Wars, that thorn was grubbed up; however, there were in the town and neighbourhood several trees raised from the thorn, which yearly budded and blowed upon Christmas Day, as the old root did: That the old Abbey was built in honour of St Joseph's coming thither: That the last Abbot of it, whose name was Whiting, was either hanged on, or tumbled down in a barrel, a very steep Hill, on the north-east side of the town, called the Tor, for building the great kitchen (which is still there standing) and saying, he would keep as good a house as King Henry the Eighth himself should: And that St Bennet's Church, one of the parish churches there, was the first church, wherein the Gospel was preached in England.' Finding my landlord's relation imperfect, and knowing him to be mistaken in some particulars; at my return home, I turned over what books I had, that treated any thing of Glastonbury, and collecting together what I can meet of it, I resolve to print it, hoping it may encourage some abler person, and one better versed in Antiquity than my self, to enlarge upon it. I find then,

2. St Joseph of Arimathea, that noble senator, so honourably mentioned by the four Evangelists, for asking and obtaining of Pilate the Body of our Saviour Christ, and afterwards burying it, was, for that noble Action, imprisoned in a 'close prison by the Jews, the very night he performed that Christian duty, and was thence miraculously

---

[1] Originally published in London, 1772.

delivered by an angel the night of our Saviour's Resurrection, which so enraged the Jews, that, they not only turned him, with St Lazarus, St Mary Magdalen, St Martha, out of Jerusalem, but, putting them in an open vessel, without stern or tackling, they turn'd them to sea, where, by God's providence, they were driven to Marseilles, a city of France upon the Mediterranean, whence St Joseph came into Great Britain, where after he had preached the Gospel he died.

3. The antiquities of Glastonbury and old historians tell us, that he came hither in or about the year of Christ 63 and that he brought over with him 12 companions, whereof one was his Son, called also Joseph. Protestant authors say, he was sent hither by St Philip the Apostle; but Papists will not allow it, and say, he was sent by St Peter, and though they own St Philip's disciples, yet they deny, that St Philip ever was in Gallia, what we now call France, and say he suffered martyrdom at Hieropolis, a city in Asia, in the year of Christ 54, nine years before St Joseph's coming hither; whereas St Peter suffered not till the year 69, which was six years after St Joseph's arrival in Great Britain. But leaving this matter to such, as love dispute and contention, we will proceed with our story.

4. There is an old book called *Sanctus Graal*, quoted by some authors, that saith, St Joseph, what of the one sex, and what of the other, brought over with him 600 persons, amongst whom (besides his son Joseph above mentioned) were his wife, his nephew Helaius, from whom (it says) our renowned King Arthur was descended, and a kinsman whose name was Peter, from whom one Loth descended, who married King Arthur's sister: That St Joseph was a king, *Rex Orcania, King of Orcania*; and that divers of this his great retinue were persons of the first rank, some whereof were also called *Reges, Kings,* &c. But Mr Cressy tells us, this Book is not to be relied on. Leaving therefore this matter as doubtful, I will go forward with what I may report with more certainty.

5. Mr Broughton from the Antiquities of Glastonbury tells us, that the first landing of St Joseph in this Island, was in Venodocia, now called North Wales, where he and his companions preaching the Faith of Christ, were not only denied all necessary things for their relief and sustenance, but their doctrine-rejected, and themselves committed to prison by the king or prince of that province, a pagan infidel. But he and his associates being freed of their imprisonment by the great mercy and providence of God to them, and seeing how fruitless a business it was like to be, to make any longer stay amongst that (then) so obstinate and obdurate a people, he came into that part of the island, called then Loegria, now England.

6. At his first arrival here, he assumed the confidence, to repair to the then British King Arviragus, to whom he gave an account of the design of his journey, which was to bring the happy news, and to offer the only assured means of eternal happiness to all that would embrace

it. This message, gravely and modestly deliver'd by one, filled with the Spirit of God, and also of a venerable presence, one that renounced all worldly designs of power or riches, professor of a religion sufficiently recommended in that it deserved the hatred of Nero, a prince then infamous beyond any ever mentioned in former histories; so wrought upon Arviragus, that he not only gave them leave to convert and save his subjects, but also extended his liberality so far, as to afford them a place of retreat, commodious for their quiet and holy devotions, and sufficient for their sustenance; that without distraction and solicitude they might attend to the worship of the true God, and the instruction of all those that were willing to take it.

7. The place Arviragus assigned them was an island, rude and uncultivated, called by the Britains for the colour of it, *Iniswitryn*, that is, *the Glassy Island*, compassed by the bay full of woods, bushes and fens, situated in Somersetshire. In succeeding time, being cleared from briars, drained and cultivated, it was by the inhabitants named Avallonia, for the plenty of apples and other fruit growing there. But in after ages, when the Saxons had possessed themselves of those parts, they resumed the former title, and called it in their own language *Glaston* or *Glascon*.

8. Mr Broughton says it is a continued tradition of the still inhabitants of Glastonbury, that when St Joseph and his companions came into England out of North Wales, they divided themselves into divers companies, and that three only at first went to Iniswitryn, whereof one was St Joseph himself. That he and his companions coming tired and weary to a hill, within half a mile of south-west of where Glastonbury now stands, rested themselves on the ridge thereof, for which reason that hill to this very day is called *Weary all Hill*, and that in the very place where they rested there sprung up a miraculous thorn tree, which every year at Christmas in the coldest year and weather, frost, snow or what ever else, never failed budding forth leaves and flowers, of which thorn I design to say more hereafter, being unwilling here to interrupt the course of my story.

9. When the rest of these holy men understood where St Joseph and his two companions had their settlement, they likewise repaired thither, and being all got together, and having earnestly implored the help of Heaven, where to make their stay and abode, they set up their rest in the adjoining place, where the late Abbey of Glastonbury stood. A little while after they had been there, they were admonished by St Gabriel the Archangel in a vision, to build a church in honour of the Holy Mother of God and Perpetual Virgin Mary: upon which they immediately built an oratory of barked alder or wicker wands, winded and twisted together, with a roof of straw, or rather, after the nature of the soil of that neighbourhood, of hay or rushes . . .

10. Some will have it, that these holy men, prevailed little by their preaching, and therefore at last gave themselves wholly to a

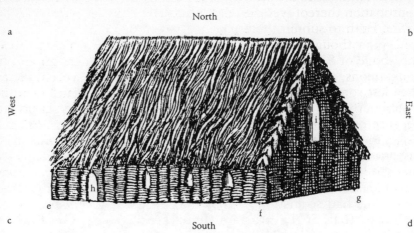

Figure 2: The Church

a. b. c. d. The compass of the church-yard. the extent whereof is not certainly known, but large enough to contain 1000 graves.

e. f. The length of the church 60 foot.

f. g. The breadth of the church 26 foot.

h. The door, the top whereof reaches the eaves of the church, which were very low.

i. The east window over the altar. Vide *Sammes's Antiquities, pp. 213, 214.*

monastical and solitary life. But this is a notion, that is contradicted by Sir William Dugdale and Mr Dodsworth in their Monasticon, who say, St Joseph and his companions converted a great multitude of pagans to the faith of Christ. And it would be an injury (I should think) to the zeal and charity of these our primitive fathers, to imagine they were willing to spare their labour and travels, to make Christ known to many, which inquired not after him. No doubt (saith a grave author) they behaved themselves, as all holy missioners did in those days, through all places exhorting men to fly from the wrath to come, and made use of their retreat, allowed them by the king, only as a place of repose, after they had been spent with toiling in God's service; in which place, being separated from worldly conversation, they might purify themselves before their deaths, that so they might be admitted into God's presence, to receive the crown of all their Labours.

11. After this manner of living they all ended their days in the Island of Iniswitryn. having bin supported by the liberality of King Arviragus, who, for their subsistence, bestowed upon each of them a hide of land, 12 hides in the whole; which donation of his was confirmed to them after his death by his two successors, Marius and Coillus, who, some report, were converted by these holy primitive Fathers to the Faith of Christ. But whoever reads Mr Broughton and Mr Cressy will find, though these princes (particularly King Arviragus)

by their kindness to the professors of Christianity, tacitly showed their approbation thereof, yet they did not receive from Heaven the gift of divine Faith to submit thereto.

12. Now though we are told, that this holy Island, which had been the abode of Saints, became, after the decease of St Joseph and his companions, a den of wild beasts, till St Lucius's days, yet 'tis certain they left some disciples behind them, either in the Island or in it's neighbourhood, or else how could St *Eluanus*, called Avalonius, because he was either born or bred at Glastonbury, and *Medivinus Belga*, that is to say, of Wells, be instructed in Christianity? and all our historians agree these two saints were Christians, before St Lucius sent them to Rome to the then Pope Eleutherius, to treat with him about his and his kingdom's conversion. Nay some go so far, as to say, these two saints had so instructed that prince, before they went on that embassy, that St Fugatius or Phaganus, and St Dervianus or Damianus, Pope Eleutherius's two legates, had nothing more to do, than baptize him. So 'tis evident St Joseph and his brethren left disciples behind them, who continued Christianity in the Isle of Iniswitryn, or its neighbourhood, till King Lucius's days, who spread it throughout all his kingdom. But to return from this digression.

13. These two holy legates Phaganus and Damianus travelling through Britain, teaching, preaching and baptizing, were informed, that St Joseph and his companions, about 100 years before, had, in some measure, spread the seed of the Christian faith in the south-western part of the kingdom, and that they at last retired themselves to Iniswitryn, and there died. Understanding whereabout this sacred place was, these holy legates, about the year of Christ 183, penetrated into this holy Isle, as Moses, the Lawgiver of the Jews, did (say my authors) into the inmost parts of the desert, where, by the divine conduct, they found an ancient church, built by the hands of the disciples of our Lord, which the supreme creator of Heaven declared by many miraculous signs, that himself had consecrated to his own glory, and to the honour of his blessed mother. The aforesaid holy men having found this oratory, were filled with unspeakable joy, and searching diligently that sacred place, they found the holy cross, the figure of our redemption, together with several other signs, declaring that that place had been formerly the habitation of Christians. After this they found the antiquity of the coming of St Joseph and his brethren thither; and also the acts and lives of them there, how religiously they lived, and how three pagan kings ministred necessaries by a certain portion of land for their maintenance. Afterwards being admonished by a divine oracle, they consider'd, that our Lord had made choice of that place above all others in Brittany, wherein he, his holy mother, and his saints should be implored on. Upon which they added another oratory, built of stone, and dedicated to the honour of our Lord and his Apostles St Peter and

St Paul. And after St Phaganus and Damianus had built that oratory, they on the top of the mountain, called (now) the Tor, raised another oratory, in honour of St Michael the Archangel, *that he might have there honour on earth of men, who, at the command of God, should bring men to eternal honours in Heaven.* This chapel also of St Michael (say my authors) St Phaganus and Damianus built by admonition and direction from Heaven; and, to stir up the devotion of the faithful, they obtained of Pope Eleutherius indulgences for all such, who devoutly visited those three holy places.

14. Nine years did these holy men live here, and, in memory of the first twelve in the time of St Joseph of Arimathea, they chose twelve of their company to dwell in that island, as anchorites, in little cells and caves, who met often together every day, that they might the more devoutly perform their divine offices; and as the three pagan kings had long before granted the said island, with its appurtenances, to the first twelve disciples of Christ, so the said Phaganus and Damianus did obtain of King Lucius, to have it confirmed for ever to these their twelve companions, and others their successors after them. Thus these two holy legates established a succession of twelve devout persons, which continued there the service of God, without interruption, till the coming of St Patrick the Apostle of Ireland to that Place.

15. St Patrick, after several years labour in his apostolic office in Ireland, retired (according to Mr Cressy) AD 439 to this Island of Iniswitryn (now become a noted school of sanctity) where he spent thirty years, or more of the later part of his life, in prayers, fasting, watching, and all other penitential austerities. The names of the twelve successors of the disciples of St Phaganus and Damianus which St Patrick found there, were, Brumban, Hiregaan, Bremwal, Wentreth, Banttoniweng, Adelwolred, Loyor, Wellias, Breden, Swelwes, Hinloernus and Hyn, all of them descended of noble families, and men of so great sanctity, that St Patrick, who was a wonder himself for piety, says, he was not worthy to untie the latches of their shoes.

16. These holy men chose St Patrick for their superior, and informed him of all they knew of the island. Whereupon, after he had reduced them to a cenobitical way, that is to say, brought his religious to live in community and in common under the same roof (for till then they lived singly in Huts, Dens and Caves), he took Brother Wellias with him, and with great difficulty they went up together the Tor, where he found the ancient Oratory of St Michael almost ruined, and finding by an old book, which he, by great search and industry, had there found out, that the chapel there had been built by revelation, and held in vast veneration by St Phaganus and Damianus, he and his companions spent there three months in fasting, prayers and watching, during which time he had, on a certain night, a vision of our Saviour

Christ himself, who signified to him, that he was to honour the same Archangel in the same place; for a testimony of the certainty of which vision his left arm withered, and was not restored, till he had acquainted the rest of his brethren below with what he had seen.

17. St Patrick's vision being thus by Miracle confirmed; his religious below were convinced that the chapel on that hill was likewise chosen by God, for the exercise of Christian devotion. Whereupon the holy men Arnulphus and Ogmar, two Irish Monks whom he brought with him thither out of Ireland, desired to go up the hill, and remain constantly there.

4

Ictis and Avallon[1]

C. R. DAVEY BIGGS

I. *The Wattle and Daub Church*

Among the traditions which are concerned with the introduction of Christianity to our island none is more tenaciously held, none seems to be based more firmly on fact, than that some years after the Resurrection of Jesus Christ Joseph of Arimathea, who had been responsible for Christ's entombment, came to Glastonbury.

Nor did he come alone. However much embroidery there may be in the legends retailed by the monkish chroniclers, there is the outstanding fact of the size of the church he built 'of wattle and daub', the ground plan of which is still preserved in the ruined Lady Chapel of the Abbey. It was no small oratory for a single anchoret, but a building sixty feet wide, reproducing the oblong shape of that 'Upper Room' which was the meeting-place in Jerusalem of the adherents of 'the New Way', and capable of accommodating even more than the hundred and twenty who were present at the election of Matthias. A man of such wealth as Joseph's was not likely to travel as a solitary refugee, and quite apart from his ship's company there would naturally be some companions of the type who, according to the tradition, made their way after landing up 'Weary-All Hill' before a settlement was made and the site of the church chosen.

How strongly the belief in the fact of Joseph's foundation of this wattle and daub building is held in the Church of England was made manifest at the time of the Lambeth Conference in 1897. A large number of bishops from all parts of the world, as well as from Great Britain and Ireland, assembled, on August 3rd, in the Abbey grounds, where an address, emphasizing that Joseph's arrival and building there were actual facts of history, was given by Dr G. F. Browne, then Bishop of Stepney; and later the whole of the Abbey grounds and ruins were bought and made the property of the Established Church of England.

So general is the acceptance of the tradition of Joseph's coming. But no one ever seemed to raise the question, 'Why was Glastonbury his choice for a home in the West?' He must have had some good reason for choosing to come up the estuary of the Brue in preference to any

[1] Privately printed pamphlets (n.d.).

of those other inlets on the south coast which are so numerous from Falmouth eastwards. And of course conditions were very different then from what they are now.

But before we start dealing with them, the reminder must be given, that in the vicissitudes of a long history, with peoples of various races and tongues succeeding each other, the same place may at different times have borne different names, and that one most interesting, but occasionally misleading, fact, in our geographical studies, is what S. R. Gardiner called 'The Palimpsest of the map of Britain'. It is obvious, for instance, that the word 'Glastonbury' is of Saxon composition and could not therefore have come into use before the Saxon occupation of Somerset, in the latter part of the seventh century; and we should expect that, through the invasion of Celts and Romans, the Iberians' Cliff Castle, at the Tor, with its adjoining peninsula, would receive a succession of fresh names given by the conquerors and the occupiers.

How difficult those fresh names might be to spell correctly from only being heard we may judge from the substitution of 'Hawaii' for 'Owhyhee' as the name of the largest of the Sandwich Islands; and we must not therefore be surprised at the same name being spelt in different ways, or at a puzzled copyist trying to make sense of what to him was unintelligible and making the confusion worse by getting further away from the original. There are numerous instances of this in connection with the Tor of Glastonbury, as will appear in due course.

But as far as the actual history is concerned we can with fair confidence distinguish fact from fable; for the period with which we have to deal hardly comes at all within 'that huge system of monastic lying in which Glastonbury had a bad pre-eminence'.[2] And since 1917, when Sir Flinders Petrie demonstrated to the British Academy the minute accuracy of geographical detail in a selected portion (Bk. I, 11, 12) of Geoffrey of Monmouth, students are finding more statements worth careful consideration in that once discredited writer.

II. *The Iberian Occupation*

The town of Glastonbury stands on the side of a hilly table-land which rises abruptly out of the flat moor, and is dominated by the Tor, a cone-shaped hill which rises to a height of five hundred feet at the south-west corner of the Isle of Avallon. The orchards and water meadows which surround the town have been reclaimed from the fens and swamps which once encircled the Tor, and made it without need of artificial protection except at the east, where a solid ridge of ground connects it with the hill at Pennard, which is a spur of the Mendips.

[2] Plummer, *Bede*, ii. 167.

Along this ridge was a road or trackway by which the island could be reached by friendly or hostile visitors, and as a means of protection against the latter there was constructed right across the isthmus from swamp to swamp the rampart of clay known as Ponter's Ball. It was three-quarters of a mile in length, and was strengthened as a defence by a ditch, which went to a depth of twelve feet below the old level of the ridge. No one who was familiar with the plan of the 'cliff-castles' on the coast of Pembrokeshire could fail to recognize that the plan of the Tor at the sea front, with Ponter's Ball as the defence from the inland, was exactly similar; and would infer that both were constructed by the same people, the Iberian 'metal-seekers' from the eastern Mediterranean, who planted their groups of 'circle, menhir, and dolmen' all the way up from Cornwall to the Orkneys on either side of what is now St George's Channel.

A glance at the Ordnance Map will show how the entrance of the Brue estuary has been silted up; though the low-lying flatland will be flooded with an exceptionally high tide, or with heavy autumn rains, even at the present time. And then the Tor stands out, as in days long since past, to the seafarer a welcome and inviting beacon, to the landsman a defence to seaward. With its levelled top, now crowned with the tower which is all that is left of a medieval chapel of St Michael, it proclaims itself as having been occupied at a time when the country was still so wet from the last glaciation that it could only be traversed by tracks along the top of the hills, terraces for the cultivation of crops of corn being hewn out from the top downwards by heavy mattocks of flint. Mattocks of this kind have been found in great numbers in Kent, where the megalithic builders have left abundant evidence of similar terraces made from the tops of the hills downward to the impenetrable swamps of the valleys.

The secret of their attraction to the Tor and its hinterland is disclosed in the rich, red soil laid bare by the plough in the area below the terraces; for that colour shows that there is abundance of iron to be had for the trouble of mining, and the 'metal-seekers' were stimulated to activity by the variety of valuable ores in the district. Only a few miles north of the Tor, is the famous cave known as Wookey Hole, where the stalactites are deeply stained with red and blue and green from the iron, lead, and copper in the soil above. Further north, at Priddy, a dolmen tells us that the Iberians worked at the lead mines long before the Romans came to the Mendips, and appropriated all metals to be the personal property of the Emperor.

According to the local tradition, our Lord visited Priddy in 'the silent years' before He entered on His public ministry; and Parry's musical setting has popularized Blake's poem based on this tradition:

> And did those Feet in ancient time
>   Walk upon England's mountains green?
> And was the Holy Lamb of God

On England's pleasant pastures seen?
And did the Countenance Divine
  Shine forth upon our clouded hills?
And was Jerusalem builded here
  Among those dark Satanic mills?

For the hills would at that period be continually clouded by the smoke from the furnaces, and the conditions of heat and darkness, under which the mining and de-silvering were done, might well justify the description 'Satanic mills'.

The Tor at Glastonbury is not the only evidence of the occupation of this district by the Iberian metal-seekers. They set up their circles of monoliths, presumably for purposes of worship, as at Staunton Drew, where there are still three in a group, one of them containing a 'cove', i.e. three monoliths formed into a shelter by a huge flat stone placed over them as a kind of roof; and they built their dolmens, to be abodes for the living or dead, as circumstances might dictate, in a chain stretching north into Gloucestershire and eastward through Wiltshire to Berkshire. The most important of these is at Stony Littleton, about three-quarters of a mile south-west of Wellow Church. It is approached through a passage forty-seven feet six inches in length, and of varying breadth, out of which three recesses, or transepts, open on each side, and an arched roof is made by setting the stones as corbels, each layer projecting forward from that below it till the passage is roughly vaulted and the chamber domed. At Maes How, which has been considered the abode of the overseer or 'nomarch' of the Orkneys, there is only one transept opening out on each side of the central avenue; that there should be three at Stony Littleton suggests how much more important and dignified was the resident in this chambered tumulus; and we must bear in mind that the area in which it is found is even today one of the most important mining districts in Somerset.

These Iberians were short in stature, about five and a half feet in height, with brown skins and dark hair, and have bequeathed these characteristics to 'the small dark Welshman, the small dark Highlander, the small dark South of Ireland man, between whom and the small dark Basque-speaking man from the Pyrenees there is no ethnological difference';[3] and their descendants, planted in the metal-bearing district of Glamorgan, known then as 'Silures', were at once recognized by Agricola's soldiers as a kindred Mediterranean race. As in their bodily frame, so also in their speech they were akin to the Basque; to them we owe apparently the names of rivers such as Severn, Wye, and Eure (the river on which York, Eboracum, stands) for which no Aryan ancestry has been found. Nor is it altogether fanciful to suppose, with these Iberian names of rivers surviving in the

[3] Professor Boyd Dawkins, *Y Cymmrodor*, v. 22.

neighbourhood, that they called the cliff-castle Tor, and that the word
Ictis itself was the name given by them to their island trade-centre. It
survives in Irish as *muir-nOict*, which in the *Annals of the Four Masters*,
under the dates of 405 and 1537 A.D., is translated 'the Ictian sea',
and is obviously from the context a name for the Bristol Channel. The
entry in 1537 AD expresses the horror caused by the suppression of
Glastonbury and other abbeys.

III. *Ictis and Avallon*

We are told that the Silures crossed the stormy seas which were,
perhaps, the predecessors of 'a Severn bore', in boats or coracles made
of osier and protected by an outer covering of hides; and the crossing
must have been robbed of some of its perils by the breakwaters
afforded in the Island of Steepholm and Flatholm which were then of
much greater size. The Brue estuary was open water until a short
distance west of the Tor, where a group of small islands lay in the way
to the larger one, known today as Avallon. These islands have for
centuries past been joined by the silt to the mainland; but their
rediscovery has led to the speculation that Avallon was really that Isle
of 'Ictis' or 'Mictis' which travellers in the second century before
Christ wrote of as being the centre of the British metal trade. Pliny, for
instance (iv. 30), quotes Timaeus as follows: 'Six days sail inland from
Britain there is an island called Mictis, in which white lead [? tin] is
found, and to this island the Britons come in boats of osier, covered
with sewn hides'; 'Timaeus historicus a Britannia introrsus sex dierum
navigatione abesse dictit insula Mictim, in qua candidum plumbum
proveniat; ad eam Britannos vitilibus navigiis, corio circumsutis,
navigare.' We know nothing of Timaeus except that he is thus quoted
by Pliny, but his statement is confirmed and expanded by Posidonius,
who travelled in Britain, presumably about the year 80 BC, and is thus
quoted by Diodorus Siculus (v. 21–22–31): 'They who dwell near that
promontory of Britain which is called Belerion, are exceedingly fond
of strangers, and from their intercourse with foreign merchants are
civilized in their habits. These people obtain tin by carefully working
the soil which produces it; this being rocky, has earthy interstices, the
produce of which is ground down, smelted, and purified. They form
the metal into masses shaped like knuckle-bones,[4] and carry it to a
certain island lying off the coast of Britain called Ictis; for as the
ground between is left dry at low tide, they carry the tin thither in
great abundance in their waggons. Now there is this singular
circumstance connected with the neighbouring islands, which lie
between Europe and Britain; for at the high tides the intervening

---

[4] The knucklebone form of ingot was for convenience of carriage. One such ingot,
of quite uncertain date, which weighs 158 pounds, was dredged up near the entrance
to Falmouth Harbour, and is now in the Truro museum. It has no definite mark or
inscription, but its shape is corroborative of the statement of Posidonius.

ground is flooded, and they seem like islands, but at the low tides when the sea recedes and leaves much space dry, they seem peninsulas. At this island (Ictis) the merchants buy the tin from the natives of Britain and carry it across into Gaul, and finally, journeying by land through Gaul for about thirty days, they convey their burdens on horses to the outlet of the river Rhone . . . A great deal of tin is carried across from the Britannic isle to the opposite coast of Gaul, and thence conveyed by merchants, on horses, through the midland Celtic country to the people of Marseilles, and to the city called Narbonne.'

Many writers have identified this island peninsula which was the seat of the British metal trade with St Michael's Mount in Cornwall, because of the mention of Belerion, the pre-Christian name of Cornwall, and because it does at the present time fulfil the condition of being an island at high tide and a peninsula at low tide; but they assume that the coast-line is the same today as it was two thousand years ago, and that is an extremely precarious assumption.

'The alluvial flat of Mount's Bay, under which the submerged forest lies, formerly extended much further seaward, and old writers mention the tradition that St Michael's Mount formerly rose as an isolated rock, in a wood. As far as can be calculated from its known rate of encroachment, the sea cannot have reached the Mount until long after the Roman period, and the legend is probably quite accurate. The Mount was surrounded by wide marshy flats, covered with alders and willows, till well within the historic period. The contradictory story that the Phoenicians traded to St Michael's Mount for tin seems to be the invention of a sixteenth-century antiquary.'[5]

And where near St Michael's Mount are the islands spoken of by Posidonius, which were only islands at high tide? Where, too, are the cart-tracks by which the metal was brought to Ictis? Not, certainly, 'in the wide marshy flats, covered with alders and willows'. But we have at Glastonbury a centre, or junction, for roads leading up from Cornwall and stretching north and west to Rollright and Arbor Low, to Kit's Coty House and Coldrum.[6]

There are, too, the islands. For if we start back from the Saxon overlordship, we find this striking and interesting fact: Kenwalch on his conquest of Somerset confirms to the Abbey of Glastonbury the possession of certain islands lying to the west, in the Brue estuary, up which it was still possible to sail. The names of these islands are thus given in Kenwalch's charter: 'The Manor of Glastonbury, with its islands, viz. Beckery, which is called "little Ireland", Westhay, Godney, Martinseye, Andresey, Clewer, Northlode, Redlake, Pamborough, and Bledney'; of which Beckery, Westhay, and

[5] Reid, *Submerged Forests*, 100, 101.
[6] R. Hippisley Cox, *The Green Roads of England*.

Martinseye are in Mere; Andresey in Stoke Gifford; Clewer, Northlode, and Pamborough in Wedmore; and Bledney in Wookey.[7]

Each rises still as a more or less conspicuous mound from the level of the silted-up marshes; and together they suggest that the statement of Posidonius that there were islands near his Ictis, which were of the same peninsula character as Ictis itself at low tide, refers to the Tor, and the islands, still traceable, west of it, in the seventh century. And when we consider the distance of the Tor from the extreme point of Cornwall, we recall Timaeus's statement, that his 'Island of Mictis was six days sail inland from Britain', and we are led to the conclusion that the island trading centre mentioned by Timaeus and Posidonius was none other than that place we now call Glastonbury. Nor is it without significance that an area between the Tor and the Brue is marked in the map facing page 35 of the first volume of Bulleid and Reid's book on the Glastonbury lake village as being named 'Actis'.

IV. *The Brue and the Loire*

Can we produce evidence that there was ever a trading centre near the Tor? To answer this question we need only refer to the account of the Lake Village discovered in 1892 at Glastonbury. The account is given by the excavators, Messrs Bulleid and Gray, in their monumental and exhaustive volumes. They conclude that the pasture fields known locally as Meare Pool occupy part of the site of a body of water which in AD 1540 is reported to have been five miles in circumference, and must have been much larger two thousand years earlier. In its area was noticed in March 1892, near the middle of the moorland lying between Glastonbury and Godney, a triangular space, three and a half acres in extent, which contained between sixty and seventy low hemispherically shaped mounds. They varied from fifteen to forty feet in diameter, with an elevation at the centre of from six to twenty-five inches above the surrounding level of the meadow, and each represented the place of a human dwelling. Of the amount of labour involved in the building of the village, we can judge from the fact that every scrap of stone, clay, and gravel had to be imported in primitive dug-out canoes, such as that discovered at Crannel Farm, three-quarters of a mile north-east of this village, and now on exhibition in the Glastonbury Museum. One dwelling-mound alone produced a hundred and fifty tons of material, and this material has been identified as having been brought from places one, two, six, and even twelve miles distant. Though discovered first, the Glastonbury lake village was of later construction than the Meare village, the method of which is copied with much exactness, and both date from the beginning of the third century before Christ. But whereas a layer of flood-soil varying from six to eighteen inches in depth, extending all

---

[7]Somerset Archaeological Society. *Feodary of Glastonbury Abbey*, 51, and note, 45.

over the area of the mounded field at Glastonbury, suggests that the inhabitants of the village may have been flooded out of their homes; the Meare village came to an end through hostile attack. About which more will be said later.

The results of the excavation show us a good deal of the daily life of a highly-civilized community on the Severn shore in the two centuries before the raids of Julius Caesar.

For instance, in one area, worked wooden timbers were found, which were suggestive of the remains of the framework of looms, seventeen combs, and over twenty spindle whorls, besides triangular 'loom-weights' of clay, and of at least three sizes, all which indicate that here was a flourishing weaving industry. But besides weaving and spinning, there was pottery making, and work in glass, bronze, and iron, as well as admirable coopering and carpentry. In one hut so many needles were found that it is thought to have been a needle factory; and perhaps each industry was pursued in its own hut or group of huts.

The inhabitants grew crops of wheat, barley, and peas, on the adjacent land, and they possessed dogs, pigs, and cattle, flocks of sheep and herds of goats, and mobs of small horses which were used for food, but also for driving and possibly riding. Their personal ornaments consisted of rings, brooches, and armlets, and beads of amber, glass, and jet. And in their lighter moments they gambled with dice that may have been derived from Italy, and amused themselves with cock-fighting, with birds probably obtained from Gaul.

For it seems clear that a trade connection had already been established between the Silures, with their osier, hide-bound boats, and the Veneti, an offshoot of the same tribe as had occupied the northern slope of the Adriatic. This offshoot had made their way through Gaul to the mouth of the Loire, and controlled the sea coast near Brest and Ushant, with an inland capital which is still called after them, Vannes. Their ships were built on the model of those of the Carthaginians, whose trade they had inherited, entirely of heavy oak; the beams, which were a foot thick, were fastened with iron nails, the thickness of a thumb; their sails were made of skins and hides, in order to stand the violence of the winds.[8] The Silures also had ships of a similar kind, and took part, as allies of the Veneti, in the famous battle off Quiberon, the first recorded sea engagement outside the Mediterranean, in which they met with a crushing defeat from the fleet of Julius Caesar. It was through this battle that Caesar was inspired further to subdue the people of Britain and acquire its great mineral wealth for Rome.

The chief trade from Britain to the Mediterranean countries, through Gaul was in tin and other minerals, but furs and skins were

[8] Caesar, *de Bello Gallico*, iii.

also in request; and the great wolf dogs, which were trained to fight for the protection of their owners and their homes, had increasingly repute in Gaul and the countries beyond. We conclude, then, that it was to this 'Venice of the West' on the banks of the Loire that the *astragali* of tin were carried by sea, to be forwarded thence to Marseilles across Gaul.

V. *Afallach and his Descendants*

Who, however, were the invaders who destroyed the Meare village?

An old map, that of Speed, published in 1610, shows the Belgae, situated west of the Meare Pool, and north of the Brue; and it appears certain that it was this Celtic tribe which, crossing from the opposite coast of France to the Solent, made their way inland and westward, to the sea, in the neighbourhood of the Tor; they established themselves on the island peninsula, which, from the name of one of their first chieftains, began to be called Afallach. The form of the Latin adjective from this name being Avallonensis, led to the variant Avallon; but even so, many years later, at the time of King Arthur, we are told that his famous sword 'Excalibur' was wrought at Afallach.[9]

For at least six centuries the descendants of Afallach held rights of property in the Tor peninsula; and their story was traced by a former librarian of the Bodleian, E. W. B. Nicholson, in a paper entitled, *The Dynasty of Cunedda*.[10]

He interpreted a genealogy found at the end of the Harleian MS of the 'Annales Cambriae' to this effect: A Belgic chieftain settled in the apple country near the beginning of the Christian era, and had a son whose name indicated his inheritance of the chieftainship; this son married a princess of the Coritanians, and their son married a princess of the Dobuni; and in adherence to the Iberian and Silurian tradition of inheritance through the mother, their son became the chieftain of the Dobuni, taking the name of Dobun; and Dobun married one of the Ambivariti, a small tribe settled in the Severn sea. Through the imperial policy of exercising rule through the local chieftains, the family, as generation succeeded to generation, became more and more attached to Rome; and owing to the inter-tribal influence it had acquired through its politic marriages, it received increasing confidence from the Roman authorities. In the first half of the third century they began assuming 'regnal' names of Roman origin, and there is ground for believing that their doing so coincided with the Caledonian expedition of Severus; that the emperor found the son of Dobun a 'teachable' lieutenant, and that when, after reconstructing the Northern Wall, he retired south, 'Docilis' (teachable) was left to occupy, as a dependent chief, that part of the country between the walls of Hadrian and Antoninus known to the Welsh as Manau

[9]Peter Roberts, *Annals of the Kings*, 142.
[10]*Y Cymmrodor*, xxi, 63–104.

Guotodin. From Docilis, a succession of four more regnal names, indicating that their bearers held rule in subordination to, or alliance with, the Roman government of South Britain, brings us to Cunedag, or Cunedda, the hero of Welsh minstrelsy, and founder of a line of kings in Wales. Of two of his great grandsons, Gwytherin and Glast, we shall hear more later on, in connection with their ancestral property on the Isle of Avallon.

THE ANCESTRY OF GLAST

Beli, *magnus*. The chieftain of the invading Belgae, who destroyed the Lake village.

Aballac (called by William of Malmesbury Avalloc) or Amalech, both archaic forms of Afallach, which means 'rich in apples' or 'apple-lander', took possession of Ictis.

Eugein = Avigenios, 'of noble birth'.

Brithguein, or Prydein, son of a princess of an East Midland tatooed tribe, Cruithni or Coritani, of which the Kymric form is Prydein.

Dubun, son of a princess of the Dobuni, a tribe settled about the head of the Severn estuary, in Gloucestershire.

Amguerit, son of an Ambivaritan mother.

Dumn = *domn*, i.e. *dominus*

Doli = Docil, i.e. *docilis*, 'teachable.'

Cein, Ceionius, a well-known Roman family name borne by a consul in 240.

Tacit, Tacitus, the name of a Roman emperior, 275–6. Appears in later Welsh as Tegid.

Patern Pesrut = Paternus (a name borne by Roman consuls in 267, 268, 269, 279), 'of the purple cloak', i.e. he was holder of the highest rank of command in the imperial army.

Aetern = Aeternus, a title borne on coins by the Emperors Diocletian (284–305) and Julian (360–3).

Cunedag.

Dunaut (4th son)	Docmail (9th son)
Ebiaun	Elno
Dinacat	Glast
Gwytherin 'ab Dingad'	
= Victorinus	

VI. *Joseph and the Metal Industry*

Long before the Belgae came the Phoenicians must have lost their monopoly of the metal trade from Britain, and it is not impossible that enterprising members of the Jewish race should have begun to take a part in it. According to a Cornish doggerel 'Joseph was a tinman', and in all the Latin versions of the Gospels of St Mark (15: 43) and St Luke (23: 50), without exception, he (Joseph of Arimathea) is called

'Decurio', which, at the time those versions were made, was the regular term in the Roman Empire for the officers placed in charge of the metal mines. He may indeed, even then, have been drawing some of the wealth upon which St Matthew lays such emphasis from the metal workings in the Mendips, as our English merchants have derived wealth from concessions arranged with the rulers of lands outside the British Dominions.

For even as being nothing more than a well-to-do and well-educated subject of the Roman Empire, he could hardly be ignorant of Caesar's historic naval battle of Quiberon, and the upshot of it — which was the desire to acquire for Rome that district which had for millennia supplied the lands east of the Mediterranean with metals. He must have known about the Isle of Ictis and its actual situation; there must have been hundreds of mariners able and eager to describe it to him, and to advise as to the route thither, and the possibilities of acquiring land. And if he had already a line of merchant vessels, and regular commerce with native rulers, how natural would it not be for him, at the time when the Christians were all scattered abroad, 'except the Apostles' (Acts 8: 1), to turn his back on the land of his own kindred, and make a home where as yet there was no Roman ruler.

So we may imagine Joseph of Arimathea came to the long-established and well-known harbour, and the Tor gave him the same beckoning welcome that it had given to un-numbered generations of immigrants from the same eastern Mediterranean. Tradition makes him land at Weary-All Hill on the north-west corner of the island, along the top of which a road ran from Street to the Lake Village: there he planted his staff which became a thorn-bush of distinct variety, and was cut down by a fanatical Puritan in 1624. Cuttings from it, however, had been made, and one of them has grown into the vigorous tree in the churchyard of the parish church, and flowers twice a year, at Christmas and in May. His wealth and trading connection made it easy for him to acquire a piece of land on the north-east of the Tor, and on it he quickly had a church built.

The houses of the Meare lake village had been built of wattle and daub, and Joseph availed himself of this, the local method of construction, which as we know from the remains of Roman merchants' houses excavated in London, was capable of receiving handsome fresco decoration on the plastered walls. It was therefore no indication of poverty or economy to build the church in this style, and as a matter of fact the church so erected lasted till the fifth century, and then only needed repair on account of the damage it received in the raids made upon the place by the Pagan Irish.

When the Romans advanced into Somerset, they took possession of the lead mines, and worked them in the interests of the government to raise revenue. By Roman law, all minerals belonged to the state, and lead pigs from most of the British mines bear the reigning emperor's name. The two earliest of the twelve exhibited in the British Museum came from the Mendips; one, dated AD 49, bears the name of Britannicus, son of Claudius; the other, dated AD 60, is inscribed, 'British lead, property of the Emperor Nero'.

Four others are stamped as coming from the mines of Lutudarum, which was in Derbyshire, near Matlock and the river Derwent, and leased apparently to a succession of Greek freed-men. Two of these pigs have been desilverized, showing from their inscriptions that the Romans were mining for silver, but finding little of it in Britain, were content to continue to work the lead.

More interesting perhaps than these 'pigs' are the leaden sealings, exactly similar to those used today still in Italy for securing a passenger's registered luggage. As they originally had cords through them, they seem to be peculiar to Britain. They had letters or devices on one or both faces. They may have been used for sealing or certifying military (i.e. government) stores, or they may have been custom marks for merchandise, as they were found in the *principia* of the Roman official at Combe Down, near Bath, in the Mendip mining area; as well as at Richborough, Felixstowe, and at other similar coastal places.

Some other exhibits in the British Museum, which belong to the first century of the Roman occupation, show how the metal industry grew in importance and spread in area; for the injuries likely to be inflicted on the eyes of the workers from the glowing masses of red-hot metal, and the sparks which might fly from them, led to the emergence of a school of medical men in Britain, who made a special study of diseases of the eye and of remedies for them. Such was Lucius Valliatinus, who practised as a physician in the Roman colony on the Esk, and there prepared his own medicines for the eye. Such was Stolus, whose eye-salve came under the notice of Galen, the court physician of the Emperor Marcus Aurelius. And these specialists used to stamp their remedies with the name of the practitioner or make, the nature of the salve and directions for its use, either on the wax fastenings of the preparation or on sticks of solid collyrium. The stamps were not unlike in size and appearance to oblong pieces of scented soap, only their inscriptions were not on the top, but on the sides, each of which, as in the case of one found at Sandy, $2\frac{1}{8} \times 1\frac{1}{2} \times \frac{3}{8}$ in., might be inscribed with a different medicine; while one found at Cirencester boldly advertises a 'heal-all'.

It is strange that the makers of these stamps seem only to have thought of using them to make an impression on soft or yielding substances. Had they made the experiment of setting their dies, while still damp and sticky from the coloured mass on which they had been impressed, on some flat surface or fabric, they would have stumbled into the discovery of printing, and achieved for the old world what was one of the mainsprings of progress in the new.

VII. *Banna Venta Bernae*

Meanwhile, as the 'pimbo', to use the Italian term for the leaden seals clamped over the knots of corded luggage, found at Combe Down, seems to indicate, the Isle of Avallon continued to thrive as a well-known place of commerce in metals; and the fame of Joseph's religious foundation grew, and attracted more and more pilgrims and settlers. Before the year AD 139, a Christian named Adiuuandus, known later as St Diuvan, was flourishing there; and some time after AD 210 another Christian, Pacandus, arrived; he became the St Mawgan, after whom a monastery on the borders of Pembrokeshire and Cardinganshire was named.

So, as the years passed, the Isle of Avallon became a strong Christian centre, with links of intimacy with the Christians of Tours of the same kind as in pre-Christian days existed in commerce between the traders of the Lake Village and 'the Venice of the West' at the mouth of the Loire. Martin, the bishop of Tours, had two sisters married in Britain, one to Gorthol, prince of the Strathclyde Britons, to whom she bore Ninian, the apostle of the southern Picts; the other, Concessa, was married to Calpurnius, the deacon *decurio*, to whom she bore Succat, otherwise known in later days as St Patrick. An inscription at Hexham records how a prefect of cavalry, named Concessinus, cut to pieces a band of Irish raiders, and McNeill[11] raises the question, from the similarity of names, whether the prefect of cavalry and Patrick's mother were of the same kin, and whether the raid in which Patrick was taken captive was not a calculated reprisal for the Hexham massacre.

There is abundant evidence, therefore, that Christian faith and worship were maintained in the neighbourhood of the Tor previously to the time when the monastic life was introduced, on stricter lines, by St Patrick, when he came at the end of his missionary toils in Ireland to Avallon. Patrick was accompanied by Bridget and other companions, who established themselves as anchorets on the little islets of the Brue estuary to which they gave their names: Andresey, Martinseye, and Becary, i.e. Bridget's Island, which was actually called 'Little Ireland.'

But what took Patrick to Avallon? Why should he have chosen that place in preference to others, in which to pass his latter days? How was it, that when he was first given land in Ireland, for the purpose of building a church, he built, at Donagh Patrick, one which was in size and shape an exact reproduction of Joseph's *vetusta ecclesia*? To state the problem clearly: is it possible that the Isle of Avallon was Patrick's birthplace?

There are four sources for the life of St Patrick; and taking first

[11] *Proceedings of the Royal Irish Academy*, xxxvii, 6, 140. Patrick had consecrated both Fiacc and Aed to be successive Bishops of Sletty.

Fiacc's hymn, we learn that the saint 'was born in Nemthur', a word which is in the dative, corresponding to a nominative *Nemthor*, and as far as signification goes may be represented by St Michael's *Tor*. The importance of Fiacc's statement is that the name he gives is that known to him as the name of Patrick's birthplace; for it seems that the author of the hymn was not the Fiacc who was a contemporary of St Patrick, but his successor, Bishop Aed, at whose 'dictation' our next authority, the life by Muirchu, was written.[12] Muirchu states that Patrick was born at a town which he knew by a constant and undoubting tradition to be called *Ventre*, i.e. *practically the same as Nemthor*, the copyist having made the common error of reading *u* for *n*. The form *Nemtrie* is actually found in the Brussels codex of Muirchu's *Life of St Patrick*. And considering the frequent interchange of *b* and *v* in Latin we may find the last syllable of *Severn* in *Bernae*. When we come to our other two authorities, St Patrick's *Confession* and *Letter to Coroticus*, what we find is *not the name but a description* of his birthplace, as a man born in London might say he was born in the metropolis. The saint admits that he cannot write good Latin, and his spelling may have been as bad as his grammar and idiom; but he insists on the fact that his father was a townsman, and it would be quite in keeping with his insistence on the social standing of his family for him to assert that his birthplace was no obscure village but 'the chief trading place of the Severn'.

The phrase he uses was obscure even to Irish writers of the seventh century, and the spelling of it differs in different manuscripts; but Dr Newport White[13] gives it as Banavem Taberniae, and Professor Eoin McNeill[14] took 'the common ground that the phrase as it exists in its various spellings is corrupt and requires reconstruction, and that in its original form it contained the word Venta' (trading-place, Chepstow). Hence McClure[15] says that the phrase would in early Irish represent 'the principal Chepstow on the Severn', i.e. the Isle of Avallon or Ictis. No other Venta, such as that in Glamorganshire, had so long a history; it fits in with Muirchu's phrase, 'not far from our sea' — the Ictian sea or Bristol Channel; and perhaps the most decisive point in the identification is that Fiacc asserts that he *learnt that Nemthur was Patrick's birthplace from Patrick himself*.

All indeed that Patrick tells us about himself locates him near the Tor. He was born of a family in which not only the Christian Faith but the Christian ministry was traditional. His father, Calpurnius, was a deacon, one of the sons of Potitus, a presbyter. The district was so thickly populated that 'many thousands' of captives were carried off

[12] Whitley Stokes, *Tripartite Life of St Patrick*, Rolls Series, cxi, 127.

[13] Newport White, *Libri Sancti Patricii*, SPCK (1918).

[14] *Proceedings of the Royal Irish Academy*, xxxviii, 6, 123. [See also note 11, p.46.].

[15] E. McClure, *English Place Names*, 130.

in the same raid as that in which Patrick was snatched from his father's suburban villa. And it was a metal producing district, for Calpurnius was a *decurio*, one of the order which the Romans used as an agent to establish a thorough system of local government, and for administration.

If Spain may be taken as typical of other parts of the empire, a *decurio* was established in every little mining centre, being charged with the care of the games, the water supply, the sanitary arrangements, and the local fortifications.

Hence Calpurnius must have been a very well-known man, and his son, as a captive, a specially valuable asset to the Irish raiders.

Patrick speaks of the raid in which he was carried off, as if there were nothing unusual in the occurrence; and there had been since the close of the third century a series of Irish raids on the Welsh coast, and of settlements inland in Wales. It was to check these, and re-establish Roman-British authority, that Cunedda, no doubt because of his influential tribal connections, was commissioned to return from the district between the walls of Solway and Clyde, in the first decade of the fifth century. The genealogy of his descendants shows a series of great political and religious leaders, who always reverted to their ancestral possessions in the Isle of Avallon. One of his great-grandsons, St Gwytherin (i.e. Victorinus), betook himself to Avallon not very long after the death of Patrick, and there founded a community house, 'Insula Victorini'.

The word 'insula' could not here mean the whole of the Avallon Island, for Avallon already had upon it Joseph's church and its surrounding buildings, and Patrick's settlement; but it was used in what may be called its military sense, for a group of soldiers' quarters and stores, such as filled each of the corners made by the roads which crossed each other through the camp, was an 'insula'.

Hence the actual meaning of 'Insula Victorini' would be 'the convent or monastery quarters of Victorinus'. This in the British language became Yneswitherim, which the passage of time reduced to Yniswitrim; and through that form it became by way of the Latin *vitreus* a plaything for the monkish fabulists, who thought the name of their foundation had something to do with *glass* and the aspect of its shallow surrounding waters.

VIII. *Glastonbury*

But the name 'Glastonbury' reveals that it belongs at least to the seventh century, for it means 'the fort of the descendants of Glast', and Glast was a military commander in high favour with King Arthur when he was fighting his twelve great battles against the heathen. Glast, who from the way in which his name has been impressed on history, had inherited the gifts and powers of his grandfather

Cunedda, was in the year AD 510 defending the important strategic point of Luitcoyt, where the Watling Street which led from London to Chester was crossed by the Iknild Way, along which the megalithic or Iberian metalseekers had travelled from St Davids to the lead mines in Derbyshire. Luitcoyt was the Roman fort of Letocetum, two miles west of the present city of Litchfield, which preserves in its first syllable the original Celtic name of the place, Letoc. It was being besieged by an Anglo-Saxon army, and Arthur coming to Glast's relief, routed them, in the tenth of his great battles, at the River Bassas, now known as Hammerwich Water, which runs below Lichfield, and has left traces of its former name in the three Staffordshire Basfords. Routed from Luitcoyt, which seems even then to have been a See city — William of Malmesbury calls it Escebtiorne (a word compounded from the Welsh *escob*, bishop, and *teign*, lordship) — the heathen determined, in their furious hatred of Christianity, to make an effort to secure and destroy the venerable sanctuary at Avallon, and moved westward; Arthur himself moved to intercept them at Mt Badon, near Bath, where in his last great battle, he inflicted on them a defeat from which they did not recover for fifty years. But he could not with certainty anticipate that issue, and so he directed Glast to go to the protection of the home of his ancestors. Accordingly Glast took the Iknild Way until it joined the Fosse, followed the Fosse to Bath, and thence took the right hand road to Wells, and so came to Avallon.

It was still a place of great importance, for its wealth in metals and the forging of them — had not Arthur's famous sword 'Excalibur' been wrought at Afallach? — and it would have been a great prize for the invaders. 'Glast on coming saw that it was rich in manifold sources of wealth' (eam multimodis bonis affluentem uidit). But even more serious was the threat of these invaders to the oldest Christian sanctuary in Britain, and every nerve therefore had to be strained for its defence. Glast seems to have repaired and strengthened Ponter's Ball, which after five hundred years of peace was still likely to be of as much value as before in checking invasion from the land side, and the marshes and the open river Brue made Avallon practically impregnable on the other three sides. But the invaders never came; the sanctuary remained inviolate; and Arthur's body was brought there by water for interment in the grave in which in AD 1191 his body was found in a massive trunk of oak. There was a slab inscribed, 'Hic iacet sepultus inclytus rex Arthurus in insula Avalonia.'

Glast remained, after Arthur's burial, as a kind of overlord in his ancestral estates, and his descendants maintained his name and fame, so that when, more than a hundred years later, the Saxons had become Christians and occupied Avallon, they not only called the town 'Glaston — but King Kenwalch gave special honour to the

Abbey, and confirmed it, in 670, in the possession of 'the adjacent islands'. These were they in which Patrick's companions had lived in Irish fashion, as anchorets, and which on that account were known by their names: as they answered to the description given by Posidonius they help us to recognize in Avallon the Isle of Ictis.

PART II
THE GLASTONBURY GRAIL

The Glastonbury Grail

Probably predating the association of Glastonbury with Arthur was belief that the site of the Abbey was built upon ground hallowed by the feet of many generations of saints and holy men — possibly even by those of Christ himself. The tradition was well founded by the Middle Ages, and lies at the heart of the claim that Glastonbury is worthy to be called 'this holiest earth'.

According to the tradition, Joseph of Arimathea, a wealthy Jewish tin trader, visited Britain on more than one occasion, on one of which his 'nephew' accompanied him. This nephew is believed by some to have been Jesus, and the visit to Britain to account for the 'missing' years between childhood and the beginning of his ministry. In various parts of Cornwall this belief has been kept very much alive; there is still a saying, current until recently among the miners in the area of St Just-in-Roseland, that 'Joseph was in the tin trade!' Such an affirmation indicates the continuing strength of the tradition as well as contributing to it.

After the events of the crucifixion of Christ legend has it that the Saviour appeared to Joseph, who had been imprisoned for his beliefs, and entrusted to him both the cup with which the first Eucharist was celebrated, and the secrets of its use. These secrets, grown with the centuries into a body of mystical lore, became the centre of the medieval Grail texts. Here also it was told how Joseph, miraculously kept alive by the dove of the Holy Spirit, was released and fled, with a small group of followers, to Britain. Here they made their way inland, eventually reaching a hill where Joseph planted his staff. The wood at once took root and burst into flower. The travellers decided to remain in this spot, found some land on which they were allowed to settle, and built the first church in which Joseph enshrined the Cup, which he had brought with him.

Thus began the legend that was to flower into the vast epic of the Grail myth. Rapidly subsumed into the body of the Arthurian mythos, it gave rise to the wondrous story of the Quest for the Cup by Arthur's knights; the Grail was not, in the end, discovered at Glastonbury, but in the mystical city of Sarras, a place outside time and space.

None the less the story remained entrenched in local tradition. It grew in the telling and people began to come to Glastonbury in search of the fabled vessel. It was, of course, never found, despite occasional claims to the contrary, being in truth more the representation of an idea than a physical object. People still come to Glastonbury in search of spiritual reality, and many find it, in their own way, interpreting the myths as they will.

In the selection of essays that follows we begin with the vision of King Arthur from the thirteenth-century romance of *Perlesvaus*, or, as it is sometimes called, *The High History of the Holy Graal*. This text, which was almost certainly written at Glastonbury, or by someone who knew the area, refers to the Abbey as 'the Holy House at the head of the Moors Adventurous' — a likely enough description when all is said. This is followed by an account of the early Joseph traditions by J. Armitage Robinson, Dean of Wells, whose investigations into the legends of Glastonbury greatly extended the depths of knowledge available.

Next comes a medieval account of the saint's life, which despite its occasionally archaic language carries the powerful charge of tradition. Finally in this section, J. W. Taylor traces the stories of Joseph and the Grail through the stages of their development into a fully-fledged legend.

5

King Arthur's Vision of the Grail [from *the High History of the Holy Graal*][1]

The authority of the scripture telleth us that after the crucifixion of Our Lord, no earthly King set forward the Law of Jesus Christ so much as did King Arthur of Britain, both by himself and by the good knights that made repair to his court. Good King Arthur after the crucifixion of Our Lord, was such as I tell you, and was a puissant King, and one that well believed in God, and many were the good adventures that befel at his court. And he had in his court the Table Round that was garnished of the best knights in the world. King Arthur after the death of his father led the highest life and most gracious that ever king led, in such sort that all the princes and all the barons took example of him in well-doing. For ten years was King Arthur in such estate as I have told you, nor never was earthly king so praised as he, until that a slothful will came upon him and he began to lose the pleasure in doing largesse that he wont to have, nor was he minded to hold court neither at Christmas-tide nor at Easter nor at Pentecost. The knights of the Table Round when they saw his well-doing wax slack departed thence and began to hold aloof from his court, insomuch as that of three hundred and three-score and six knights that he wont to have of his household, there were now not more than a five-and-twenty at most, nor did no adventure befal any more at his court. All the other princes had slackened of their well-doing for that they saw King Arthur maintain so feebly. Queen Guenievre was so sorrowful thereof that she knew not what counsel to take with herself, nor how she might so deal as to amend matters so God amended them not. From this time beginneth the history.

It was one Ascension Day that the King was at Cardoil. He was risen from meat and went through the hall from one end to the other, and looked and saw the Queen that was seated at a window. The King went to sit beside her, and looked at her in the face and saw that the tears were falling from her eyes. 'Lady,' saith the King, 'What aileth you, and wherefore do you weep?' 'Sir', saith she, 'And I weep, good right have I; and you yourself have little right to make joy', 'Certes, Lady, I do not.' 'Sir,' saith she, 'You are right. I have seen on this high

[1] *The High History of the Holy Graal*, trans. from the French by Sebastian Evans (London, J. M. Dent, 1899).

day, or on other days that were not less high than this, when you have
had such throng of knights at your court that right uneath might any
number them. Now every day are so few therein that much shame
have I thereof, nor no more do no adventures befal therein. Wherefore
great fear have I lest God hath put you into forgetfulness.' 'Certes,
Lady,' saith the King, 'No will have I to do largesse nor aught that
turneth to honour. Rather is my desire changed into feebleness of
heart. And by this know I well that I lose my knights and the love of
my friends.' 'Sir,' saith the Queen, 'And were you to go to the chapel
of S. Augustine that is in the White Forest, that may not be found save
by adventure only, methinketh that on your back-repair you would
again have your desire of well-doing, for never yet did none
discounselled ask counsel of God but He would give it for love of him
so he asked it of a good heart.' 'Lady,' saith the King, 'And willingly
will I go, forasmuch as that you say have I heard well witnessed in
many places where I have been.' 'Sir,' saith she, 'The place is right
perilous and the chapel right adventurous. But the most worshipful
hermit that is in the Kingdom of Wales hath his dwelling beside the
chapel, nor liveth he now any longer for nought save only the glory of
God.' 'Lady,' saith the King, 'It will behove me go thither all armed
and without knights.' 'Sir,' saith she, 'You may well take with you one
knight and a squire.' 'Lady,' saith the King, 'That durst not I, for the
place is perilous, and the more folk one should take thither, the fewer
adventures there should he find.' 'Sir,' saith she, 'One squire shall you
take by my approval, nor shall nought betide you thereof save good
only, please God!' 'Lady,' saith the King, 'At your pleasure be it, but
much dread I that nought shall come of it save evil only.' Thereupon
the King riseth up from beside the Queen, and looketh before him and
seeth a youth tall and strong and comely and young, that was hight
Chaus, and he was the son of Ywain li Aoutres. 'Lady,' saith he to the
Queen, 'This one will I take with me and you approve.' 'Sir,' saith she,
'It pleaseth me well, for I have heard much witness to his valour.' The
King calleth the squire, and he cometh and kneeleth down before him.
The King maketh him rise and saith to him. 'Chaus,' saith he, 'You
shall lie within tonight, in this hall, and take heed that my horse be
saddled at break of day and my arms ready. For I would be moving at
the time I tell you, and yourself with me without more company.'
'Sir,' saith the squire, 'At your pleasure.' And the evening drew on,
and the King and Queen go to bed. When they had eaten in hall, the
knights went to their hostels. The squire remained in the hall, but he
would not do off his clothes nor his shoon, for the night seemed him
to be too short, and for that he would fain be ready in the morning at
the King's commandment. The squire was lying down in such sort as
I have told you, and in the first sleep that he slept, seemed him the
King had gone without him. The squire was sore scared thereat, and
came to his hackney and set the saddle and bridle upon him, and did

on his spurs and girt on his sword, as it seemed him in his sleep, and issued forth of the castle a great pace after the King. And when he had ridden a long space he entered into a great forest and looked in the way before him and saw the slot of the King's horse and followed the track a long space, until that he came to a launde of the forest whereat he thought that the King had alighted. The squire thought that the hoof-marks on the way had come to an end, and so thought that the King had alighted there or hard by there. He looketh to the right hand and seeth a chapel in the midst of the launde, and he seeth about it a great graveyard wherein were many coffins, as it seemed him. He thought in his heart that he would go toward the chapel, for he supposed that the King would have entered to pray there. He went thitherward and alighted. When the squire was alighted, he tied up his hackney and entered into the chapel. None did he see there in one part nor another, save a knight that lay dead in the midst of the chapel upon a bier, and he was covered of a rich cloth of silk, and had around him waxen tapers burning that were fixed in four candlesticks of gold. This squire marvelled much how this body was left there so lonely, insomuch that none were about him save only the images, and yet more marvelled he of the King that he found him not, for he knew not in what part to seek him. He taketh out one of the tall tapers, and layeth hand on the golden candlestick, and setteth it betwixt his hose and his thigh and issueth forth of the chapel, and remounteth on his hackney and goeth his way back and passeth beyond the grave-yard and issueth forth of the launde and entereth into the forest and thinketh that he will not cease until he hath found the King.

So, as he entereth into a grassy lane in the wood, he seeth come before him a man black and foul-favoured, and he was somewhat taller afoot than was himself a-horseback. And he held a great sharp knife in his hand with two edges as it seemed him. The squire cometh over against him a great pace and saith to him, 'You, that come there, have you met King Arthur in this forest?' 'In no wise,' saith the messenger, 'But you have I met, whereof am I right glad at heart, for you have departed from the chapel as a thief and a traitor. For you are carrying off thence the candlestick of gold that was in honour of the knight that lieth in the chapel dead. Wherefore I will that you yield it up to me and so will I carry it back, otherwise, and you do not this, you do I defy!' 'By my faith,' saith the squire, 'Never will I yield it you! rather will I carry it off and make a present thereof to King Arthur.' 'By my faith,' saith the other, 'Right dearly shall you pay for it, and you yield it not up forthwith.' Howbeit, the squire smiteth with his spurs and thinketh to pass him by, but the other hasteth him, and smiteth the squire in the left side with the knife and thrusteth it into his body up to the haft. The squire, that lay in the hall at Cardoil, and had dreamed this, awoke and cried in a loud voice: 'Holy Mary! The priest! Help! Help, for I am a dead man!' The King and the Queen heard the cry, and the chamberlain leapt up and said to the King: 'Sir, you may well be moving, for it is day!' The King made him be clad and shod. And the squire crieth with such strength as he hath: 'Fetch me the priest, for I die!' The King goeth thither as fast as he may, and the Queen and the chamberlain carry great torches and candles. The King asketh him what aileth him, and he telleth him all in such wise as he had dreamed it. 'Ha,' saith the King, 'Is it then a dream?' 'Yea, sir,' saith he, 'But a right foul dream it is for me, for right foully hath it come true!' He lifted his left arm. 'Sir,' saith he, 'Look you there! Lo, here is the knife that was run into my side up to the haft!' After that, he setteth his hand to his hose where the candlestick was. He draweth it forth and showeth it to the King. 'Sir,' saith he, 'For this candlestick that I present to you, am I wounded to the death!' The King taketh the candlestick and looketh thereat in wonderment for none so rich had he never seen tofore. The King showeth it to the Queen. 'Sir,' saith the squire, 'Draw not forth the knife of my body until that I be shriven.' The King sent for one of his own chaplains that made the squire confess and do his houselling right well. The King himself draweth forth the knife of the body, and the soul departed forthwith. The King made do his service right richly and his shrouding and burial. Ywain li Aoutres that was father to the squire was right sorrowful of the death of his son. King Arthur, with the approval of Ywain his father, gave the candlestick to St Paul in London, for the church was newly founded, and the King wished that this marvellous adventure should everywhere be known, and that prayer should be made in the church for the soul of the squire that was slain on account of the candlestick.

King Arthur armed himself in the morning, as I told you and began to tell, to go to the chapel of St Augustine. Said the Queen to him: 'Whom will you take with you?' 'Lady,' saith he, 'No company will I have thither, save God only, for well may you understand by this adventure that hath befallen, that God will not allow I should have none with me.' 'Sir,' saith she, 'God be guard of your body, and grant you return safely so as that you may have the will to do well, whereby shall your praise be lifted up that is now sore cast down.' 'Lady,' saith he, 'May God remember it.' His destrier was brought to the mounting-stage, and the King mounted thereon all armed. Messire Ywain li Aoutres lent him his shield and spear. When the King had hung the shield at his neck and held the spear in his hand, sword-girt, on the tall destrier armed, well seemed he in the make of his body and in his bearing to be a knight of great pith and hariment. He planteth himself so stiffly in the stirrups that he maketh the saddlebows creak again and the destrier stagger under him that was right stout and swift, and he smiteth him of his spurs, and the horse maketh answer with a great leap. The Queen was at the windows of the hall, and as many as five-and-twenty knights were all come to the mounting-stage. When the King departed, 'Lords,' saith the Queen, 'How seemeth you of the King? Seemeth he not a goodly man?' 'Yea, certes, Lady, and sore loss is it to the world that he followeth not out his good beginning, for no king nor prince is known better learned of all courtesy nor of all largesse than he, so he would do like as he was wont.' With that the knights hold their peace, and King Arthur goeth away a great pace. And he entereth into a great forest adventurous, and rideth the day long until he cometh about evensong into the thick of the forest. And he espied a little house beside a little chapel, and it well seemed him to be a hermitage. King Arthur rode thitherward and alighteth before this little house, and entereth thereinto and draweth his horse after him, that had much pains to enter in at the door, and laid his spear down on the ground and leant his shield against the wall, and hath ungirded his sword and unlaced his ventail. He looked before him and saw barley and provender, and so led his horse thither and took off his bridle, and afterwards hath shut the door of the little house and locked it. And it seemed him that there was a strife in the chapel. The ones were weeping so tenderly and sweetly as it were angels, and the other spake so harshly as it were fiends. The King heard such voices in the chapel and marvelled much what it might be. He findeth a door in the little house that openeth on a little clister whereby one goeth to the chapel. The King is gone thither and entereth into the little minster, and looketh everywhere but seeth nought there, save the images and the crucifixes. And he supposeth not that the strife of these voices cometh of them. The voices ceased as soon as he was within. He marvelleth how it came that this house and hermitage were solitary, and what had become of the hermit that dwelt therein. He drew nigh the altar of the chapel and beheld in front thereof a coffin all discovered, and he saw the hermit lying therein all clad in his vestments, and seeth the long beard down to his girdle, and his hands crossed upon his breast. There was a cross above him, whereof the image came as far as his mouth, and he had life in him yet, but he was nigh his end, being at the point of death. The King was before the coffin a long space, and looked right fainly on the hermit, for well it seemed him that he had been of a good life. The night was fully come, but within was a brightness of light as if a score of candles were lighted. He had a mind to abide there until that the good man should have passed away. He would fain have sate him down before the coffin, when a voice warned him right horribly to begone thence, for that it was desired to make a judgement within there, that might not be made so long as he were there. The King departed, that would willingly have remained there, and so returned back into the little house, and sate him down on a seat whereon the hermit wont to sit. And he heareth the strife and the noise begin again within the chapel, and the ones he heareth speaking high and the others low, and he knoweth well by the voices, that the ones are angels and the others devils. And he heareth that the devils are distraining on the hermit's soul, and that judgement will presently be given in their favour, whereof make they great joy. King Arthur is grieved in his heart when he heareth that the angels' voices are stilled. The King is so heavy, that no desire hath he neither to eat nor to drink. And while he sitteth thus, stooping his head toward the ground, full of vexation and discontent, he heareth in the chapel the voice of a Lady that spake so sweet and clear, that no man in this earthly world, were his grief and heaviness never so sore, but and he had heard the sweet voice of her pleading would again have been in joy. She saith to the devils: 'Begone from hence, for no right have ye over the soul of this good man, whatsoever he may have done aforetime, for in my Son's service and mine own is he taken, and his penance hath he done in this hermitage of the sins that he hath done.' 'True, Lady,' say the devils, 'But longer had he served us than he hath served you and your Son. For forty years or more hath he been a murderer and robber in this forest, whereas in this hermitage but five years hath he been. And now you wish to thieve him from us.' 'I do not. No wish have I to take him from you by theft, for had he been taken in your service in such-wise as he hath been taken in mine, yours would he have been, all quit.' The devils go their way all discomfit and aggrieved; and the sweet Mother of our Lord God taketh the soul of the hermit, that was departed of his body, and so commendeth it to the angels and archangels that they make present thereof to Her dear Son in Paradise. And the angels take it and begin to sing for joy *Te Deum laudamus*. And the Holy Lady leadeth them and goeth her way along with them. Josephus maketh remembrance of this history and telleth us that this worthy man was named Calixtus.

King Arthur was in the little house beside the chapel, and had heard the voice of the sweet Mother of God and the angels. Great joy had he, and was right glad of the good man's soul that was borne thence into Paradise. The King had slept right little the night and was all armed. He saw the day break clear and fair, and goeth his way toward the chapel to cry God mercy, thinking to find the coffin discovered there where the hermit lay; but so did he not! Rather, was it covered of the richest tomb-stone that any might ever see, and had on the top a red cross, and seemed it that the chapel was all incensed. When the King had made his orison therein, he cometh back again and setteth on his bridle and saddle and mounteth, and taketh his shield and spear and departeth from the little house and entereth into the forest and rideth a great pace, until he cometh at right hour of tierce to one of the fairest laundes that ever a man might see. And he seeth at the entrance a paled bar, and looketh to the right or ever he should enter therein, and seeth a damsel sitting under a great leafy tree, and she held the reins of her mule in her hand. The damsel was of great beauty and full seemly clad. The King turneth thitherward and so saluteth her and saith: 'Damsel,' saith he, 'God give you joy and good adventure.' 'Sir,' saith she, 'So may He do to you!' 'Damsel,' saith the King, 'Is there no hold in this launde?' 'Sir,' saith the damsel, 'No hold is there save a most holy-chapel and a hermit that is beside St Augustine's chapel.' 'Is this then St Augustine's chapel?' saith the King. 'Yea, Sir, I tell it you for true, but the launde and the forest about is so perilous that no knight returneth thence but he be dead or wounded; but the place of the chapel is of so great worthiness that none goeth thither, be he never so discounselled, but he cometh back counselled, so he may thence return on live. And Lord God be guard of your body, for never yet saw I none aforetime that seemed more like to be good knight, and sore pity would it be and you were not, and never more shall I depart me hence and I shall have seen your end.' 'Damsel,' saith the King, 'Please God, you shall see me repair back thence.' 'Certes,' saith the damsel, 'Thereof should I be right glad, for then should I ask you tidings at leisure of him that I am seeking.' The King goeth to the bar whereby one entereth into the launde, and looketh to the right into a combe of the forest and seeth the chapel of St Augustine and the right fair hermitage. Thitherward goeth he and alighteth, and it seemeth him that the hermit is apparelled to sing the mass. He reineth up his horse to the bough of a tree by the side of the chapel and thinketh to enter thereinto, but, had it been to conquer all the kingdoms of the world, thereinto might he not enter, albeit there was none made him denial thereof, for the door was open and none saw he that might forbid him. Sore ashamed is the King thereof. howbeit, he beholdeth an image of Our Lord that was there within and crieth Him of mercy right sweetly, and looketh toward the altar. And he looketh at the holy hermit that was robed to sing mass and said his *Confiteor*, and seeth at his right hand the fairest Child that ever he had seen, and He was clad in an alb and had a golden crown on his head loaded with precious stones that gave out a full great brightness of light. On the left hand side, was a Lady so fair that all the beauties of the world might not compare them with her beauty. When the holy hermit had said his *Confiteor* and went to the altar, the Lady also took her Son and went to sit on the right hand side towards the altar upon a right rich chair and set her Son upon her knees and began to kiss Him full sweetly and saith: 'Sir,' saith she, 'You are my Father and my Son and my Lord, and guardian of me and of all the world.' King Arthur heareth the words and seeth the beauty of the Lady and of the Child, and marvelleth much of this that She should call Him her Father and her Son. He looketh at a window behind the altar and seeth a flame come through at the very instant that mass was begun, clearer than any ray of sun nor moon nor star, and evermore it threw forth a brightness of light such that and all the lights in the world had been

together it would not have been the like. And it is come down upon
the altar. King Arthur seeth it who marvelleth him much thereof. But
sore it irketh him of this that he may not enter there-within, and he
heareth, there where the holy hermit was singing the mass, right fair
responses, and they seem him to be the responses of angels. And when
the Holy Gospel was read, King Arthur looked toward the altar and
saw that the Lady took her Child and offered Him into the hands of
the holy hermit, but of this King Arthur made much marvel, that the
holy hermit washed not his hands when he had received the offering.
Right sore did King Arthur marvel him thereof, but little right would
he have had to marvel had he known the reason. And when the Child
was offered him, he set Him upon the altar and thereafter began his
sacrament. And King Arthur set him on his knees before the chapel
and began to pray to God and to beat his breast. And he looked
toward the altar after the preface, and it seemed him that the holy
hermit held between his hands a man bleeding from His side and in
His palms and in His feet, and crowned with thorns, and he seeth Him
in His own figure. And when he had looked on Him so long and
knoweth not what is become of Him, the King hath pity of Him in his
heart of this that he had seen, and the tears of his heart come into his
eyes. And he looketh toward the altar and thinketh to see the figure of
the man, and seeth that it is changed into the shape of the Child that
he had seen tofore.

When the mass was sung, the voice of a holy angel said *Ite, missa est.*
The Son took the Mother by the hand, and they evanished forth of the
chapel with the greatest company and the fairest that might ever be
seen. The flame that was come down through the window went away
with this company. When the hermit had done his service and was
divested of the arms of God, he went to King Arthur that was still
without the chapel. 'Sir,' saith he to the King, 'Now may you well
enter herein and well might you have been joyous in your heart had
you deserved so much as that you might have come in at the beginning
of the mass.' King Arthur entered into the chapel without any
hindrance. 'Sir,' saith the hermit to the King, 'I know you well, as did
I also King Uther Pendragon your father. On account of your sins and
your deserts might you not enter here while mass was being sung. Nor
will you to-morrow save you shall first have made amends of that you
have misdone towards God and towards the saint that is worshipped
herewithin. For you are the richest King of the world and the most
adventurous, wherefore ought all the world to take ensample of you in
well-doing and in largesse and in honour; whereas you are now an
ensample of evil-doing to all rich worshipful men that be now in the
world. Wherefore shall right sore mishap betide you and you set not
back your doing to the point whereat you began. For your court was
the sovran of all courts and the most adventurous, whereas now is it

least of worth. Well may he be sorry that goeth from honour to shame, but never may he have reproach that shall do him ill, that cometh from shame to honour, for the honour wherein he is found rescueth him to God, but blame may never rescue the man that hath renounced honour for shame, for the shame and wickedness wherein he is found declare him guilty.'

Figure 3: 'St Joseph of Arimathea' from a window in Langport church.

6

Joseph of Arimathea[1]

J. ARMITAGE ROBINSON

The Early Tradition

Of Joseph of Arimathea, as we have already said, William of Malmesbury knows nothing. But in the introductory chapter by another hand, prefixed to the *De Antiquitate* in the middle of the thirteenth century, we hear for the first time that at the head of the twelve disciples whom St Philip sent over from Gaul he placed, as it is said (*ut ferunt*), Joseph of Arimathea. We are further told that the pagan king to whom they came was not willing to accept their teaching, yet as they had come from far he gave them the island of Yniswitrin. Afterwards he and two other kings in succession gave each of them a portion of land; and these portions afterwards came to be known as the Twelve Hides. At the bidding of the archangel Gabriel they built a church of wattles in honour of the Blessed Mary, thirty-one years after the Passion of our Lord and fifteen after the Assumption of the Virgin. This was the first church in the land, and it was dedicated to His Mother by the Lord Himself. After these first disciples had fallen asleep, the place was deserted until the days of King Lucius, when the chapel was discovered and repaired by Phagan and Deruvian, the missionaries from Rome. The story had been told thus, as we have seen, in St Patrick's charter — the only new point made here being the bare mention of Joseph of Arimathea as the leader of the original band.

A long marginal note to the first original section of the *De Antiquitate*, added by an early hand, says: 'That Joseph of Arimathea, the noble counsellor, with his son Josephes and many others, came to Greater Britain (which is now called Anglia) and there ended his life, is attested by the book of *The Deeds of the famous King Arthur*.' For this statement reference is made to 'the Quest of Lancelot de Lac', and to 'the Quest of the vessel which there they call the Holy Grail'. Another early note says: 'For this chapter see the whole of the fourth book, and most of the fifth, of the Brut (*Bruti*).' The reference here is to the *Historia Regum Britanniae* of Geoffrey of Monmouth (capp. iv, v.).

So much for the *De Antiquitate* in its latest and most expanded form.

[1] from J. Armitage Robinson, *Two Glastonbury Legends* (Cambridge University Press, 1926).

Figure 4: 'St Joseph of Arimathea' by Horace Knowles

Our next authority is John of Glastonbury, from whom we may see the extraordinary amplification of the story which had taken place before the end of the fourteenth century. His book was published by Hearne in 1726; and copies of it are now so rare outside the great libraries that we shall be justified in giving a somewhat full account of what he has to tell us in this connexion.

First, we note that he had before him the enlarged edition of the *De Antiquitate*, just as we have it today; for he states in his prologue that William of Malmesbury wrote an account of the abbey 'from the coming of St Joseph' down to the time of Henry of Blois; but, as we have seen, the coming of St Joseph is only barely mentioned, with an *ut ferunt*, in the introductory chapter which belongs to the latest stage of the enlargement.

After he has given the Bounds of the Twelve Hides, he goes on to speak of 'the Saints who rest in the church of Glastonbury' (p. 16). Here, after embodying a few sentences from *De Antiq.*, p. 27, he inserts at the head of the list Joseph of Arimathea and his son Josephes. On p. 29, after a few lines from William of Malmesbury (*De Antiq.*, p. 42), he comes back to the subject of burials, and quotes a prophecy of Melkin the British bard. This is a queer piece of semi-poetical prose, intended to mystify and hardly capable of translation into English.

> Avalon's island, with avidity
> Claiming the death of pagans,
> More than all in the world beside,
> For the entombment of them all,
> Honoured by chanting spheres of prophecy:
> And for all time to come
> Adorned shall it be
> By them that praise the Highest.
> Abbadaré, mighty in Saphat,
> Noblest of pagans,
> With countless thousands
> There hath fallen on sleep.
> Amid these Joseph in marble,
> Of Arimathea by name,
> Hath found perpetual sleep:
> And he lies on a two-forked line
> Next the south corner of an oratory
> Fashioned of wattles
> For the adoring of a mighty Virgin
> By the aforesaid sphere-betokened
> Dwellers in that place, thirteen in all.
> For Joseph hath with him
> In his sarcophagus
> Two cruets, white and silver,
> Filled with blood and sweat
> Of the Prophet Jesus.
> When his sarcophagus
> Shall be found entire, intact

In time to come, it shall be seen
And shall be open unto all the world:
Thenceforth nor water nor the dew of heaven
Shall fail the dwellers in that ancient isle.
For a long while before
The day of judgement in Josaphat
Open shall these things be
And declared to living men.

Of this supposed pagan prophecy we shall have to say something later, especially in connexion with the *duo fassula* — the 'two cruettes' of the metrical *Lyfe of Joseph of Armathia*.

After this John of Glastonbury goes on to speak of King Coel, Caradoc of Cornwall, King Arthur, and a host of others. Then (p. 48) we are given 'a Treatise concerning Joseph of Arimathea, drawn from a certain book, which the Emperor Theodosius found at Jerusalem in Pilate's Judgement Hall.' This title guides us at once to the early apocryphal book known by the name of *Gesta Pilati*, or the Gospel of Nicodemus. This work had long been popular in England, and an Anglo-Saxon version of part of it goes back, it is said, to the beginning of the eleventh century. From this book we are now given an extract, which contains all that is there related as to Joseph of Arimathea. It may be summarized as follows:

> The Jews, hearing that Joseph had buried the body of Jesus, sought to take him and Nicodemus and certain others. When they opened the cell he was not there. It was presently (after the Ascension) found that he was in his own city of Arimathea. The high priests were rejoiced at the discovery, and sent a letter of invitation by some of his friends, asking him to come in peace. On his return to Jerusalem they asked him to explain how he got away. Four angels had lifted the cell into the air, whilst he stood in prayer; and the Lord had appeared to him. Joseph had saluted Him as *Rabboni Elias*. He was told that it was not Elijah, but Jesus: and the Lord at his request took him to the Sepulchre and shewed him the grave-clothes. 'Then I knew that it was Jesus, and I worshipped Him, and said, Blessed is He that cometh in the Name of the Lord.' They then went together to Arimathea, and he was bidden to abide there till the fortieth day. The Lord then said, 'I will go to My disciples,' and with these words He disappeared.

All this is taken almost word for word from the Latin version of the Gospel of Nicodemus.[1] But that book has no more to tell us of the story of Joseph of Arimathea.

Our writer now proceeds to say that Joseph became a disciple of Philip the apostle, who baptized him and his son Josephes. Afterwards he was appointed by St John to attend on the Blessed Virgin (in Jerusalem), while that apostle was busy at his work in Ephesus; and so

[1] Tischendorf. *Evangelia Apocrypha*, ed. 2, cc. 11, 12 and 15.

it came about that he was present at her Assumption. The ground of this last statement would appear to be one of the Latin forms of the *Transitus Mariae*, or the Passing of Mary, which claims to be written by Joseph of Arimathea himself.[2]

The narrative then proceeds (p. 51):

> In the fifteenth year after this he went to St Philip in Gaul, taking with him Josephes, whom the Lord had consecrated a bishop in the city of Sarath. For when the disciples were dispersed throughout the world after the Lord's Ascension Philip (as Freculfus tells us in the fourth chapter of his second book) went to the kingdom of the Franks, where he converted and baptized many. Then the apostle, desiring that the word of God should be spread abroad, sent twelve of his disciples to preach in Britain, placing at their head his favourite disciple Joseph of Arimathea, together with his son Josephes.

The last two sentences come from the thirteenth-century introduction prefixed to William of Malmesbury's book, save for the mention of Josephes in the final clause. What follows is a further extension of the story, and here the source of it is told us (p. 52):

> There came with them (as it is read in the book which is called *The Holy Grail*) six hundred and more, both men and women, who all took a vow to abstain from matrimonial intercourse until they should have entered the land that was appointed for them. This vow all failed to keep, save one hundred and fifty; and these at the Lord's command crossed the sea on the shirt of Josephes on the night of the Lord's Resurrection, and reached land in the morning. When the rest repented and Josephes prayed for them, a ship was sent by the Lord, which King Solomon had curiously wrought in his day to last till the times of Christ. And so they reached their fellows on the same day.

We need not pursue in detail the story of their adventures. Joseph was imprisoned by the perfidious king of North Wales. After his release by the king of Sarras, he and Josephes and ten others passed through Britain, where Arviragus was reigning, in the sixty-third year from the Incarnation of the Lord. This king, though he rejected their message, gave them the island of Yniswitrin, that is, the Glassy Isle. Here we are back again with the introduction prefixed to William of Malmesbury's book, save for the explanation of the name Yniswitrin. But four rude Latin verses follow, which introduce the name of Avalon.

> Avallon is entered by a band of Twelve:
> Joseph, Armathea's flower, is chief of them;
> And with his father cometh Josephes.
> So to these Twelve Glastonia's rights are given.

The lines are said to be by a certain metrical writer. The story of the

---

[2] Tischendorf, *Apocalypses Apocryphae*, 113 ff.; MS C.

building of the chapel follows as before. Joseph in due course is buried among his companions on the two-forked line next the oratory. The place became deserted and waste, until the Blessed Virgin chose that her oratory should once again be brought to the memory of the faithful.

Next follows (p. 55) the writing found in *The Deeds of King Arthur*, which we have already mentioned as being one of the early marginal notes to the *De Antiquitate*.

Then comes over again the prophecy from the book of Melkin, as we have had it already, save that Melkin is here described as having been 'before Merlin.'

Presently (p. 56) a quotation is given us, from a source not mentioned, which traces the descent of King Arthur from the kindred of Joseph through his nephew Helaius. Another quotation declares that from Petrus, Joseph's cousin, was descended Loth, who married Arthur's sister, and whose sons were Walwan (i.e. Gawain) and three others.

Such is the lore of Glastonbury at the end of the fourteenth century concerning Joseph of Arimathea. We are now in a position to trace from the outset the successive stages of its development.

(1) Isidore of Seville († 638) says that St Philip preached Christ to the Gauls, and led the barbarous peoples, near neighbours of darkness and bordering on the tempestuous Ocean, to the light of knowledge and the harbour of faith.

(2) This is repeated (c.830) by Freculfus, bishop of Lisieux (Bk. II, c. 4).

(3) The anonymous biographer of St Dunstan (writing c.1000) records the legend that the first preachers of Christ in Britain found at Glastonbury a church built by no skill of man, and consecrated by our Lord Himself to the honour of His Virgin Mother.

(4) William of Malmesbury (c.1130), though he knows this story, will not commit himself further than to say that, if St Philip preached in Gaul as Freculfus said, then it was not incredible that he should have sent disciples into Britain.[3]

(5) The charter of St Patrick (c. 1220) marks a further development of the legend. The new points are that we now have twelve disciples of St Philip and St James; that they build the church at the bidding of the archangel Gabriel; and that three pagan kings give them twelve portions of land.

(6) This is again developed shortly before 1250, by the final reviser

---

[3] It is important for the tracing of the growth of the legend to recall that between (4) and (5) the Great Fire of 1184 had intervened, followed as it was by the claim to the discovery of St Dunstan's remains and of King Arthur's body with the inscription which identified Glastonbury with Avalon.

of William of Malmesbury's book, in an introductory chapter which says that the leader of St Philip's disciples was Joseph of Arimathea, and that he arrived AD 63, in the fifteenth year after the Assumption of the Blessed Virgin.

(7) To this final edition of the *De Antiquitate* two marginal notes have been added, perhaps before the end of the thirteenth century. One tells us (p. 7) that Joseph was accompanied by his son Josephes and many others, and that he died on the island. The other (p. 45) gives the names of the three kings as Arviragus, Marius and Coillus, adding that the only son of the last of these was Lucius, the first Christian king of Britain. The former note mentions the Grail Legend as its source; the latter is derived from Geoffrey of Monmouth.[4]

All this lay before John of Glastonbury, when at the end of the fourteenth century he recast the earlier history of the abbey. By him we are now given for the first time an orderly account of the full legend of Joseph of Arimathea as it was told at Glastonbury:

(1) The simplest form of St Joseph's early story — taken over word for word from the Gospel of Nicodemus.

(2) His attendance on the Blessed Virgin and his presence at her Assumption — from the *Transitus Mariae*.

(3) His connexion with St Philip who sends missionaries to Britain — an addition to the story which had been told in St Patrick's charter.

(4) The voyage to Britain on the miraculous shirt of his son Josephes; his imprisonment by the king of North Wales, and his release by King Mordrains — from 'the book which is called *The Holy Grail*'.

(5) His arrival at Glastonbury, his work and his burial there — Glastonbury additions to the legend of the Grail.

The most notable point about the Joseph story, as thus fully developed by the Glastonbury monks, is that, though confessedly based to a large extent on 'the book which is called *The Holy Grail*', it knows nothing of the Grail itself.

The origin of the Grail legend, after all that has been written about it, remains obscure. But as the tales in connexion with which the Grail first makes its appearance are Celtic tales, it is now generally believed that the Grail itself has its prototypes in the mystic cauldron of unfailing supply and the magic cup of healing, which are also elements of Celtic mythology. When the Grail first appears in the romances it is as a marvellous vessel which passes round to feed the guests, or else as a cup which miraculously revives or heals. It is one of a group of talismans, which the hero must seek, and the meaning of which he must discover, as a condition of success. It is speedily Christianized and is linked with the name of Joseph of Arimathea, who is made to

[4] The further extension of the legend — 'The Holy Thorn' and the Miracles (1502) — will come before us later.

bring it to Britain. It is the Sacred Dish of the Last Supper in Jerusalem. Joseph had begged it of Pilate after the Lord's arrest. He had held it to catch the drops of the Sacred Blood from the Cross. By an easy transition it becomes the Sacramental Cup of the Last Supper. Joseph was fed by it during the forty years of his imprisonment by the Jews, from which he was at last released by Vespasian. Joseph brought it with him on his travels, and when he came as the first Christian teacher to Britain it fed his hungering companions. It passed down in the line of his descendants who were kings or famous knights. Where was it? Who might see it? Then comes the search for it — the Quest of the Holy Grail. Arthur and his Round Table provide the heroes of this highest, holiest Quest.

Thus far Glastonbury has neither part nor lot in the matter. But the name of Avalon, already linked with Arthur, is occasionally mentioned or vaguely suggested in the Grail romances, though Joseph himself is not definitely brought thither. Joseph's part is played when he has accounted for the presence of the Grail in Britain. But Glastonbury, which at the beginning of the thirteenth century had claimed twelve disciples of St Philip as the first builders of its church of wattles, was ready by the middle of that century to place Joseph of Arimathea at their head, and to take over from the legend of the Grail the tale of his miraculous arrival in Britain.

But with the Grail itself Glastonbury would have nothing to do. It deliberately excised it from the story. It substituted the simpler version of Joseph's first imprisonment which it found in the Gospel of Nicodemus, in place of the later story of the imprisonment for forty years and the release by Vespasian,[5] into which the romances had introduced the Grail as the means of his sustenance. It felt no qualms about accepting Josephes and his miraculous shirt, the persecution by the king of North Wales and the miraculous deliverance: but it left out all mention of the part played in these stories by the Grail. It even went so far as directly to exclude it by a counter-tradition, which declared that Joseph had brought two cruets filled with the blood and sweat of the Lord, and that these two cruets were buried with him in his grave.

All this is in harmony with the fact that the Holy Grail was purely an invention of the romances, and never at any time received ecclesiastical sanction. It was probably felt that the very conception was inconsistent with the reverence due to the Blessed Sacrament. Be that as it may, the fact remains that the Glastonbury tradition to the very end, though it borrowed what it wanted from 'the book which is called *The Holy Grail*', makes no claim, no allusion even, to the Grail itself.

[5] As found in the *Vindicta Salvatoris* (Tischendorf, *Acta Apocrypha*, 471.)

Figure 5: 'The Arms of Joseph of Arimathea'

Figure 6: 'A Ship from the East' by Horace Knowles

7

The Lyfe of Joseph of Arimathea[1]

Ihesu, the royall ruby, moost hye of renowne,   [leaf 1, back]
Rested in Mary the mayde / for her humylyte;   Jesus became
And fro the realme of rightwysnes / descended down   incarnate,
To take the meke clothyng / of our humanyte.   4
The .v. welles of pyte to open, Adam restored he
On the crosse, & for vs shedde / his precyous blode;   and shed His
There was the boke vnclapsed / of perfyte charyte,   blood, being
With Longis spere smyten / hangyng on the rode.   8   smitten by Longinus' spear.

His precyous body / on the crosse beyng deed,
Sore it greued his dyscyples / euery-chone;   His disciples were
And in the olde bokes, as we rede,   grieved.
That amonge all other there was one,   12
His hert was perysshed with very compassyon.
His name called Ioseph / the lorde of Aromathy,   Joseph of
He went to pylate & full humbly desyred hym   Arimathea asks
To haue the body of Ihesu / hym for to bury.   16   for His body.

And pylate graunted hym all his askyng,
Than Ioseph retourned / with countenaunce demure,
And prayed Nycodymus / to go with hym   Nicodemus and
For to take downe / our lordes precyous body.   20   Joseph take Jesus down.
So Ioseph layde Ihesu / to rest in his septulture,
And wrapped his body / in a clothe called sendony;   Joseph wraps
Ryche was it wrought, with golde & sylke full pure,   Christ's body in
Ioseph of a mayd it bought / in Aromathy cyte.   24   'sendony'.

But yet whan Ioseph Ihesu downe toke,
The syde that the wound was on / lay to his brest;   The blood of
The colde blode / that was at our lordes herte rote   Christ falls upon
Fell within Iosephes sherte / & lay on his chest.   28   Joseph's shirt.
Truly as holy scripture sayth / there dyde it rest   [leaf 2]
At the holy place / aboue his stomake,
And whan our lorde / in the sendony was drest,   Joseph collects
Thys blode in two cruettes / Ioseph dyd take.   32   the blood in two cruets.

[1] Originally published in *Joseph of Arimathie*, ed. W. W. Skeat (London, Early English Text Society, 1872).

The Iewes herd say / that Ioseph Ihesu had buryed,
They thought that Nycodemus & he shulde repent;
The[y] went to pylat / & sayd they wer greued,
Ioseph & Nycodemus for them both they sent.   36
Than came they to pylat, to knowe all his entente,
& sayd they had buryed ihesu / as he gaue them
     lette;
'I-wys,' sayd all the jewes / that there were present,
'He shall curse the tyme / that his body dyd remeue.'

The Jews send for
Joseph and
Nicodemus.

and accuse them.

'Why,' sayd Ioseph, 'iesu was goddes owne sonne,
That ye bounde lyke a thefe / & hyng on the rode;
Also to the hert with a sharpe spere / ye hym stonge,
& with .iii. nayles made hym shede his giltles blode.
I wote well, he neuer dyd yll / but euermore gode;   45
He made the blynde to se / & heled some of lepry;
He resed Lazarus / also / by his worde,
This is true,' sayd Ioseph / 'ye knowe as well as I.'

'Ye have slain
Jesus,' said
Joseph,

'who healed
men, and raised
Lazarus.'

The Iues put Ioseph / in a stronge prison of stone,   49
In that darke house / by hym-selfe he lay.
Lyght he coude not se / for wyndowe had it none,
The[y] locked the dore / and than went theyr way.   52
Cayphas and Anna / of that kept the kay,
And sealed the dore / also / they thought to be sure;
For 'Ioseph shulde dye' / playnly dyd they say,
But paycyently all theyr truble / dyd he endure.   56

The Jews put
Joseph in a dark
prison.

Calaphas and
Annas keep the
key on it.

Than Ihesu Christ / at his resurrection
To Ioseph apered / about hye mydnyght,
And rered all the foure corners / of that pryson,
The walles he susteyned / by his great myght.   60
Ioseph, that / meruayled / seyng so great a lyght,
A full precious water / our lorde threwe in his face,
Before that hour / he sawe neuer so swete a syght.
'Who is there?' sayd Ioseph / 'art thou Elyas?'   64

[leaf 2, back]

Christ appears to
Joseph and
raises his prison.

Joseph sees a
great light.

He asks if it is
Elias.

Our lorde spake to Ioseph / & bad hym nat fere,
He sayd, 'aryse' / & toke hym vp by the hande;
'I am Ihesu / whom thou buryed in the sepulture.'
'If thou be' / sayd Ioseph / 'that here doth stande,
Gyue me the rychest / treasour / of this lande,   72
The clothe / that is called the Sendony.'
Ihesu led hym to the sepulture / & there it fonde;
'Holde, isoeph,' sayd ihesu / 'that couerture of my
     body.'   72

Christ reveals
Himself to
Joseph.

and gives him the
cloth in which He
was buried.

There ihesu bad ioseph to his owne place wende,
And sayd, 'kepe thou thy house / dayes fully forty;
Farwell,' sayd our lorde, 'Ioseph, my frende,
Where euer thou becom / peace be with the; 76
I go to my disciples / that longe after me.'
Ioseph wept for joy / that was of yeres olde,
Saynge / 'o Ihesu, worshypped may thou be;
For thy grace, I haue spyed / is better than golde.' 80

Christ tells
Joseph to stay at
home 40 days.

Joseph weeps for
joy.

Ioseph kept his house, as our lorde bad,
And on the morowe cayphace went to the pryson;
No body be there founde; than was he full sad. 83
'Where is Ioseph?' sayd anne, 'I trowe he be gon!
I marueyle,' he sayd; 'the seales were hole eche one,
And yet he out of the house is gone!'
For wo they all wyst nat what to done, 87
Sayeng, 'he that conuayed hym was a false felone.'

Caiaphas cannot
find Joseph.

Annas says he is
gone.
[leaf 3]

So worde they had that in Armathya cyte
Ioseph was / than sent they to hym gretyng
By theyr letters made full craftely,
Him lowly prayeng that theyr writing 92
He wolde² ouer-se, and as [touchyng] any thyng
That was done to hym, they were wo therfore;
And prayed to Ioseph, his louers he wolde bryng,
For they wolde be frendes with hym for euermore. 96

They hear that
Joseph is in
Arimathea,

and pray him to
come to Jerusalem.

This matter to shorten, Ioseph thyder Went,
And shewed them how theyr lorde delyuered hym
Out of the pryson; 'suche grace god me sent.'
'Well,' sayd the Iewes, 'we meruayle of one thyng,
How he gate [thee] out with all his connyng.' 101
Ioseph sayd, 'he lyfted the house fro the grounde.'
They sayd, 'by what crafte was it hanging,
That it fell nat in sonder, but stode styll sounde?'

Joseph tells them
how he was
released,

and how Christ
lifted the prison
off the ground.

'Well,' sayd Ioseph, 'this was a great wonder, 105
Whan the sharpe spere to his hart was pyght,
To se great rockes and stones breke a-sonder,
The sonne darked & withdrewe his lyght. 108
The earth trymbled by his great myght;
All these were maruaylous,' sayd Ioseph than;
'Deed bodyes in theyr graues were sene with sight;³
Wherefore I dare say, he is very god and man.' 112

Joseph reminds
them of the
wonders at the
Crucifixion.

when the dead
bodies rose.

² *Printed* holde.
³ *Printed* sihgt.

Now here how Ioseph came into englande;   [leaf 3, back]
But at that tyme it was called brytayne.
Than .xv' yere with our lady, as I vnderstande,   Joseph was 15
Joseph wayted styll / to scrue hyr he was fayne;   116   years with Mary,
So after hyr assumpcyon, the boke telleth playne,   but after her
With saynt Philyp he went into fraunce,   Assumption went
   to France with St
His sonne and his wyfe to serue god with payne,   Philip.
Fayne for to folowe vertuous gouernaunce.   120

Ioseph had a sonne whose name was Iosephas,   His son,
That our lorde a bysshop dyd consecrate,   Josephas, was
   made bishop by
A vertuous lyuer the boke sayth that he was,   Christ.
Phylip bad them go to great brytayn fortunate.   124
So to the see they went, of ioye seperate,   500 of his
For of them there were .v. C. & mo   company set out
In that company, bothe erly and late,   to go to Britain.
Taryeng for passage / togyder forto go.   128

A shyp they toke, as I ynderstande,   They take ship,
And passed without peryll ouer the salt streme;
Into the hauen they all aryued to lande,
But yet of brytayne they fayled theyr course clene. 132
They fortuned to a countre of a tyraunt kene,   but land in
Called wales, there was a kyng that tyme;   Wales on Easter
   eve, 31 years after
They landed all, as the boke telleth, on an ester   the Passion.
   euyn,
xxxi. yere after the passyon, about the houre of
   nyne.

Whan the kyng knewe that they dyd lande,   137   The king puts
He toke Ioseph and all his felowes truly,   Joseph and his
   fellows in prison.
And put them in pryson great and strong;
Than they all prayed to god almyghty,   140
And he herde theyr prayers lyghtly,   [leaf 4]
That they were delyuered in short space;
He thought his seruauntes sholde nat in peryl lye,   God condescends
Than he sent them confort by his great grace.   144   to deliver them.

Our lorde apered to a kyng in the west,   Christ appears
That named was Mordrayous in dede,   to king
   Mordrayous,
Bydding hym for to make hym prest,
With all his myght in to wales to spede;   148
Sayng, 'there be my seruauntes, that of helpe nede,   and tells him to
Go thou theder and bere thy[4] swerde in thy hande;   go to Wales.
That proude kyng that me doth nat drede
Thou shalt hym ouercome and all his lande.'   152

[4] *Printed* they.

Than the kyng, after his vysion sene,
Thought in hast his deuer to do;
So vp he rose in the mornyng,
All his lordes he called hym to.   156
He sayd, 'in to wales in dede must I go;
Now thyder wyll I hye me with all my might;
God to me appered, and bad me do so,
Agayne the prince of that countre for to fight.'   160

King Mordrayous obeys,

and prepares to go to Wales.

In all hast he dysposed his householde,
And to a lorde he toke the realme to gouerne,
To delyner goddes scruauntes he sayd he wolde;
'I knowe no maner man that shall we werne.'   164
In his journey he hyde, he thought not to turne
Tyll he came to the place there Ioseph was.
Many a towne in wales dyd he burne,
The prynce of that countre herd therof in space;   168

He makes over his own kingdom to a lord.

He burns some Welsh towns, and frightens the king.

And to Mordrayous he sent a messangere,
Prayng hym to come in with peace.
He sayd, 'this lande is poore, therefore I hym fere,
Besechyng his goodnesse this stryfe to sease;   172
And I wyll hym gyue a lady perelesse,
Myn owne doughter, by name called Labell,
Precyously arayed in cloth of rychesse;' —
He bad the messangere all this vnto hym tell.   176

[leaf 4, back]

The king of Wales submits,

and offers him his daughter, named Labell.

Than went the messangere vnto Mordrayous,
And sayd all, as is before tolde:—
'Syr kyng, my lorde the prayeth to be gracious
Vnto him, and not so fyerse and bolde;   180
And ye shall haue his doughter with plentie of golde,
With all the prysoners that in his pryson be,
Ioseph & his felowes, both yong and olde.'
Than sayd Mordrayous, 'he shall haue peace with
    me.'

A messenger comes to Mordrayous,

saying that Joseph shall be released.

On a day these kynges togeder both dyd mete,
Mordrayous toke Labell to his wyfe;
Eche saluted other with wordes swete,
And loued togyder the terme of theyr lyfe.   188
For Mordrayous was doughty with swerd & knyfe,
That all landes nere hym dyd dowt.
Ioseph was delyuered from daunger blyfe,
With his felawes, all the hole rowt.   192

Mordrayous marries Labell

Joseph is released.

Than hyther into brytayne Ioseph dyd come,
And this was by kyng Aueragas dayes;
So dyd Ioseph and also Iosephas his sonne,
With many one mo, as the olde boke says.   196
This kynge was hethen & lyued on fals layes,
And yet he gaue to Ioseph au[i]lonye,
Nowe called Glastenbury, & there he lyes;
Somtyme it was a towne of famous antyquyte.⁵   200

Joseph comes to Britain in the days of Arviragus,

[leaf 5]

who gives to Joseph Avilion, now called Glastonbury.

There Ioseph lyued with other hermyttes twelfe,
That were the chyfe of all the company,
But Ioseph was the chefe hym-selfe;
There led they an holy lyfe and gostely.   204
Tyll, at the last, Ihesu the mighty,
He sent to Ioseph thaungell gabryell,
Which bad hym, as the writyng doth specify,
Of our ladyes assumpcyon to bylde a chapell.   208

Here Joseph and 12 hermits lived.

Gabriel tells Joseph to build a chapel to Our Lady.

So Ioseph dyd as the aungell hym bad,
And Wrought there an ymage of our lady;
For to serue hyr great deuocion he had,
And that same ymage is yet at Glastenbury,
In the same churche; there ye may it se.
For it was the fyrst, as I vnderstande,
That euer was sene in this countre;
For Ioseph it made wyth his owne hande.   216

Joseph does so.

Our Lady's image is still at Glastonbury.

The rode of northdore of london also dyd he make,
Moche lyke as our lorde was on the rode done;
For this Ioseph fro the crosse hym dyd take.
And loke howe a man may make by proporcion   220
A deed ymage lyke a quycke, by cunnynge;
So lyke the rode of northdore Iesu henge deed,
For Ioseph made it nere semyng
Vnto our lorde enclynynge his heed.   224

He also made a crucifix.

now the 'Rood of Northdoor'.

Than Ioseph there abode, prechyng the fayth,
Tyll by the course of nature he dyed;
Thus the olde boke recordeth and sayth,
But in dede his body at Glastenbury doth abyde. 228
Our lorde for hym well doth prouyde,
Likely there to be sought with many a .M.;
The name of Glastenbury wyll sprede full wyde
To men & women of many a straunge lande.   232

[leaf 5, back]

Joseph dies.

He is buried at Glastonbury,

where he is sought by many a thousand.

⁵ *Printed* autyquyte.

By whose prayer god sheweth many myrakyll,
Proued the .xviii. yere of henry our kyng;
In doltyng parysshe, there was sicke longe whyle
Two yonge women of the pestelence, lamentyng,   236
Which passed the cure of men in eche thynge.
Theyr prayer makyng to joseph of Aramathye,
So began to recouer, & brought theyr offryng
On Symone day & Iude vnto Glastenbury.   240

And syth god there hath shewed many a myrakyl,
I lacke tyme & season all to expresse;
But yet all that do vysyte that holy habytakyll,
It is euer lyke newe to them that call in distresse.   144
Four C. yere ago / the boke bereth wytnes,
So longe there hath rested that holy body;
And nowe pleaseth it god, of his goodnesse,
Great myracles for hym to worke, as ye may se.   248

Many be there holpen through our lordes myght;
A chylde of welles raysed fro deth without dout.
Lame ar there heled, the blynde restored to sight;
One that had the fransy to his wytte was brought.
The vykary of welles, that thyder had sought,
On the tenth day, that many men dyd se,
Where .iiii. yere afore he stande nor go mought,
Released he was of part of his infyrmyte.   256

There is continuaunce of grace, as it is shewed
On a woman of banwell, the wyfe of Thomas Roke,
whyche was tempted by the fende & greatly styred;
With hyr husbandes knyues she cut hyr throte,   260
And doubtlesse, as true men do report,
She slewe hyr selfe, so greuous was the wounde.
For wo hyr husband wyst not whether to resort,   263
Whan he sawe hyr all blody & his own knife found.

This wofull man, seynge his wyfe thus lye,
Whiche with his knyfe had done that wofull dede,
Vnto his neyghbours he cryed full pyteously,
Hym for to helpe in that tyme of nede.   268
The wounde to sewe fast he began to spede,
Besechynge our lorde and holy Ioseph,
This woman to saue, and so hertely prayed,
That anone after she began to drawe brethe.   272

In the 18th year of our king Henry, two women of Dolting parish were healed of the pestilence, and offered at Glastonbury on St Simon's day.

Many miracles have happened there.

His body has lain there 400 [P 1400] years.

A child, of Wells, was raised to life there.

[leaf 6]
The vicar of Wells was cured of lameness.

The wife of Thomas Roke, of Banwell,

cut her throat with a knife.

Her husband cried out for help.

He sewed up the wound, prayed to Joseph, and she recovered.

And they yet say, that the stytches brake,

The stitches broke, but the flesh closed.

That the flesshe / closed, and that was wonder;
She was confessed / hoseled / eneled, and spake,
Therefore, good men, this in your myndes ponder;276
yet lyueth, & in the .ix. day of apryl came she
   thyder,

She came to Glastonbury on the 9th of April.

And went before the honourable procession.
The same knyfe she offred vp all blody there;   279
Now thanked be god & Ioseph, she is hole &
   sounde.

The .ix. day of Aprill, Iohn Lyght, gentylman,

[leaf 6, back]

Dwellynge besyde Ilchestr at lyghtes care,
His wyfe had vpon her a feuer quartayn,

John Light, of Ilchester, had a wife who had a quartan fever.

By the space of two yere vexed gretly;   284
No medycyne nor phisyke that coude do her remedy;
[She prayed to Ioseph to hele her of her payne],[6]
And promysed thyder her offrynge deuoutly,
Than was she delyuered of her dysease certayne.   288

She recovered.

The tenth daye of Apryll, that was than sonday,
A chylde was smyten with a plage all deed,

The 10th of April, a Sunday, a child died of the plague.

And to euery mannes syght an houre so he lay
His moder hertely to sent Joseph prayed,   292
And bowed[7] her offryng, in her hert sore afrayed.
The chylde recouered and had his hele,

The child recovered, and made an offering on St Mark's day.

And on saynt marke daye there they offred,
Hole and sounde; no herme dyde he fele.   296

The .xv. day of Apryll one Robert Browne,
Of yeuell, that at ylchester was prysoner,

On the 15th of April, Robert Browne of Yeovil,

He was delyuered by proclamatyon,
And went to gader his fees for the kepar.   300
The prysoner about his legge had a fetter;
He prayed ioseph to helpe him, as he was not gilty,

had a fetter on his leg, which fell off.

And sodenly the fetters sprange fro hym there,
In myddes of the market-place of Glastenbury.   304

Iohñ Gyldon, gentylman, of port melborne,
The syde of his mouth was drawen to his eare;

John Gyldon, of Milborne Port, was paralysed.

His lyft syde and his arme was benome,
That he of his lyfe stode in great fere;   308
Speke coude he nat nor hymselfe stere.
He prayed to Ioseph, promysyng his offryng,

[leaf 7]

So of his sykenes he was delyuered clere,

He was healed by Joseph.

Saue onely of an hurte in his lefte arme.   312

[6] A line omitted. Supplied from conjecture.
[7] *For* vowed?

The .xx. day of apryll, Iohñ popes wyfe of comtone,
Had a yong chylde, that was taken sodenly,
And so contynued and coude not be holpen;
His moder prayed to god and Ioseph deuoutly,   316
Her offrynge promysed, than founde she remedy.
The chylde recouered, & had his lymmes at wyll.
Lo! ye well dysposed people, here may ye se,
That there is nothynge to god impossyble.   320

The 20th of April, the wife of John Pope, of Comton, had a sick child.

He recovered.

yonge walter sergaunt, dwellynge in Pylton,
His chylde in the pestylence was in Ieopardy,
And sore panged that he myght not meue hym,
So that to theyr syght he appered deed veryly.   324
This wofull moder, as the neyghbours testefy,
Prayed to Ioseph and of the chylde the mesure,
And promysed to do her offrynge truly;
Than shortly after the chylde dyde recure.   328

The child of Walter Sergeaunt, of Pilton, was nearly dead.

He recovered.

Also Alys, wyfe to Walter benet, dwellyng in welles,
Infect with the frenche pockes a yere and more,
And doubtlesse, as her owne neyghbours telles,
Her fete were so paynfull and sore,   332
That go coude she not but as she was bore.
Thyder was she brought in-to the chapell,
Verely she was heled, and lefte her styltes thore,
And on her fete wente home resonably well.   336

Alice, wife of Walter Bennet of Wells, was quite lame.

She left her stilts in the chapel.

Iohñ Abyngdons wyfe, of welles, had a sykenesse,
Moost paynfull with a sore called a fistula;
So long it[8] contynued that she laye spechelesse,
And her lymbes dyde rotte, truly they do say,   340
So that with a knyfe the peces were cut away.
At last she thought she had sene Ioseph in pycture,
How he toke god fro the crosse, & to hym dyde pray,
Her for to hele, and than began she to recure.   344

[leaf 7, back]

The wife of John Abingdon, of Wells, had a fistula.

She was healed.

All the myracles to shewe it were to long,
There is many mo full great that I do not reherse.
As pestylence, purpyls, and agonys strong,   347
With megrymes also, & men that haue lyen
    specheles.
And this I knowe well, both in prose, ryme, & verse,
Men loue nat to rede an ouer longe thyng;
Therefore I entende this matr to short & sease,
I pray you all to marke well the endynge.   352

Many more miracles happened there.

I intend to cut this short.

[8] *Printed* is.

ye pylgrymes all, gyue your attendaunce
Saynt ioseph there to serue with humble affectyon,
At Glastenbury for to do hym reuerence;
Lyft vp your hertes with goostly deuocyon,　　356
Therwith conceyuyng this brefe compylacyon;
Though it halte in meter of eloquence,
All thyng is sayd vnder correctyon,
And wryten to do holy Ioseph reuerence.　　360

All ye pilgrims, serve St Joseph at Glastonbury.

This treatise is in Joseph's honour.

ye lettred, that wyll haue more intellygence
Of the fyrst foundacyon of Ioseph there,
The olde bokes of Glastenbury shall you ensence,
More plainly to vnderstande this forsayd matere.　364
To you shall declare the hole cronycle clere,
Wryten full truly with a notable processe.
Make ye no doute, nor be not in fere,
As olde clerkes thereof bereth wytnesse.　　368

Learned men may consult the books at Glastonbury.

[leaf 8]

Ye need not have any doubts.

Sothely Glastenbury is the holyest erth of england,
Rede saynt Dauydes lyfe, and there may ye se,
That our lorde it halowed with his owne hande;
For Dauyd by myracle proued it, parde.　　372
Chryst made through his handes two holes truely,
Than went Dauyd, and his masse began;
And, after sakeryng, the holes dyd shyt; 'a!' sayd he,
'This church was halowed by a better than I am!'

Read St David's life,

and you will find a miraculous story about Glastonbury.

Great meruaylles men may se at Glastenbury,
One of a walnot tree that there dooth stande,
In the holy grounde called the semetory,　　379
Harde by the place where kynge Arthur was founde.
South fro Iosephs chapell it is walled in rounde,
It bereth no leaues tyll the day of saynt Barnabe;
And than that tree, that standeth in the grounde,
Spreadeth his leaues as fayre as any other tree.　384

There is at Glastonbury a walnut-tree near Arthur's tomb,

which bears no leaves till St Barnabas day.

Thre hawthornes also, that groweth in werall,
Do burge and bere grene leaues at Christmas
As fresshe as other in May, whan the nightyngale
Wrestes out her notes musycall as pure as glas;　388
Of all wodes and forestes she is the chefe chauntres.
In wynter to synge yf it were her nature,
In werall she myght haue a playne place,
On those hawthornes to shewe her notes clere.　392

Three hawthorns at Werrall bear green leaves at Christmas.

The nightingale might sing there at Christmas.

Lo, lordes, what Ihesu dooth in Ianuary,
Whan the great colde cometh to grounde;
He maketh the hauthorne to sprynge full fresshely.
Where as it pleaseth hym, his grace is founde;   396
He may loose all thing that is bounde.
Thankes be gyuen to hym that in heuen sytteth,
That floryssheth his werkes so on the grounde,
And in Glastenbury, *Quia mirabilia fecit*.   400

[leaf 8, back]

Jesus makes the hawthorn bud in January.

Thanks be to Him who works miracles at Glastonbury.

St Joseph and Glastonbury[1]

J. W. TAYLOR

The Bible of Glastonbury

The counterpart, or rather 'complement', of the Provençal tradition is to be found in Aquitaine, in Brittany and in England.

In the Provençal legends, as we have seen, the name of St Joseph of Arimathea occurs as that of one member of the group of Eastern missionaries who come to the Rhone Valley in the neighbourhood of Marseilles, but one who simply passed through on his way to Britain.

Again we find his traces at Limoges (the ancient Lemovices and Augustoritum). The old Aquitaine legends concerning St Martial, the supposed first missionary Apostle of Limoges, which have a definite history reaching, at least, as far back as the tenth century (*Fastes Episcop*, vol. ii, p. 104), mention the name of St Joseph of Arimathea incidentally. St Martial, accompanied by his father and mother (Marcellus and Elizabeth), St Zaccheus (the publican of the Gospels) and St Joseph of Arimathea — all Hebrews — are represented as arriving at Limoges in the first century. St Martial is said to have remained at Limoges; the name of St Zaccheus is permanently associated with the romantic village and pilgrimage of Rocamadour, while that of St Joseph has no local resting-place.[2]

Again we find traces of the disciples or companions of St Joseph at Morlaix in Brittany. The local tradition here is that Drennalus, a disciple of St Joseph of Arimathea and first bishop of Treguier, preached the Gospel in this district about AD 72 (*North-Western France*, Augustus Hare).

Again, we find faint legendary traces of the presence of St Joseph of Arimathea in Cornwall. He is represented as coming in a boat, as bringing the infant Jesus with him and as teaching the Cornish miners how to purify their tin. But here, too, St Joseph had no settled resting-place.

[1] Originally published as Part of the Coming of the Saints by J. W. Taylor, (London, Methuen, 1906).

[2] In addition to the legend we find quasi-historical references to the mission of St Martial in ecclesiastical literature: 'Martialis, Lemovicum in Gallia episcopus et apostolus, una cum St Petro (ut volent) ex Oriente Romani venit, indeque ab eo in Gallias amandatur; ubi Lemovicensibus, Turonnensibus, aliisque ad-fidem conversis, abiit (ut exactis ejus liquet) Ann. 74 (G. Cave, *Script, Eccles, Hist, Liter, Basileae*, 1741, vol. i, 36).

Yet, again, we find his name at Glastonbury. Not only so, but the little town and adjacent country appear to be filled with ancient memories and traditions of his mission, in very much the same way as the Rhone Valley seems to be filled wth traces of the family of Bethany.

'Weary all Hill', the winter thorn, the story of the Holy Grail (or cup) he is said to have brought with him, the chalice spring, and last, but not least, St Joseph's chapel, all remain traditionally associated with his reputed coming to the Britons. In short, the tradition here is not only a report of his coming but of his life, his labours, and his end.

But this is not all. The old romances or history — romances of the Middle Ages, compiled to a large extent from old records in the Abbey of Glastonbury — appear to carry us further still.

St Joseph of Arimathea is never represented as coming to Britain alone, but as accompanied by other Hebrews, and notably his son 'Josephes'. These companions and relations are said to have intermarried with the families of the British kings or chieftains, and from them, by direct descent, in something like four hundred years, are said to have arisen the greater heroes of King Arthur's Court — the Knights of the Round Table.

About the middle of the first century AD the western country on both sides of the Severn was held by the British in comparative security, being outside the main lines of Roman conquest, and it was purposely to these (as we are told) that St Joseph and his companions came.

Now in ancient British records — the very oldest we possess — a Christian mission of about this date is definitely mentioned. Gildas, who lived early in the sixth century, wrote as follows(referring to Great Britain):

> These islands received the beams of light — that is, the holy precepts of Christ — the true Sun, as we know, at the latter part of the reign of Tiberius Caesar, in whose time this religion was propagated without impediment and death threatened to those who interfered with its professors.
> These rays of light were received with lukewarm minds by the inhabitants, but they nevertheless took root among some of them in a greater or less degree, until the nine years' persecution by the tyrant Diocletian, when the Churches throughout the whole world were overthrown. All the copies of the Holy Scriptures which could be found were burned in the streets, and the chosen pastors of God's flock butchered, together with their innocent sheep, in order that (if possible) not a vestige might remain in some provinces of Christ's religion (*History of Gildas*, sections 8, 9).

The account of Eusebius is quite in accordance with this. He writes: 'Tiberius . . . threatened death to the accusers of the Christians: a Divine providence infusing this into his mind, so that the Gospel, having freer scope at its beginning, might spread everywhere over the world.' Speaking of the events from AD 37–41, he goes on to say: 'Thus . . . the doctrine of the Saviour, like the beams of the sun, soon irradiated the whole world. Throughout every city and village Churches were found rapidly abounding and filled with members from every people' (*Eccles. Hist.*, bk. ii, chaps. ii, iii).[3]

As Tiberius Caesar died in AD 37 this very much antedates the earliest received record of any Christian mission to this country, but the date need not be insisted on too rigidly; the more especially as the news of the death of one emperor and his succession by another would often take years before it filtered to the farthest corners of the Roman Empire and its dependencies. What we do know is that through the reigns of Tiberius, Claudius and the earlier years of Nero there was but little or no hindrance to the spread of the Gospel, and that troops were continually passing between Britain and Rome during all this time. No persecution of any importance reached Great Britain until the reign of Diocletian (AD 285) when, according to the Venerable Bede, 'The persecution was more lasting and bloody than all the others before it, for it was carried on incessantly for the space of ten years with burning of Churches, outlawing of innocent persons and slaughter of martyrs. At length it reached Britain also, and many persons, with the constancy of martyrs, died in the confession of their faith' (bk. i, cap. vi).[4]

Such persecutions would — and did, no doubt — destroy nearly all the earliest written records. In many places they not only did this but practically wiped out (as they were intended to do) the existing Christianity of the day, so that fresh missions had to be undertaken in later years, but none the less the earlier message most certainly had been delivered, and the second coming brought a revival of the older teaching rather than a new and original message.

This is the more easily understood when we remember that the earliest missionaries appear to have gone directly to the peoples of the various nations, and did not, so far as we can judge, seek to influence them through their conquerors.

---

[3] Messrs. Haddan and Stubbs (and some other critics) speak of Gildas as copying Eusebius and applying his remarks to Britain without reason or authority. A close examination of the writings of both does not support this view, for Gildas and other old English writers, who follow him in their statements that 'the British were very slow to receive the gospel, and that it made but little progress among them for many years', strike a special note which cannot be found in other writers on the spread of early Christianity. This certainly supports some definite historical source for the account (see also William of Malmesbury).

[4] In this persecution they not only destroyed the churches, but they prejudiced Church history beyond recovery, for as Velserus observes. 'They burnt all the monuments which concerned the Christian Church' (Wm. Borlase, *Antiquities of Cornwall*, Oxford, Jackson, 1754).

In Britain, for example, the original message must have been delivered to the native Britons directly and not by means of Roman intercourse (or only accidentally in this way), for we have the historical evidence of Tertullian who, writing at the latter end of the second century, speaks of the 'places of the British inaccessible to the Romans' as having been already won for Christ. But by what route leading to a district 'inaccessible to the Romans' could the early Christians of the first or second century have brought the news of the Gospel?

A complete answer to this question is found in the writings of Diodorus Siculus, who lived in the time of Augustus: it was the route of the tin traders.

The passage describing this ancient British industry of tin mining and tin smelting is as follows (bk. v, cap. ii):

> They that inhabit the British promontory of Belerium, by reason of their converse with merchants, are more civilized and courteous to strangers than the rest. These are the people that make the tin, which with a great deal of care and labour they dig out of the ground; and that being rocky, the metal is mixed with some veins of earth, out of which they melt the metal and then refine it. Then they beat it into four square pieces like a die and carry it to a British isle, near at hand, called Ictis. For at low tide, all being dry between them and the island, they convey over in carts abundance of tin. But there is one thing that is peculiar to these islands which lie between Britain and Europe: for at full sea they appear to be islands, but at low water for a long way they look like so many peninsulas. Hence the merchants transport the tin they buy of the inhabitants of Gaul, and for thirty days' journey they carry it in packs upon horses' backs through Gaul to the mouth of the river Rhone.

And again:

> This tin metal is transported out of Britain into Gaul, the merchants carrying it on horseback through the heart of Celtica to Marseilles and the city called Narbo (Narbonne, vol. v, cap. 2) (*Diodorus Siculus*, Booth's trans., vol. i, p. 311).

So that, before Christ was born, we find the very route exactly described by Diodorus that was afterwards traditionally chosen by St Joseph of Arimathea.

We can retrace it step by step. From Marseilles up the Rhone as far as Arles or farther; then the thirty days' journey across Gaul, through the country of the Lemovices to the sea-coast; the stopping at Limoges; the arrival in Brittany at Vannes or Morlaix; the four days' sailing in the traders' vessels (Diodorus) across the English Channel to Cornwall and, finally, the journey inland to the British stronghold.

This well-known journey of the tin merchants presents no difficulty from the mouth of the Rhone to Cornwall, and it is only the journey beyond it — the inland journey from Cornwall to Glastonbury — that would call for the courage and determination of the explorer in an unknown land.[5]

The recognition of this route as almost certainly the route of the early missionaries, gives a special force to the Cornish tradition. Cornwall was not really Christianized until the end of the fifth or beginning of the sixth century, and then mainly by Christian missionaries from Ireland, so that we should not (prima facie) expect to find any tradition of St Joseph here. Yet here is the tradition of the actual coming of St Joseph preserved through all the centuries, and not only so, but the coming is especially associated with the old industry of the tin workers.

The legend is that 'Joseph of Arimathea came in a boat to Cornwall and brought the child Jesus with him, who taught him how to extract tin and purge it of its wolfram. When tin is flashed the tinner shouts, "Joseph was in the tin trade" ' (*Cornwall*, S. Baring-Gould, p. 57).

Again, 'There is a traditional story that Joseph of Arimathea was connected with Marazion when he and other Jews traded with the ancient tin-miners of Cornwall'' (*Guide to Penzance, Land's End and Scilly*, 5th edition, London, Ward, Lock & Co.).

Anyone who knows the eastern coast of Cornwall, the 'promontory' of the Lizard and Land's End, including Mount's Bay, cannot fail to identify Ictis with St Michael's Mount. It is close to all the old tin-mining region and still answers exactly to the description of Diodorus. Every day, at low tide, the carts go across from the mainland to the Mount over the sand or by the old immemorial causeway, and every detail corresponds to the ancient history.

The only alternative offered is that of the Isle of Wight, and this is so far from the tin-producing region, and so very unlikely to have been accessible by land within two thousand years, that it is surprising to find anyone bold enough to suggest its claims as worthy of consideration.

All the best authorities, including the late Professor Max Müller, accept the identification of St Michael's Mount with Ictis, and there can hardly be any reasonable doubt that they have the best grounds for doing so.

Whatever may have happened to the far Cornish coast toward Scilly — the supposed old Lyonesse — it is very evident that little or no change has taken place in Mount's Bay from immemorial times. We find quaint old pictures of the Mount in medieval times and histories of it under the Norman kings. 'Edward the Confessor found monks here serving God, and gave them by charter the property of the

[5] On closer study of the probable route it even appears that the last part of the journey was by no means dangerous or through an unknown country. There is an old tradition that a trading route existed from pre-Roman times between the tin mines of Cornwall and the lead mines of the Mendips. Traces of this 'way' may perhaps still be found in the 'Here path' over the Quantocks.

Mount.' Long before this it is said that St Kayne, or Kenya,[6] who lived in the latter end of the fifth century, went to pilgrimage to St Michael's Mount in Cornwall' (Borlase, *Antiquities*, p. 351 and notes; Carew, p. 130; and Capgrave, p. 204). So that the Mount through the whole of the Christian era has remained very much as we see it today, and from the very earliest times it was regarded as sacred and as a place of pilgrimage.

All the adjacent country is rich in remains of old mining works and debris. Some of these, like those of the Ding-Dong Mine, may be traced to a high antiquity; others, though long neglected, belong rather to medieval or almost modern times. The oldest rude pits containing smelted tin are called 'Jews' houses', there being a tradition that the tin mines were in very remote periods 'wrought by the Jews with pickaxes of holm, box and hartshorn — tools sometimes found among the rubble of such works' (Edwards).

'There is scarcely a spot in Cornwall where tin is at present found that has not been worked over by the "old men", as the ancient miners are always called; . . . upon whatever spot the old miner has worked there we are told the Phoenician has been or the Jew has mined. The existence of the terms "Jews' houses", "Jews' tin", "Jews' leavings", "attall" and "attall Saracen", prove the connection of these strangers with the Cornish mines' (Hunt, *Romances of the West*).

From the supplement to Polwhele's *History of Cornwall* (Falmouth, 1803) we find that the oldest smelting-places are called 'Jews' houses', the old blocks of tin occasionally found are called 'Jews' pieces', and the stream works of tin that have been formerly deserted by the labourers are called 'Jews' works' or 'atall Saracen'. 'The Jews appear to have called themselves or were called by the Britons of Cornwall "Saracens".'

Now, although the ancient presence and influence of the Jew in Cornwall is marked and undeniable — names and places like 'Bojewyan' (abode of the Jews), 'Trejewas' (Jews' village) and 'Market Jew' being well-known examples of such influence, and these, as well as the historical 'Jewish windows' in St Neot's church and other Jewish monuments and memories abundantly supplementing the older traditions of the 'Jews' houses' and 'Jews' leavings' — it is by no means easy to fix the date of the earliest Jewish appearance and influence on the country.

In the reign of King John we know that the Jews were working or farming the tin mines, not as slaves but as masters and exporters,[7]

[6] Kenia, 'daughter of Braganus Prince of Brecknock'. She died on the eighth day before the Ides of October, AD 490 (Cressy's *Saints*).

[7] In the time of King John, the tin mines (were) farmed by the Jews for 100 marks,' and later, 'the Jews being banished they' (the tin mines) 'were *neglected*' (Camden's *Britannia*, vol. i, p. 9).

and whether the bulk of the Jewish traditions date from this time or from a much older period it is difficult to determine.

The tin used by the Greeks came from the 'Cassiterides', and these islands were 'situated in the extremes of Europe toward the West' (Herodotus, 400 BC). Mr Copeland Borlase, the best authority on the subject, unhesitatingly states that Cornwall is the country indicated by Herodotus. The earliest workers of the tin mines here, however, are really unknown.

They do not appear to have been the British themselves, nor do they appear to have been the Phoenicians, who were the commercial traders or middle-men rather than the actual workers of the tin. For, although occasional Phoenician antiquities have been discovered in Cornwall, there are no traces here of any genuine Phoenician graves. The oldest graves that have been found — those of the Harlyn Bay discoveries, near Padstow — are remarkable as showing that the earliest settlers in Cornwall and, as some think, the first tin workers, were buried exactly like the prehistoric Egyptians, in a crouching position on the left side with the knees almost touching the chin.[8]

All the graves have slanting lids, a method of covering still in common use among the Turks; and the race here buried, though prehistoric in Cornwall, need not be regarded as belonging to any very remote antiquity, but may have lived at any time from 400 BC to near the Christian era. Gold, bronze and iron ornaments, and Roman pottery have been found either within or in close proximity to these early graves.[9]

Such evidence and tradition as we have seem to point to the settlement in Cornwall of some pre-British Eastern race, who worked the tin mines, were buried, like some of the old Egyptians, in a crouching position on the side, and left an obscure but ineffaceable impress on the language, customs and work of the land and (by inter-marriage?) on the very race or races that succeeded them.[10] By the time of Diodorus or Christ these as well as the true Phoenician traders may have lost some of their chief national characteristics, and the

[8] Mr J. B. Cornish, of Penzance, writes: 'The idea that these (Harlyn skeletons) are the remains of the pre-Cornish tin workers is my own explanation of the mystery that whereas we know that tin was worked in and exported from Cornwall in the time of Julius Caesar, on the other hand the earliest of modern historical records and all subsequent evidence go to show that the Cornish people themselves did not work the metal.'

[9] *Harlyn Bay and the Discoveries of its Pre-historic Remains*, by R. A. Bullen, BA, London Swan, Sonnenschein & Co., 1902. See also British Museum, Egyptian Room No. 1. No. 3, 275.

[10] It is noteworthy than John of Fordun, the Scottish historian (1384–87), describes the original Irish or 'Scots' as coming from Egypt. Bede, on the other hand, speaks of Great Britain as containing five nations — the English, Britons, Scots, Picts, and Latins — and says that it was the Picts who came from Scythia by sea and settled in Ireland and the adjacent coasts of Britain.

natives of the Cassiterides, mentioned by Strabo (44 BC) as 'bartering their tin, lead and skins for pottery, salt and brazen manufactures', were probably a mixed race or some combination of the British and the tin workers who had lived for so many ages in 'Belerium' that they possessed equal rights to the British tribes around them though still retaining marked traces of an Eastern if not Semitic origin. In the old records of the Saints we read of Solomon. 'Duke of Cornwall', as living about AD 300. This not only suggests the presence of a Jewish population of tin workers, but that one of this race held a position of some local headship or Sovereignty.

Certainly the oldest traditions of the 'houses' and 'leavings' of the 'Jews or Sarasins' suggest a race of workers who kept themselves more or less distinct from the tribes around them, and whose tools of 'holm and box and hartshorn' point to a time long anterior to the dates of the Norman kings.

That they were an Eastern race seems to be borne out by the antiquarian studies of Mr Bellows, of Gloucester, who in his travels in the Trans-Caucasus discovered specific 'Cornish' implements and customs in common use in this distant country, no similar pattern or use being known of elsewhere.

The shovel or spade and pick which he found used in the East at Tiflis and used by the miners of the Kedabek mines in the Caucasus are (he says) of exactly the same patterns as the ancient Cornish shovel and pick used in tin mining. He also says that at Akstapha, near Tiflis, 'what we call Cornish cream' was set before him, and adds, 'This helps to show, I think, that the Cornish people had their ways of making cream from Asia' (John Bellows, Kegan Paul, 1904, p. 210).

Mr Bellows does not commit himself to anything beyond this, but it is remarkable that a distinguishing feature of the population of the Caucasus, especially in the neighbourhood of Tiflis, is the ancient Hebrew origin of many of their customs and habits, and the strong Hebrew traditions found there regarding the ancient coming of the Jews to the Caucasus. The well-known Hebrew writers and compilers of the Jewish Encyclopaedia state: 'It is certain that among the peoples of the Caucasus the Jewish type is everywhere represented, and that even among Christian and Mohammedan tribes many Jewish habits and customs have been preserved to the present day . . . Many of the villages bear Hebrew names, and the marriage and funeral ceremonies correspond in many respects with those of the ancient Hebrews . . . Some of the Caucasian Jews claim to be descendants of the tribes which were taken captive by Nebuchadnezzar, while others are equally certain of their descent from the Israelites who were taken from Palestine by Shalmaneser.'

Those who have studied the ancient Cornish language, and particularly Dr Pryce, of Redruth, who in 1790 published his *Essay to Preserve the Ancient Cornish Language*, profess to have found in it strong indications of an Eastern impress or origin, Dr Pryce's opinion being that 'Cornish and Breton were almost the same dialect of a Syrian or Phoenician root' (Preface of *Archaeologia Cornu-Britannica*, W. Pryce, MD, 1790).[11]

This Eastern element or origin has generally been put down to the Phoenician trade with Cornwall, but the Phoenicians themselves were, as we have seen, only commercial travellers or visitors, and it seems far more likely that the old Jewish or 'Sarasin' tin workers of 400 BC and downwards, were the men who really left their impress on the race.

For the thoughtful visitor and student may well question whether it has really gone today. The language is dead, but the Eastern look of the old villages — such as Mousehole, beyond Penzance and Newlyn — the Eastern use and breed of the Cornish donkey, the facial and other characters of the people — so akin and yet so different from the red-haired men of Wales — the black hair and eyes, the profoundly nervous constitution — nervous with an intellectual antiquity and strain that tends toward disease as well as progress — the genuine indifference to, or delight in, long sea voyages, and the spirit of adventure in the fibre and the blood[12] — all of this seems to separate the Cornish from the rest of their British family, and increases the interest of the inquirer into the nature and origin of the 'old men', 'the Jews' and 'Sarasins', who are now mysteriously lost but have apparently left such strong and virile traces behind them. If they were of Jewish extraction, it is not improbable that they came from the great Jewish colonies of Egypt, which were originally contemporaneous with the Babylon dispersion to the Caucasus, and this would account for the alternative name of Saracen as applied to them by the British.[13]

If they were Jews — and the old name is more likely to have lived unaltered than any history — it is only reasonable to suppose that those who were connected in any way with the Phoenician tin trade would be cognizant of this Jewish colony in the Cassiterides. Much as St James the Greater would necessarily know of the Jews who had been banished to Sardinia, so St Joseph might hear and know of the Jewish tin workers, and his mission would be undertaken, in the first

[11] In Jago's *Glossary* 'Punic' (Phoenician) and Cornish sentences are compared. So late as 1730 the Cornish dialect near Penzance and the Breton dialect at Morlaix were so similar that a Cornish boy, using the Cornish language, was able to make his wants known at Morlaix better than when using the same language at home (see Jago's *Glossary*, p. 21, and Pryce's Essay).

[12] 'Many Cornishmen seem to think less of a voyage to America or the Cape than of a railway journey to London' (local conversation).

[13] Some of the older writers mention the Jews as coming out of Egypt, and appear sometimes to regard them as Egyptians (Strabo). Compare the speech of the 'chief captain' to St Paul — 'Art thou not that Egyptian?' (Acts 21: 38).

place, to preach the glad tidings of the coming of the Saviour to the 'lost sheep' of his own race.

If we turn to the account of the journeyings of St Joseph, as given in the *Morte d'Arthur*, we come to some interesting details which seem to harmonize rather curiously with local tradition and nomenclature.

The narrative (bk. xiii, cap. 10) brings St Joseph and his son to 'Sarras', where the 'Saracens' under 'Tolleme la Feintes', are fighting against the Britons under King Evelake. King Evelake is apparently a local king belonging to one of the provinces of Great Britain, and the Saracen, 'which was . . . a rich king and a mighty', is spoken of as marching to meet him, so that the encounter must necessarily have been reported — or imagined — as taking place on this side of the Channel. Moreover — and this is of further interest — King Tolleme the 'Saracen' is said to have been the 'cousin' of King Evelake, so that although they were at war with each other and apparently of different nationality, ties of marriage had taken place between the 'Saracens' and the ancestors of King Evelake. Surely there are some fragments of history underlying this tale of the journey of St Joseph!

Are not the rich 'Saracens' the Jewish or Jewish-Egyptian tin workers of the Cassiterides, and do we not gather, as the tale progresses, that these turned a deaf ear to the message of St Joseph, while King Evelake and, later on, the greater king of Glastonbury (Arviragus?) were kindly disposed towards his company and more or less won over by the teaching of St Joseph and his son?[14]

Both 'Saracens' and British were probably by no means so uncultivated and barbarous as many have imagined.

Diodorus Siculus, although writing before the time of our Lord, describes them as civilized and courteous to strangers. He writes: 'They are of much sincerity and integrity, far from the craft and knavery of men among us, contented with plain and homely fare, and strangers to the excess and luxury of rich men.' His description, too, of their work shows that they had then made very considerable progress in the useful arts and in commerce. From other descriptions (of the British) we read that their ordinary clothing was of 'tartan, spun, coloured and woven by themselves. The upper classes wore collars and bracelets of gold and necklaces of amber. The chiefs were armed with helmets, shields and cuirasses of leather, bronze or chain mail, while their many weapons of defence — darts, pikes and broadswords — were often richly worked and ornamented' (Conybeare, *Roman Britain*, pp. 48–50).

The Druids, who were the ministers of religion, education and jurisprudence among the Britons, appear to have possessed some

[14] The name of the Saracen leader, 'Tolleme la Feinte', meaning 'Tolleme the False', seems to suggest that he had usurped the name and title of Ptolemy, a name which might well have special attraction for an Egyptian Jew at this date (see *Morte d'Arthur*, bk. xiii, cap. X).

knowledge of the Greek language as well as that of their native tongue. Some of them sang to the music of harps (Diodorus). They professed to understand the movements of the stars (Pomponius Mela). They studied natural science and ethics (Strabo), and especially taught the doctrine of the Immortality of the Soul.

Again, in contrast to what is sometimes taught regarding British weakness and isolation at this date, we know that the coast was plentifully supplied with ports and harbours, that there was very considerable shipping, that much of the land was cultivated with corn, that a definite British coinage had existed for some two centuries before the Christian era (Brit. Museum), and that in spite of the small chieftaincies into which the government was broken up, the British 'kings and princes lived for the most part in peace and amity with one another, and the Romans had the utmost difficulty in subduing them'.

Some of these leaders were men of considerable cultivation and ability — men who would have been conspicuous in any age or country for character, for intellect and wit. This is abundantly shown by the remarkable and eloquent speech of Galgacus, the leader of the British forces in the battle with Agricola in AD 84. Tacitus, the historian, in his Life of Agricola, has preserved the whole of this wonderful address, and it would probably be difficult even in modern times to find language better chosen, more impassioned in its pathos, or more refined in its irony and satire.

It must necessarily not only have been spoken by a man of very considerable intellectual force, but have been addressed to men who could understand and appreciate his arguments. It has been assumed by many writers that this address has been 'put into the mouth' of Galgacus by Tacitus. It bears the impress of a strong individuality, and is much more likely to have been directly repeated and preserved. Compare, too, with this the strikingly similar terse and epigrammatic speech of Caradoc before Claudius in Rome. 'Kill me,' he said, 'as all expect, and this affair will soon be forgotten; spare me, and men shall talk of your clemency from age to age.'

In much of this we have had the finger of actual history or of existing monuments to guide us. Beyond this we have some old but mostly undated writings, chronicles of the twelfth century, romances of the fifteenth century, and some monuments both in Wales and Somerset (then equally the strongholds of the British), which are more or less in harmony with the traditions we have found in Provence and in England.

The most connected account of the British mission of St Joseph is that given by William of Malmesbury, the historian of Glastonbury.

This was probably written about 1126, and from it I have taken the following:

In the year of our Lord, 63, twelve holy missionaries, with Joseph of Arimathea (who had buried the Lord) at their head, came over to

Britain, preaching the Incarnation of Jesus Christ. The king of the country and his subjects refused to become proselytes to their teaching,[15] but in consideration that they had come a long journey, and being somewhat pleased with their soberness of life and unexceptional behaviour, the king, at their petition, gave them for their habitation a certain island bordering on his region, covered with trees and bramble bushes and surrounded by marshes, called Ynis-wytren (and later Glastonbury). Afterwards two other kings, successively, although pagans, having information of their remarkable sanctity of life, each gave of them a portion of ground, and this, at their request, according to the custom of the country, was confirmed to them — from whence the 'twelve Hides of Glastonbury', it is believed, derive their origin.

These holy men, thus dwelling in this desert place, were in a little time admonished in a vision by the Archangel Gabriel to build a church in honour of the Blessed Virgin, in a place to which they were directed. Obedient to the Divine precept, they immediately built a chapel of the form of that which had been shown them: the walls were of osiers wattled together all round.

This was finished in the one-and-thirtieth year (AD 64) after our Lord's Passion, and though rude and misshapen in form, was in many ways adorned with heavenly virtues; and being the first church in this region, the Son of God was pleased to grace it with particular dignity, dedicating it Himself in honour of His Mother.

These twelve saints serving God with peculiar devotion in this place, making addresses to the Blessed Virgin, and spending their time in watching, fasting and prayer, were supported in their difficulties by the assistance and appearance of the Blessed Virgin (as it is reasonable to believe); and for the truth of this matter we have St Patrick's charter and the writings of the ancients to vouch for us.

The foregoing is an abridged account from Malmesbury's history. It will be noticed that he takes his authority from 'the writings of the ancients', which he is said to have found in the Abbey Library, and very probably from the history of one Melchin, who wrote about the year AD 560; and who is quoted by John of Glastonbury as follows: 'The disciples . . . died in succession and were buried in the cemetery. Among them, Joseph of Marmore, named of Arimathea, receives perpetual sleep, and he lies in linea bifurcata near the south corner of the oratorio, which is built of hurdles.'[16]

The history of this 'oratorio of hurdles', or wattled church, said to have been built by St Joseph of Arimathea; the building of the great church of St Peter and St Paul to the east of it, so as not to interfere with the integrity of the older church; and the history of the Abbey buildings surrounding them is very remarkable.

[15] Compare Gildas 'received with lukewarm minds by the inhabitants'.

[16] Melchin, or Melkyn, is said to have lived before Merlin, and to have recorded the coming of St Joseph in a book (see the *Flores Historiarum*, London, 1890, p. 127).

Figure 7: 'Glastonbury Abbey' from a print by A. Coney, 1817

Professor Freeman writes:

The ancient church of wood or wicker, which legend spoke of as the first temple reared on British soil to the honour of Christ, was preserved as a hallowed relic, even after a greater church of stone was built by Dunstan to the east of it. And though not a fragment of either of those buildings still remains, yet each alike is represented in the peculiar arrangements of that mighty and now fallen minister. The wooden church of the Briton is represented by the famous Lady Chapel, better known as the chapel of St Joseph; the stone church of the West Saxons is represented by the vast Abbey church itself. Nowhere else can we see the works of the conquerors and the works of the conquered thus standing though but in a figure, side by side. Nowhere else, among all the churches of England, can we find one which can thus trace up its uninterrupted being to days before the Teuton had set foot upon English soil. The legendary burial-place of Arthur, the real burying-place of Eadgar and the two Edmunds, stands alone among English minsters as the one link which really does bind us to the ancient Church of the Briton and the Roman 'The Origin of the English Nation', by Professor Freeman, *Macmillan's Magazine*, 1860, p. 41).

The most remarkable feature of the Glastonbury buildings is this continued representation of the wooden church of the Britons by the Lady Chapel or chapel of St Joseph. For, through all the ages since the wattled church was first erected, and through all the vicissitudes affecting the later buildings of the Abbey, the approximate size and shape of the first British church appear to have been religiously maintained.

There is, perhaps, nothing really corresponding to this to be found in Christendom. Every effort seems to have been made to preserve the original church, 'the first ground of God, the first ground of the saints in Britain, the rise and foundation of all religion in Britain, the burying-place of the saints, built by the very disciples of our Lord.'[17]

First we are told it was encased with boards and covered with lead, then it appears to have been built over in stone, the interior being beautified with all manner of costly gifts, among which we read of an altar of sapphire presented by the Patriarch of Jerusalem.

All that was best in Great Britain came to it and, for a time, all who were noblest and kingliest sought to be buried here. Speaking of this oldest church, dedicated, as we have seen, to St Mary, but later known as the Chapel of St Joseph, William of Malmesbury says: 'Here are preserved the human remains of many saints, nor is there any space in the building that is free from their ashes, so much so, that the stone pavement and, indeed, the sides of the altar and the altar itself above

[17] In the charter granted by Henry II (1185) for rebuilding Glastonbury, he styles it 'the mother and burying-place of the saints, founded by the very disciples of our Lord' (Hitchings, *History of Cornwall*, vol. i, p. 349); and in the charter of Edgar it is said to be 'the first church in the kingdom built by the disciples of Christ' (Conybeare's *Roman Britain*, p. 254).

and below, is crammed with the multitude of the relics. Rightly, therefore, is it called the heavenly sanctuary on earth, of so large a number of saints is it the repository.'

In 1184, it and the greater churches to the east of it — all the Abbey buildings — were destroyed by fire, and only a few of the treasures and relics were preserved.

Still, within two years the old church of St Mary (or Chapel of St Joseph) was rebuilt, 'where, from the beginning the "Vetusta"[18] has stood, with squared stones of the most perfect workmanship, profusely ornamented'; and lest there should be any later interruption or misconception of the old tradition, a brass plate was subsequently fixed to a pillar in the monk's churchyard, and on the south side of the chapel containing a representation of the original church of wattles, its dimensions (60 ft in length and 26 ft in breadth), and an inscription in Latin. The plate (or a copy of the original) is still preserved. It is of an octagon form, 10 in by 7 in; the holes by which it was riveted to the stone still remain. The old Latin inscription which covers it in black letters is of uncertain date, but said to be not later than the fourteenth century. It records the arrival of the first missionaries with Joseph of Arimathea in the year 31 after our Lord's Passion, and the Divine dedication of this first church to the Blessed Virgin. It records also the addition of a chancel at the east end of this church, and 'lest the place and magnitude of the (original) church should be forgotten by this augmentation, a column was erected on a line passing through the two eastern angles of that church protracted to the south, which line divided the aforesaid chancel from it'.

What was the reason of this continued careful preservation of the exact dimensions of the 'Vetusta Ecclesia', for which I think there is scarcely any parallel to be found elsewhere?

If you go to Glastonbury today, still you see it. Shameful as has been the wreckage of the churches, the 'Chapel of St Joseph', dedicated to the Blessed Virgin, that was finished in 1186, has suffered least; and there today is the site and shape of the little church of St Joseph, 'the first ground of God . . . built by the very disciples of our Lord'. Its dimensions correspond roughly — roughly, for computations vary, and the size of the original church would necessarly be increased by its over-building — but, allowing for this, its dimensions correspond roughly with those of the Jewish tabernacle, and one cannot help wondering (if there is any truth in the legend) whether St Joseph did not so design it, and impress upon all who helped him the value and significance of its shape and size.[19]

[18] 'Vetusta', or 'Vetusta Ecclesia', the ancient church.

[19] The latest and perhaps the best computation of Tabernacle measurements (by the Revd W. S. Caldecott) makes the length of the Tabernacle from the beginning of the inner court to the extreme limit of the 'Holy of Holies' 55½ ft, or to the centre of the Great Altar of Sacrifice nearly 60 ft. The width of the covered portion or tent of the Tabernacle would be exactly 24 ft (see Caldecott's *Tabernacle*, pp. 171, 183).

Standing on the half-pace or chancel steps of the ruins of the Abbey church, and looking from the choir-lawn down the long nave-lawn with the Chapel of St Joseph at its farthest limit — whether intended so or not — one sees what I have ventured to call the Bible of Glastonbury.

There — reputedly built by Jewish builders — stood the original wattled church or Lady Chapel, built as the Tabernacle was set up, and as the Temple was built, with the House of God to the west of the sacred enclosure; and, opening out from it, directly continuous with it, toward the east where we are standing grew the great church — or what has been the great church — of St Peter and St Paul, one of the greatest, or perhaps the very greatest, of all English churches.

The sins of greed and cruelty have wrecked it — sins of both king and people — for until seventy years ago it is said that the stones were carted away at a shilling the cart-load, and the coffins were melted down for cisterns; but it is the great church which has suffered most. St Joseph's Chapel, though shattered and broken, is still standing and remains — if one may carry the illustration further — a type of that Jewish recognition and obedience of the Moral Law which often stands, thank God! when Christian faith is lost, and within the portals of which the honest heart may still find shelter until Faith returns and the Christian altar is again set up, as one hopes to see it yet, in the ruined Abbey church at Glastonbury.

For now, as of old, 'The fear of the Lord is the beginning of wisdom.'

The chain of traditions marking the journey of St Joseph, the story of his mission at Glastonbury, and the historical writings referring to British Christianity in the first two centuries, are not without very considerable confirmations from the old Welsh records and traditions regarding British saints.

Three Jewish missionaries are definitely mentioned in these, though by their British names only, as bringing the Gospel into Britain at the close of the first century. The names of the missionaries are given as Ilid,[20] Cyndaf and Mawan, and the account is the more remarkable since all the names involved and the setting or story of the mission (from the British standpoint) are entirely different from those of William of Malmesbury, and yet in main essentials the two stories are in agreement.

Mawan, according to one of the copies of the Silurian Catalogue, is said to have been a son of Cyndaf, and Cyndaf (by his British name signifying chief, or head, or patriarch) is evidently recognized as the leader of the mission, and one who must have been honoured by the British in order to have been given this title. Both Cyndaf and Ilid are

---

[20]   'Hast thou heard the saying of St Ilid?
       One come of the race of Israel,
       There is no madness like extreme anger.'
       (Chwedlau y Doethion, Iolo-morganwg MS)

definitely stated to have been 'men of Israel', and the account of their coming, together with Mawan, the son of the noble Cyndaf, is obviously directly paralleled in the later monkish record of the coming of St Joseph and his son Josephes.

The actual references in Welsh literature are not easy to consult. Some are found in the third series of Triads published in the Myvyrian Archiaology, and others (according to Rees) are to be met with in the Silurian copies of 'Achau y Saint' (*Essay on the Welsh Saints*, by Professor Rees, London, 1836).

In the Welsh account the coming of the Hebrew missionaries is associated with the return from captivity in Rome of 'Bran the Blessed' (Bran Vendigaeth), for which there is but little or no good foundation, and also with the coming of Arwystli Hen, or Aristobulus, an Italian or Roman Christian (Rees), for whose presence in Britain and work as 'bishop of the Britons' we have the additional authority of the Greek martyrologies and the list of Hippolytus[21]

Accordingly, although the 'setting' of the story in the British account is one in which a king of the Britons is supposed to share with Hebrew and Roman missionaries, the glory of bringing the Faith to Britain, the coming of the mission, its character as composed of several members, and the details that the Jewish head of the mission was accompanied by his son, are absolutely identical in the two versions.

After examining both in the light of such contemporaneous or later history as is available, one is bound, I think, to admit that where there are discrepancies the balance of probability lies with the historian of Glastonbury.

There does not appear to have been any national or general acceptance of Christianity in Britain for over a hundred years after the coming of St Joseph, although British missionaries (Mansuetus, Beatus and Marcellus) preached the Gospel in foreign countries during the century intervening. Mansuetus (St Mansuy), an Irish or Caledonian Briton, became bishop of Toul in Lorraine, and is said to have died in AD 89.[22] His Commemoration is on 3 September. Suetonius Beatus is said to have been converted in Britain, baptized by 'Barnabas', a companion of Aristobulus, and to have afterwards become the Apostle of the Helvetians. He died at 'Under seven' in

---

[21] Cressy states that 'St Aristobulus', a disciple of St Peter or St Paul in Rome, was sent as an Apostle to the Britons, and was the first Bishop of Britain; that he died in Glastonbury, AD 99, and that his Commemoration or Saint's Day was kept in the church on 15 March (Rees, *Welsh Saints*, p. 81).

[22] This is confirmed by a second-century Christian sarcophagus which has been discovered at Malaincourt, in Lorraine, and which bears an inscription indicating (according to M. l'Abbé Narbey) that it was the tomb of one of St Mansuy's friends who accompanied him from Ireland (see *Acta Sanctorum*, Supplement, vol. i, pp. 313, 343, 349).

Helvetia, AD 110.[23] His Commemoration or Saint's Day is on 9 May. Marcellus, the first British martyr (though not martyred on British soil), became 'bishop' of Tongres and Triers and is said to have been martyred in AD 166.[24]

These are remembered as British missionaries, and it is impossible to believe that they could have wandered about preaching the Gospel if their own country had meanwhile remained ignorant of the Faith. There can be but little doubt that Gildas is right in picturing the Britons as very slow in receiving Christianity, though it was brought to them in the very earliest years; and those in whom the Faith 'took root' at Glastonbury naturally turned (as Christ had commanded them) to those who were ready to receive their message, even at the cost of long journeys to distant cities and to far countries.

The 'Vetusta Ecclesia' of Glastonbury remained as a witness for the Faith; but it was not until the year of the great Gallican persecution at Lyons and Vienne in AD 177 (when several of the Gallican Christians would probably find refuge in Britain) that we find any indication of a national Christianity.

Then, according to several accounts, which probably have some basis in fact, a local king of the Britons, called Llewrwg, or Lucius, accepted the Faith, established an archbishopric in London, and wrote to Pope Eleutherius asking for counsel and direction in the government of his people.

Considerable doubt has been thrown on the existence and history of King Lucius, but without any adequate reason. Pope Eleutherius, a Greek, is said to have occupied the See of Rome from AD 177 to 192.

Two letters of his have been preserved in the records of the Church of Rome (Mansi). One is to the Christians of Lyons and Vienne at the time of the great persecution, and the other is directed to Lucius, King of Britain. This is in answer to a request from King Lucius for instruction in the right way of governing his people. This letter, and the occasion which called for it, appears to be in strict harmony with what we know of Roman occupation at this date, and of the

---

[23] This is confirmed by local traditions and the cave of St Beatus on the borders of Lake Thun. St Beatus is remembered as a British missionary; the site of his first church is still shown, and the district around Interlaken, 'Unterseen' and Beatenberg is fairly full of old traditions regarding him.

[24] This is confirmed by one of the traditional records of the bishops occupying the see as given by F. Godfrey Henschen, in his *De Episcopatu Tungrensi* (*Acta Sanctorum*, v. 20). The list is as follows: 1. Maternus, 2. Navitus, 3. Marcellus, 4. Metropolus, 5. Severinus, 6. Florentius, 7. Martinus, 8. Maximus, 9. Valentinus and 10. Servatius. Maternus is said to have lived in the Apostolic age, being sent by St Peter as first missionary priest, so that Marcellus may well have finished his work as third in succession among the Tungri. Tongres is the ancient Aduatica, the capital of the 'Tungri'. mentioned by Caesar in his Commentaries. It was certainly the seat of a bishop about AD 300. Trier (Reéves) sent Agroesius, a bishop, and Felix, an exorcist, to the Council of Aries in AD 314.

opportunity it afforded a native chieftain or king (living in amity with his overlord) or admiring and envying Roman discipline and order.

It is also in essential harmony with the Welsh account in the 35th Triad (Third Series), which records how the native king bestowed 'the freedom of country and nation with privilege of judgement and surety on all those who might be of the Faith of Christ, and how he built the first Church at "Llandaff" '(?). The only question that arises is whether the last word is not a mistake for Llundain, or London.

For, whether founded by Lucius or not, it must have been at this time or shortly after that the bishopric of London was instituted. About a hundred years afterwards it was the chief episcopal see; and the chief church in the kingdom is said (by an old tradition) to have stood on the present site of St Peter's, Cornhill.[25]

However this may be, there can hardly be any doubt that it was toward the end of the second century that British Christianity received its main impetus, and that up to this time its progress had been slow. From the writings that have come down to us it may reasonably be gathered that few converts were made by the original missionaries, but that their holy lives (and possible descendants) had kept the memory of their religion green and fragrant, and that the Church of Glastonbury still remained a monument of their devotion. After they were dead further Christian teachers and guides were sent for, and these were astonished to find a Church already provided by God (as it was said), for the conversion of souls.

This keeps to very ancient authority and is a very probable résumé of the facts so far as these can in any way be gathered together.

From this date the British Church must have grown rapidly in numbers and importance, for at the end of the following century or the beginning of the next (300-305), when the great Diocletian persecution had begun, a great number of British Christians, according to Gildas, suffered for their faith, and among these Alban, Amphibalus, Julius, Aaron, Stephanus and Socrates are remembered by name as martyrs. Julius and Aaron are said to have been inhabitants of Caerleon-upon-Usk (the city of Legions) and churches

---

[25] The episcopal succession of the old London see, according to Jocelyn of Furness (twelfth century), quoted by the late Bishop Stubbs in *Episcopal Succession in England*, Oxford, 1859 (p. 152), is as follows:

NB — Compare the names in Cressy.

1. Theanus.	1. Theanus, about 185.
2. Elvanus.	2. Elvanus.
3. Cadar.	3.
4. Obinus.	4.
5. Conon.	5.
6. Palladius.	6.
7. Stephanus.	7. Stephanus, d. 300.
8. Iltutus.	8. Augulus, d. 305.
9. Theodorus.	9. Restitutus, about 314.

in the neighbourhood were dedicated to their memory. These have been now destroyed, but there is still a chapel of Llanharan, in Glamorganshire, which probably owes its name to the British — or Hebrew-British — saint who suffered in the Diocletian persecution.

In spite of, or perhaps by reason of, this very persecution 'the blood of the martyrs being the seed of the Church', the years immediately succeeding appear to show the British Church at the acme of her prosperity. The archbishopric of London became powerful and comparatively wealthy, Restitutus, who held the see in AD 314, heading the British contingent to the great Council of Arles. One of his colleagues, 'Adelphius' of Caerlon-upon-Usk, identified by Professor Rees with St Cadfrawd,[26] a British saint of this period, appears to have belonged to the chief royal family of the Britons, being descended, like Lucius, from Bran and Caractacus, while (about the same time) in the far west of Cornwall where, if our theory be right, 'Saracen or Jewish' influence was paramount, we read that Kelvius, son of Solomon, Duke of Cornwall, not only accepted Christianity but became a Christian priest,[27] and 'Moses', said to be a Briton, but presumably of some Hebrew relationship, became an 'Apostle to the Sacracens'.

With the resignation of the Imperium by Diocletian in 305, and the consequent elevation of Constantius, a new era dawned for the Catholic Faith. Constantius had married Helena, a British princess (?), already favourable to Christianity, and when he died the following year (AD 306), at York, and was succeeded by his son Constantine, both mother and son became known adherents of the Cross.

It was under this banner, and as the first Christian emperor, that Constantine won his last great battle at the Milvian Bridge in AD 312.

So that the highest British influence — and this in more than one direction — the highest Roman influence — that of the Emperor himself — and even the highest unknown Jewish or Saracenic influence of the West Country, appear to have been alike enlisted at this date in the cause and spread of Christianity.

It is small wonder, therefore, that the national British Church during the first half (at least) of the fourth century somewhat suddenly increased in power and influence, until it seemed to enfold the whole of the land within its communion.

The Church of Britain became great, both at home and abroad, holding independent but sisterly relationship to the Church of Rome and bound by closer ties — by ancient intercommunication, custom

[26] The Welsh or British 'Cadfrawd' means 'brother in battle', for which the Greek 'Αδελφο'ς or Latin-Greek Adelphius would be a natural synonym, the more warlike prefix 'Cad' being dropped on adopting a religious life.

[27] He is said afterwards to have been appointed as bishop to the see of Anglesea, where he died in AD 370 (Cressy's *Church History*).

and liturgy — with the Churches of Gaul, and again (through these) with the Churches of Asia.[28]

According to Geoffrey of Monmouth, at the beginning of the fourth century, there were three archbishops — those of London, of York and of the City of Legions (Caerleon-upon-Usk) — and under these there were twenty-eight bishops with their dioceses (*Hist.*, bk. iv, cap. xix).[29]

However extraordinary this statement may appear, it must not be contemptuously or lightly dismissed as incredible, for it seems to be directly confirmed by the records of the Council of Arles in AD 314, when Restitutus of London, Eborius of York, and Adelphinus of Caerleon attended as chief representatives of the British Church. These bishops evidently represented the three great provinces of Britain and were not casually chosen. Again, we have the authority of Athanasius that bishops from Britain were present at the Council of Sardica in Illyria, in AD 347, and that of Supicius Severus, that several bishops from Britain were present at the Council of Ariminum (in Italy) AD 359.

Of the four hundred bishops of the Western Church there assembled he writes: 'Unto all . . . the Emperor had ordered provisions and appointments to be given. But that was deemed unbecoming by the Aquitans, Gauls and Britons; and refusing the Imperial offer they preferred to live at their own expense. Three only from Britain, on account of poverty, made use of the public gift after they had rejected the contribution offered by the others; considering it more proper to burden the exchequer than individuals' (*Sulpitii Severi Historiae*, 1, ii, c. 55).

These three, though forming, probably, only a small minority of the British bishops present, show by the fact of their poverty that in some parts, at least, the life of the priesthood had become difficult, and by the end of the century we find that the period of success had been followed by one of failure and danger. For the sudden success and influence of the British Church was undoubtedly largely political and connected with the accession of Constantine to the Imperial purple. Among the great mass of the people the Christianity of the day was probably largely nominal and withered with the slow decadence of Roman authority and influence. Among the few it was a passion and a life worthy of the best ages of Christendom, and showing distinctive features characteristic of its special origin.

About AD 400, or slightly later, we come to the very earliest period touched by the literature of contemporaneous British Christianity.

[28] The ruined chapel at Tintagel and some other old western churches were dedicated to the memory of *St Julitta of Tarsus*, but the immediate link of association appears to have been lost.

[29] For further information on Caerleon see *The Legacy of Arthur's Chester*, by R. B. Stoker.

This literature, as found in the scattered writings of St Patrick, is so remarkable and has been so little regarded in its bearing on the history and religious life of the period, that some extended notice of it seems necessary in order to bring out its value and full significance.

St Patrick was born about AD 387, from an extended ancestry of Christians, his father, Calpurnius, having been a deacon, and his grandfather, Potitus, a priest, so that he must have had a good practical acquaintance with the Christianity not only of his own age, but with that of previous ages.

His 'Confession' in the Book of Armagh, his 'Epistle to Coroticus' and his wonderful 'Hymn of the Deer's Cry', are the chief writings which have been preserved to us, and we may find in these many valuable sidelights regarding British life and Christianity reaching back to the very beginning of the fifth century.

In his 'Confession' we find a brief word-picture of the British Church when he was sixteen years of age (about AD 400). It is that of a Church which had been powerful but had lost its first glory and love, and was now becoming decadent. He writes: 'We had gone back from God and had not kept His commandments and were not obedient to our priests, who used to warn us for our salvation.'

In the hymn of the 'Deer's Cry' we find the Church fighting against the influence of the Druids, and in the conditions under which this was written, and in those which called forth the 'Epistle to Coroticus', when this (local) king had suddenly made a raid on St Patrick's converts, destroying many and carrying others into slavery, we get a historical picture of the life and times exceedingly similar to that portrayed in the (later) books of the Arthurian legends. But it is the hymn of the 'Deer's Cry' which demands the most attention, standing out, as it does, beyond and apart from all other contemporaneous Christian literature.

According to the account in the 'Liber Hymnorum' (eleventh century):

> Patrick made this hymn in the time of Laoghaire, son of Nial. The cause of making it . . . was to protect himself with his monks against the deadly enemies who were in ambush against the clerics. And this is a corselet of faith for the protection of body and soul against demons and human beings and vices. Every one who shall say it every day with pious meditation on God, demons shall not stay before him.
>
> It will be a safeguard to him against every poison and envy; it will be a comna to him against sudden death; it will be a corselet to his soul after dying.
>
> Patrick sung this when the ambuscades were sent against him by Laoghaire that he might not go to Tara to sow the Faith, so that there seemed before the ambuscaders to be wild deer . . . and Faed Fiada is its name.

ST PATRICK'S HYMN OF THE 'DEER'S CRY'
(c. AD 450)

I bind myself today to a strong virtue,
An invocation of the Trinity. I believe in
A Three-ness with confession of an One-ness
In the Creator of the Universe.

I bind myself today to the virtue of
Christ's birth with His baptism.
To the virtue of His crucifixion with His burial,
To the virtue of His resurrection with His ascension,
To the virtue of His coming to the Judgement of Doom.

I bind myself today to the virtue of ranks of Cherubim,
In obedience of angels,
In service of archangels,
In hope of resurrection for reward,
In prayers of patriarchs,
In predictions of prophets,
In preachings of Apostles,
In faiths of confessors,
In innocence of holy virgins,
In deeds of righteous men.

I bind myself today to the virtue of Heaven,
In light of sun,
In brightness of snow,
In splendour of fire,
In speed of lightning,
In swiftness of wind,
In depth of sea,
In stability of earth,
In compactness of rock.

I bind myself today to God's virtue to pilot me,
God's might to uphold me,
God's wisdom to guide me,
God's eye to look before me,
God's ear to hear me,
God's word to speak for me,
God's hand to guard me,
God's way to lie before me,
God's shield to protect me,
God's Host to secure me.

Against snares of demons,
Against seductions of vices,
Against lusts of nature,
Against every one who wishes ill to me
Afar and anear,
Alone and in a multitude.

So have I invoked all these virtues between me and these.

Against every cruel merciless power which may come against my body
    and my soul,
Against incantations of false prophets,
Against black laws of heathenry,

Against false laws of heretics,
Against craft of idolatry,
Against spells of women, and smiths, and Druids,
Against every knowledge that defiles men's souls.

Christ to protect me today
Against poison, against burning,
Against drowning, against death-wound,
Until a multitude of rewards come to me!

Christ with me, Christ before me,
Christ behind me, Christ in me,
Christ below me, Christ above me,
Christ at my right, Christ at my left,
Christ in breadth, Christ in length, Christ in height!
Christ in the heart of every one who thinks of me,
Christ in the mouth of every one who speaks to me,
Christ in every eye who sees me,
Christ in every ear who hears me.

I bind myself today to a strong virtue, an invocation of the Trinity.
I believe in a Three-ness with confession of an One-ness in the Creator
    of the Universe.
Domini est salus, Domini est salus, Christi est salus.
Salus tua Domine, sit semper nobiscus.[30]

What is it that gives this hymn its peculiar power and charm?

Is it not the cultivated Hebrew model on which the construction of the hymn is based, and the late Hebrew note which rings mysteriously and repeatedly through all the gradations of this strange prayer-poem?

The old angel invocations brought from Persia are translated into Christian phraseology or, rather, turned into the material for a purely Christian hymn; and the whole is in strange accord with such influence and impress as might well be handed down from the teaching of the high-born 'men of the race of Israel' mentioned in the old Welsh writings, and left (perhaps by St Joseph) in the oldest liturgies of Glastonbury.

East and West seem both to be united in this hymn, and through the long line of St Patrick's Christian ancestry and through the traditions of Glastonbury, where St Patrick is said to have spent a good proportion of his life, we may perhaps trace living notes of that music which made the harp of Erin to sound in unison with that of the descendants of King David.

From the distinctly Hebrew invocation of 'Creator of the Universe' at the beginning of the hymn — through the 'ranks of Cherubim', 'angels' and 'archangels', 'patriarchs' and 'prophets' of the second part, down to the final measure of

---

[30] Version by Whitley Stokes in his *Goidelica*, and quoted by Dr Magnus Maclean in the *Literature of the Celts*.

Christ before me,
Christ behind me, Christ in me,
Christ below me, Christ above me,
Christ at my right, Christ at my left.

the Hebrew form or modelling, and sometimes the very words of the 'Cry', recall the voices of the later Hebrew poets and prayer writers as they invoked the protection of the great Creator and His holy angels.[31]

A much less romantic but more direct connection between St Patrick and St Joseph is that afforded by the old tradition that it was St Patrick who drove the venomous reptiles out of Ireland, for it is worthy of note that there is another legend regarding this which gives the first place to St Joseph of Arimathea.

According to Ussher (vols. v, vi and xvii),[32] it is stated to have been through the wisdom and advice of St Joseph of Arimathea (learnt from the teaching of King Solomon) that Ireland was freed from venomous reptiles (vol. vi, p. 300). If St Patrick was the Saint who accomplished the work, the source of his knowledge is directly attributed to St Joseph.

So through all the whole course of the British Church, the history of which, I venture to think, was very much as I have described: first, difficult; secondly (under kingly protection and encouragement), exceedingly prosperous; thirdly, decadent or largely nominal; and finally, oppressed or militant, we seem to find repeated traces of a quite special Hebrew influence, almost regal in its claims and associations; lofty, refined and poetic in its bearing on thought and on literature, and bravely aristocratic in its consciousness of high lineage and of moral strength.[33]

---

[31]Compare with the old Hebrew invocations:
O Lord our God, King of the Universe!
Let me not be affrighted by thoughts,
    Bad dreams or evil imaginations.
Protect us and remove from us foes, pestilence, sword, hunger, and
    troubles.
Remove Satan from before and behind us.
In the shadow of Thy wings shalt thou hide us.
God our Keeper and our Preserver!
        St Michael on my right hand;
        St Gabriel on my left hand;
        St Raphael in front of me;
        St Uriel behind me;
        The majesty of God above me.

[32] On the authority of Valdes.

[33] What is the source of the curious minor chanting of the 'hwyl' in the impassioned religious sermons of the Welsh? The only thing it really resembles (and resembles very closely) is the minor chanting of the Hebrew Rabbis in the public reading of the *Psalms*. Anyone who has heard both cannot fail to be struck by the striking likeness between these methods of quaint prose-poem singing.

And if we seem to find traces of this in the Christian names and scanty records of the earlier centuries there can be no mistake about its insistence in the work of the later writers — the history romancers or legend reciters of the thirteenth, fourteenth and fifteenth centuries.

All the extensive literature of the 'Grail-Quest', which dates from about 1200 onwards, is grouped around the tradition of St Joseph and his son Josephes who came to Glastonbury, bringing the Holy Cup of the Last Supper with them, and full of the idea that these were the ancestors of those great knights who formed the flower of Arthur's court.

In the 'Grand St Grail', one of the earliest of these histories, we are told that after the death of St Joseph and Josephes the keeping of the Holy Grail was confided to Alain, the son of Brons and cousin to Josephes. At Alain's death his brother Josue becomes Grail keeper, and after him six kings, the last of whom is Pelles.

The daughter of King Pelles has a son named Galahad, who becomes the special hero of the Holy Grail. His father is said to have been Lancelot, and this makes him ninth or tenth in descent from the time of St Joseph.

Galahad is one of the knights of King's Arthur's Round Table, and it is worthy of note that the ten generations described as intervening between the times of St Joseph (AD 60–90) and King Arthur (500) are seriously consistent with such measure of history as may well underlie the romance.

In the most readily accessible books of the 'Sangréal' (apart from the *Morte D'Arthur*), *The High History of the Holy Grail*, which was probably compiled about 1220 from the book of Josephes in the Abbey Library at Glastonbury and has been translated by Dr Sebastian Evans, it is impossible not to recognize the important and essential part played by this Hebrew lineage or descent. Every book bears witness to this, and the very names of many of the knights or their associates seem to imply their Jewish origin. Elinant of Escavalon, Joseph, Josephes, Lot, Joseus, Josuias (p. 249), Galahad (?), Alain (?), Petrus, Brons or Hebron, Bruns Brundalis, Urien, Jonas (ii, 39), Pelles and Pelleas and Ban may be taken either as examples of Hebrew names or as indicating some special Hebrew association.[34] (The sons of Bani or Ban returning with Ezra to Jerusalem were 648. Pelias (or Pelleas) put away his wife at the command of Ezra.)

However apocryphal many of the legends may be regarding them, their names are, I believe, the names of historical persons, and the stories of their lives are in rough harmony with that imperfect militant Christianity which was not only the ideal of the medieval compilers, but may well have been the actual achievement of these distant descendants of the Judean Maccabees.

[34] See Apocrypha, 1 Esdras 5:12, 37; 9:34.

In the *Morte D'Arthur*, which contains almost entire the *Quest of the Sangréal* (Quête del St Graal'), and in the *High History of the Holy Grail*, we find curious and startling digressions regarding King David, King Solomon and Judas Maccabees. These are mixed with the legends of the Arthurian Knights, and no direct explanation is offered or has been offered for their presence.

But if, as many of the old writers affirm, King Pelles, Sir Perceval, Sir Lancelot and Sir Galahad might be considered as descendants of these Hebrew kings, their chief ancestors being St Joseph of Arimathea himself and the Brons or Hebron who married the sister of St Joseph (Sir Percyville, Robert de Borron, Grand St Graal, *High History*, etc., and others), not only do these interpolations become less unintelligible, but the fusion of cultivated Hebrew with Celtic stock may to some extent account for that wonderful achievement in moral ideal and Christian chivalry which characterizes the story of King Arthur's court and the quest of the Holy Grail.

Mr Alfred Nutt, who has made a special study of the Grail legends, considers them to be essentially British in origin, and suggests that they were carried from Britain to France at the time of the Celtic immigration into Brittany (between the fourth and sixth centuries). He professes to trace their beginnings from pre-Christian or Pagan times in Britain, but recognizes that the Joseph of Arimathea history is undoubtedly one of the conversion of Britain. Regarding this he writes:[35]

> If what may be called the Joseph of Arimathea Early History be considered closely, it will be seen that in both its two main forms it is essentially a legend of the conversion of Britain. Both forms start with Joseph, but at a later stage go widely asunder. In Borron, it is kinsmen of Joseph, Brons, or Alain, or Petrus who are the leaders of the evangelizing emigration: it is to them that the Holy Vessel is confided. In the Grand St Graal Quête version Joseph's son, Josephes, is the leading spirit, and the fortunes of the Grail are bound up with those of Joseph's direct descendants or with the converted heathens Mordrains, Nasciens and their kin. This second is the popular version, the one which affected the later stages of the Conte del Graal. The fact that what may be called the Vulgate Early History (whether in its Brons or Josephes form) is in reality a conversion of Britain legend is important when we recollect that the personages of the Conte del Graal and allied versions are British and that the scene of the story is Britain.

Later on, in a somewhat lengthy argument, which is very difficult to follow, Mr Nutt appears to advance several theories in explanation of the Grail legends. None of these, however, are very illuminating or satisfactory, and although Mr Nutt appears (in Celtic and medieval romance) to acknowledge an historic King Arthur who 'died in the

---

[35] *The Legends of the Holy Grail*, pp. 39, 40.

first third of the sixth century', he attempts nowhere to explain that insistence on Hebrew lineage and wonderful atmosphere which may be regarded as among the distinguishing features of the legends of the Holy Grail. In the *High History* this Hebrew relationship is repeatedly mentioned. Sir Perceval; his mother Yglais; his sister, Dindrane; Sir Lancelot, the hermit knight; Joseus; King Pelles, the Fisher King; and the King of the Castle Mortal, are all represented as being directly of the lineage of Joseph, and in one or two passages this appears to include Gawain and King Arthur also. In the Grand St Graal we read that Gawain was the son of Lot of Orcaine, and that King Lot was descended from Petrus. If so (as Gawain was the nephew of King Arthur), the King himself and nearly all his Table Round are represented as having Hebrew relationship and being for the most part of Hebrew lineage.

For my own part, after reading Mr Nutt's book and heartily acknowledging his work and scholarship, I turn with greater confidence to the simple accounts given us in the old Histories.

If the medieval writers had not found the historical groundwork of their writings already recorded for them, they would never have dreamed of Jewish characters as types of British knighthood. There was not so much love for the Jew in medieval times that his people or the descendants of Briton and Jew should be exalted as the greatest heroes of contemporary fiction. The medieval romancers only invented new and prolonged adventures for recognized heroes whose reputed lineage and even names they did not dare to alter.

There is, after all, but little reason to disbelieve the tale we are told by the compiler of the *High History*, viz., that the Latin original, written by a scribe named Josephus, was in the Abbey Library of the Isle of Avalon (or Glastonbury), *where the bodies of King Arthur and Guinevere were buried*, and that the names and relationship of the chief actors and the main outlines of their adventures were regarded as historical and worthy of belief.[36]

[36] 'About 1280 the trouveur, Sarrazin, cites the Grail (li Graaus) in verification of the then accepted truism that King Arthur was at one time Lord of Great Britain. This appeal to the Grail as the authority for general belief shows that it was at that time recognized as a well-spring of authentic knowledge' (Sebastian Evans in his epilogue to the *High History of the Holy Grail*).

PART III
THE ZODIAC OF TIME

THE ZODIAC OF TIME

It might be thought that the association with the premier King of Britain and the Holy Cup of the Last Supper would be sufficient to keep the name of Glastonbury firmly in the consciousness of pilgrims both of the literary and the spiritual; however, another theme has come to the forefront in recent years.

In 1929 the artist Katherine Maltwood was asked to draw a map illustrating the itinerary of the Grail-Quest for the Everyman edition of *The High History of the Holy Grail*. This set her off on a long quest that lead to some surprising conclusions. In 1935 she announced that she had discovered traces of a vast terrestrial Zodiac, hidden in the landscape around Glastonbury, which mirrored the structure of the thirteenth-century Arthurian text. Having published several pamphlets on the subject, she followed this up with *Glastonbury's Temple of the Stars*. The book caused something of a sensation, and has continued to be the subject of argument ever since. Further work on the subject has been done in more recent years by Mary Caine,[1] and by a body of tireless researchers who have left no stone unturned in their efforts to establish the existence of this, and other, terrestrial zodiacs carved out of the very shape of the land itself. Historians and archaeologists have, predictably, dismissed the matter as pure fantasy, and it must be said that much of the evidence collected by Mrs Maltwood and her followers tends towards the far-fetched. However, there may well be reason to suspect that belief in the Zodiac dates from an earlier time.

The celebrated astrologer, map-maker, magician, and antiquarian, Dr John Dee, visited Glastonbury on a number of occasions around the year 1582. He was apparently drawn to the spot by the belief that his amanuensis, Edward Kelly, had, through psychic means, discovered a vase containing some of the elixir of life in the grounds of Glastonbury Abbey! According to the writer Richard Deacon, in his book on Dee,[2] the great man had already made a map of the area and made the following comments upon it: 'the starres which agree with

---

[1] Mary Caine, *The Glastonbury Zodiac: Key to the Mysteries of Britain* (Devon: Grael Communications, 1978).

[2] Richard Deacon, *John Dee* (Muller, 1968).

the reproductions on the ground do lye onlie on the celestial path of the Sonne, Moon and planets, with the notable exception of Orion and Hercules . . .'

Unfortunately, the exact source for this quotation has failed to come to light despite a prolonged search. However, there is no doubt that Dee did visit the area and that he was deeply fascinated by both Arthurian traditions and those of the Grail. With Kelly, who was undoubtedly a gifted psychic, at his side it is not beyond reason that Dee became aware of the traces of a group of archetypal guardians buried in the landscape around the Tor and that this gave rise to his belief in a zodiac.

Whether Katherine Maltwood picked up on the same idea, or knew of Dee's association with the place, seems unlikely. Many of the paths or roadways that are supposed to border the outlines of the giant figures date from no earlier than the Middle Ages, which would seem to undermine the theory of their great antiquity.

In the end the whole matter of the Glastonbury Zodiac must stand or fall on its own merits. For the present collection I have included Mrs Maltwood's own account, much abridged from her original book, which none the less outlines her theory clearly. To this is appended two articles, the first by Ronald Hever, himself a sometime resident of Glastonbury and a considerable mystic, and the second by Ross Nichols, late Chief of the Order of Bards, Ovates and Druids, who explores the subject in more general mythological terms.

The Itinerary of the Somerset Giants[1]

KATHERINE MALTWOOD

Introduction

THE SOMERSET GIANTS
BY LT COL HARWOOD STEELE, MC

I have recently examined from the air what I believe to be one of the most remarkable, and least known, discoveries of our time — the so-called Somerset Giants in what is named The Temple of the Stars. The Giants consist of the Signs of the Zodiac, in outline and partly in relief, laid out in a circle ten miles in diameter near Glastonbury, in the country associated with King Arthur, the centre of the circle being at Butleigh. They somewhat resemble other ancient giants — Uffington's White Horse, Wisconsin's effigy mounds and Ohio's Great Serpent.

With minor variations, all the familiar Signs are accounted for, and ten are annually outlined in the familiar sequence. If a modern planisphere of the correct scale be placed back-to-back[2] with a map of the Giants and the stars of the Signs be pricked through, these stars, in almost every instance, fall into the corresponding figures on the map. The exceptions fall in their vicinity. Also present are the Ship, Whale, Dove, Little Dog, and other symbols. The Great Dog stands near by, but does not synchronize with the appropriate stars. The Giants are formed by natural and artificial waterways, ancient tracks and hills which, with occasional old earthworks, model some of the figures in partial relief.

It is not necessary to fly over the Giants to distinguish them. Mrs K. E. Maltwood, FRSA, an Englishwoman now living in Canada, discovered them before the war by studying Ordnance maps and observing from high points while trying to identify on the ground scenes and episodes of the Arthurian cycle. Laymen with the map alone can trace them too. At least, like children with a picture puzzle, they can revel in separating most of the figures from the maze of irrelevant roads, streams and other features wherein (presumably by the accident of haphazard construction by men not in the secret and the design of men who were) they lie coyly and charmingly concealed yet in plain view. Air observation and air photographs like those of the discoverer, amplify the map, revealing several Giants with such

---

[1] Privately printed for the author by Victoria Printing and Publishing Co. (Victoria, BC, n.d.).

[2] The reason why the pattern is at the opposite hand to that on a planisphere is because a planisphere is intended to be held between the observer and the stars. Thus the stars were made to 'fall' straight down upon the ground.

dramatic clarity that, when I showed them to aviators, they expressed the greatest surprise.

The theory of the origin, age and significance of the Giants is this: the priests of ancient times were the custodians of scientific knowledge — including astronomy — shrouded in symbolism the meaning of which they revealed only to their initiates. The knowledge symbolized in the Zodiac was brought to Britain by Sumer-Chaldean priests who, to preserve it for ever in a manner readily visible to initiates but not to others, laid out the Zodiac as a great Nature Temple of the Stars. The Zodiacal myths are an allegory of the Sun's annual wanderings among the Signs. In these myths, the (Sun) God escapes death in a sacred ship. The ancient British priesthood, incorporating the Sumer-Chaldeans, called this ship — and, eventually, the associated Zodiac — the Caer Sidi. Still later, the whole cult, with the priesthood's confined circle of arts and sciences, became the Cup of Wisdom.

The central God subsequently became Arthur, perpetuating the real or imaginary chief who defended the Britons from the heathen and who, like the sun after his epic annual decline, would come again. When Joseph of Arimathea[3] brought Christianity and the Holy Grail to Britain, the Grail inevitably absorbed the Cup of Wisdom — hence its association with Glastonbury. Similarly, the astronomical myths became the adventures of a great Christian King Arthur and his knights (the sun and constellations), the round Zodiac merged into the Round Table and the country of the Giants into the Kingdom of Logres, Arthur's Kingdom; while the Quest of the initiates for the Cup of Wisdom (i.e. knowledge) became the Quest of the Holy Grail.

Nearly five thousand years, by the discoverer's estimate, have passed since the Giants were outlined. The component parts of the puzzle were preserved. Yet its existence was forgotten until Mrs Maltwood realized that the Arthurian adventures could be connected with the ground of the Kingdom and therefore that, being part of the transformed Zodiacal myths, they must connect with the Zodiac on that ground. Her discovery is supported, directly or indirectly, in many quarters.

In his *Celtic Researches* (1804) Edward Davies established the links between the Zodiacal myths, the ancient British priesthood and the Arthurian cycle.

Morte D'Arthur states that 'there was a day assigned betwixt King Arthur and Sir Mordred that they should meet upon a down beside Salisbury and not far from the seaside', where they fought 'the last

---

[3] Joseph of Arimathea. 'The Councils of Pisa, Constance, Siena and Basle all ruled that the English Church took precedence of all others, as being founded by Joseph of Arimathea. 'This was corroborated by such authorities as Clemens Romans, Polydore, Irenaeus, Archbishop Usher, Stillingfleet, Fuller and Genebrand.' — B. M. Moffat.

Great Battle of the West' — Arthur, wounded but escaping death, then retiring to near-by Avalon. The Persians called November Mordad, meaning the Angel of Death. The Scorpion marks November, when the approaching Winter solstice threatens the sun with extinction; Archer and Scorpion stand side-by-side in this heaven and the Somerset Giants representing them meet near Salisbury; while over the Somerset Archer flies the Dove, a reminder that, according to Druidism, the Sun God's spirit escaped as a bird from his head, vanquishing death!

Time and nature may have caused irregularities in certain Somerset Giants, or they may be unfinished, others, wonderfully clear and symmetrical, support the discoverer's case — notably the Twin, Bull, Ram, Fishes, Archer, Dove and Great Dog.

Coincidence? By the law of chance the twelve ancient Zodiacal figures in the Somerset design could take their proper sequence in the circle by accident only through one chance in 479 million. The possibility that accident formed the figures seems, on similar grounds, remote.

Whatever its origin, age and significance, the preservation of this wonderful curiosity should no longer be left to chance. Now that the war is over the opportunity should be taken to submit Mrs Maltwood's claims to expert examination. If they are substantiated, as I believe they would be, these links with the distant past should be safeguarded for all time.

A Two-Days' Tour of the Giant Zodiac in Somerset, England

First Day

THE SCORPION

Let us suppose that I am staying at the George Inn, Castle Cary, and that I take my car to Castle Cary Station, GWR, to meet two or three people who have travelled down from London on purpose to get some idea of the Effigy Giants. We drive first to Alford Church, which is situated on the left shoulder of the giant Scorpion (that Scorpion which Gilgamesh met when he went to seek his friend Enkidu) for in the Church there is an early bench-end depicting a scorpion about to sting a human head symbolizing the sun; also a stained glass window representing the Cup, which reminds us we are in quest of the Holy Grail.

We continue along the main road to the first turning on the right, and cross the bridge at the Mill over the river Brue, where we notice how the river outlines the top of the Scorpion's body and right claw. Then drive down the right side of the Scorpion, via Hornblotton Green village to the Roman Fosseway. Here we turn sharp right along

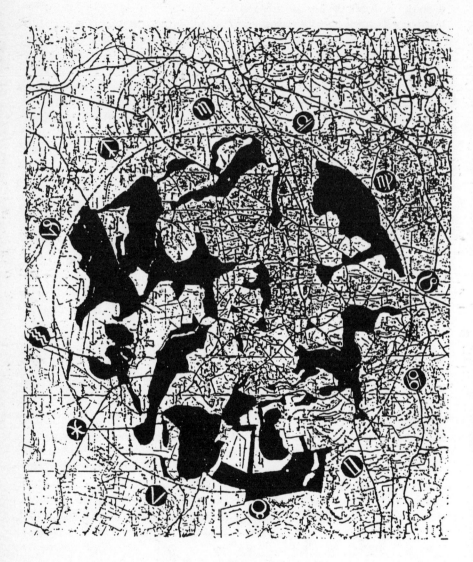

Figure 8: 'King Arthur's Round Table of the Zodiac', Somerset, England

the Fosseway to the first turning on left, to Stone. Stone lies in White Stone Hundred. In the north west corner of the first field, on the opposite side of the road from the farm house, is where the Royal Star Antares fell which marked, no doubt, the foundation stone of the whole layout of this nature Zodiac, dating it by the Autumnal Equinox as between 4000 and 2000 BC. The Stone was probably of the lovely Orange-Oolite found here. From Stone we continue along Stone Lane outlining the left side of the tail of the Scorpion, as far as College Green, where the 'sting' rises in a spring that feeds Par Brook, and flows on over the small of the back of Hercules. (King Arthur's stars are the stars of Hercules, riding the horse of the Archer.)

THE ARCHER'S HORSE

Here we leave the Scorpion and reach the left knee of King Arthur near West Bradley, follow the under part of his leg, then turn to the right down the chest of his horse, to West Pennard. All this time we have been in the Vale of Avalon 'where lies King Arthur', and towering up in front of us stands the famous Isle of Avalon. The superbly drawn figure of the Archer King Arthur should be reserved for some future visit, when all the other effigies have been thoroughly mastered, because, till this perplexing country of Sea Moors is familiar, much valuable time would be lost at this juncture, and the Dove and three Enclosures at the Centre of the effigy circle, should be visited at the same time as the Giant King. His horse Pennard Hill, rising to a height of 400 feet, lies due east of us.

THE GOAT

The main Glastonbury road outlines the back of the Goat. At West Pennard we turn sharp left, up the neck of the Goat to Ponter's Ball. This is the horn of Capricornus, it is one of the best known 'earthworks' in the Grail Area. Though a most important prehistoric landmark, about three quarters of a mile long, it is not so interesting as the 'camp' earthworks on Dundon Beacon Hill, because they actually model the ear of the Giant Orion, whilst this horn is perfectly straight. After walking along Ponter's Ball (on the left hand side of the main road, where the knee of Hercules nearly touches the earthwork) notice the raised path, on the right hand side of the Glastonbury road, that outlines the profile of the Goat's face.

THE PHOENIX OF THE ISLE OF AVALON
THE WATERCARRIER

We continue along the main road till we come to the right-hand turning to Chalice Well, which is at the foot of the pilgrim path up the Tor. Here we are indeed on hallowed ground, if we consider the feet of many saints that have passed this way, since Christ was born, though probably it was even more hallowed in pre-Christian times.

The well is at the top of the garden on the left, but we drink of the holy water that flows over the 'blood' stained stone lower down. The construction of the huge blocks of stone, visible when the well is emptied, was considered by experts to be of the Pyramid age. This Chalice Well Blood Spring is the Urn of the Watercarrier.

Now refreshed, we climb to the top of Glastonbury Tor, 500 feet high, by the Pilgrim path which outlines the beak of the Phoenix. The figure of King Arthur lies below, to the south east, but trees make it difficult to trace at this distance; however the great Fish of Wearyall Hill stands out against the setting sun, whilst the drawing of the Goat's magnificent back and horn can be seen under the Tor on the east side; the outstretched wings of the Phoenix point to the north. If we are not nearly blown off by the wind — in which case we seek the shelter of St Michael's tower — the mist called 'the White Lady of Sedgemoor' may be covering the land with her heaving mantle of invisibility, reminding us that this is the ancient haunt of ghosts, and that this Cauldron of Wisdom 'will not boil the food of a coward'. However it is also 'The Cauldron of Renovation', and in the little town of Glaston (lying on the Phoenix tail) we shall be refreshed in mind and body, for the Abbey grounds, where stood the world famous Wattle Church of St Joseph of Arimathea, are full of inspiration, and stories of her saints can be had in plenty; also the Church in the High Street is worth a visit as well as the Pilgrim Inn and the Court House.

Second Day

THE FISH OF WEARYALL HILL ANCIENTLY CALLED THE SALMON'S BACK

From Glastonbury we drive along the south side of Wearyall Hill and get out at the little gate on the right to stand on the spot where St Joseph of Arimathea planted his staff, cuttings of which still bloom at Christmas tide; the place is marked by an inscribed stone. To the north we look down on the famous Lake Villages, for which, supposedly, this hill stood as their Fish god, for legend says an enormous salmon lies buried here. On leaving the Fish, we cross Pomparles Bridge, by the Fish's mouth, from whence King Arthur is said to have cast away his sword. The arm of the effigy King Arthur crosses the river Brue four miles up stream.

THE WHALE

We are now upon the Whale's tail, the uncertain movements of which made the passage of the bridge so 'perilous' for the Knights of King Arthur, hence its name. From the top of Glaston Tor the drawing of the effigy Whale can be traced by following the course of the river on its under side; it can also be seen from the Salmon's Back.

THE RAM LAMB

The unromantic little town of Street stands in the Ram's head, so we drive on down its face and back, to Walton, and at the first turning on the left, make for the old stone windmill tower on Walton Hill. Here there is an interesting view over King Sedgemoor, on which can be seen the remarkably straight lines of the Giant Orion's ship (just west of the Dundon Hills). It is entirely delineated by water ways, and lies below the Giant who presents his back to us from this standpoint.

Now, following the road to Marshall's Elm, we outline the top of the hind leg, and the under side of the bent back fore leg; a quarry marking the knee at the cross roads. Here we leave the Ram Lamb.

The Ivy Thorn Woods opposite are National Trust property, and used to be sweet with primroses and bluebells in the Spring, when all the song birds shouted together; so let us pause there to read — lest we forget — this 'Quest of the Sangraal' by R. S. Hawker, the Cornish mystic.

> Forth gleamed the east and yet it was not day:
> A white and glowing horn outrode the dawn;
> A youthful rider ruled the bounding rein,
> And he in semblance of Sir Galahad shone;
> A vase he held on high; one molten gem,
> Like massive ruby or the chrysolite;
> Thence gush'd the light in flakes; and flowing, fell
> As though the pavement of the sky brake up,
> And stars were shed to sojourn on the hills
> From gray Morwenna's stone to Michael's tor,
> Until the rocky land was like a Heaven.
> Then saw they that the mighty quest was won:
> The Sangraal swooned along the golden air:
> The sea breath'd balsam, like Gennesaret
> The streams were touched with supernatural light,
> And fonts of Celtik rock stood full of God!

We have now completed half our circular tour of King Arthur's Round Table, for we are opposite the Scorpion which marked the Autumnal Equinox at Stone when this 'Heaven on Earth' was laid out. The continuation of the Walton Hill road runs direct from the Bull's horn to Castle Cary, via the tuft on the Lion's tail (the triangular enclosure by Christian's Cross), or should we wish to return to Glastonbury we take the road to the left at Marshall's Elm and thus complete the drawing of the shoulder, neck and head of the Ram Lamb.

THE BULL

But, weather and time permitting, the most mysterious, legend rich and oldest effigies lie ahead of us. As we mount up onto the Bull's head we look down upon its time honoured eye, and the hoof which marked the Spring Equinox of 2700 BC and rejoice with the birds that this spot was chosen by the ancient astronomers to immortalize their

May Day festivities, it still retains endless enchantment. Nightingales, black birds and many others, sing their reiterating Hallelujah chorus, whilst the Lion and the Bull with heraldic gestures, guard the young Sun Giant of the Spring. For unto us a child is born, unto us a son is given, and his name shall be called Wonderful! the Prince of Peace!

So we follow the road straight up Collard Hill, which forms the Bull's neck, to the Hood monument, which stands on its head. There is a fine view of Glastonbury Tor from here, and to the south we can peep into the Giant Child's ear which is turned upwards, listening to the music of the spheres. Further along the road we come to the great earthwork of the Bull's horn, on the right hand side, its tip pointing to the entrance to Butleigh Wood on the left. From the gate a track leads to the place of the star Capella, which is a star shaped space in the wood at the tip of the second horn, now overgrown. On returning to the Hood monument, we take the first turning to the left down a steep hill, that outlines the Bull's face, as far as the remains of Compton Cross, which marked the elbow of the Giant Orion's upraised arm.

The Giant Orion or Twin

We must take the lane to Dundon Church in order to find the path past the school, up to Dundon Beacon Camp, which forms the great ear of the Giant child. It is overgrown to such an extent that we may have to break in some other way. On the opposite side of the hill, due east, the red cliffs of Gilling Down should be noticed. Once in the Camp, we find what is left of the Tumulus forming the Beacon, excavated 100 years ago, and then walk all round the earthworks, trying to follow the drawing of the great ear. A double bank leads to the spring, now piped down the hill.

Having enjoyed the view over King Sedgemoor and Bridgwater Bay into Wales, we make our way down to Dundon Church again by the Giant's chin, where the car waits to pick us up to go to Hurst Farm which stands on the Bull's hoof. Farther on, on the right hand side of the farm road, is the Duck Decoy. The Royal Star Aldebaran falls on this important landmark. It marked the Spring Equinox of about 2700 BC.

Another interesting feature are the clearly cut linches forming the Giant's ribs, high on Lollover Hill. To reach them we return to the Church, which is haunted by a Knight holding a sword (so the Vicar told me; was it Orion's famous sword I wonder?), and take the tiny path below the vicarage leading to Lollover lane. Each rib is four to five feet high, beautifully carved and sharp in drawing; there are six of them. From this elevation we can see the great 'rhyne' outlining the mast of the Giant's Ship, upon which the Bull rests his hoof; and also the bent up knee and finely drawn back of this Giant Child.

Returning to the Church, we drive round the face and high forehead of the Giant to the main Somerton road, and then turn sharp right, noticing the little hill on the right hand side of the road forming the Little Dog's head. An important Romano-British Villa stood in the field just in front of this Littleton Hill; it was warmed by means of lead water pipes which also supplied baths from a never failing spring. The tessellated pavements that were found, like those at Pitney, should have been preserved; fortunately there are drawings of them at Taunton Castle Museum, and in the Victoria County History. At one time the Little Dog's head was of great importance, as it lies near the Ecliptic Circle of this Zodiac, with the heads of the Lion, Twin, Bull and Ram, hence the legendary interest of this lovely valley through which we are now passing.

The Lion of Cats-Ash Hundred

Castley Hill forms the Lion's right paw, raised above the main road, to the left after passing the Littleton houses. The bridge to the right over the Cary river leads to the Lion's left paw, upon which stands the ancient county town of Somerton. The Church has a wonderful roof of carved dragons and an altar table with interesting carved legs, but my 'Guide to Glastonbury's Temple of the Stars' tells all about these Somerton treasures and so many other things about the Lion and Virgin that I suggest we browse for a while over cider or Somersetshire cream in this old world setting. The Red Lion and the White Hart Inns both stand in the market square with its town hall and market cross and beautiful octagonal church tower.

Now from Somerton we return by the bridge by which we came, over the Cary; it is this river that outlines the ribs and hind leg of Leo, so turn right along the body of the Lion via Charlton Mackrell Church, and then leaving the Lion effigy, drive through Charlton Adam, to Stickle Bridge.

The Virgin

At Stickle Bridge on the Roman Fosseway, the Virgin grasps her Wheatsheaf 'Kern Baby'; a mile and a half further on, the Fosseway crosses the East Lydford road at Cross Keys Inn; here we turn sharp right, back to Castle Cary Station from which we started.

Those who are steeped in Arthurian, or for that matter, legendary lore of either land or sky, are able to visualize the Somerset Giants, despite their enormous size (eight of them are exactly the same measurement, 6000 yards, which is proof in itself that they could not be fortuitous); so come with me, 500 feet up Castle Hill, to gaze over the 'forbidden Land of Logres', and drink in the mystery and enchantment of this 'Cauldron of Wisdom', whilst the sun sinks down into the western sea only to rise again as King Arthur in a golden Dawn.

At the time of the wars of Alexander, 334 BC, the haughty Celtic envoys concluded their mission to him by saying 'We fear no man:

there is but one thing we fear, namely, that the sky should fall on us.'
T. W. Rolleston remarks: 'The reference to the falling of the sky seems
to give a glimpse of some primitive belief or myth of which it is no
longer possible to discover the meaning. One is reminded of the folk-
tale about Henny Penny who went to tell the King that the sky is
falling.'

The national oath of the Celts was: 'If we observe not this
engagement may the sky fall on us.' Now in 'Tain Bo Cuailgne' of the
book of Leinster (twelfth-century manuscript) we find: 'Heaven is
above, and earth beneath us, and the sea is round about us. Unless the
sky shall fall with its showers of stars on the ground where we are
camped . . . we shall not give ground.' This survival of a peculiar oath-
formula for more than a thousand years, and its reappearance after
being first heard of among the Celts of Mid-Europe, in a mythical
romance of Ireland, is certainly most curious (See *Myths and Legends of
the Celtic Race*), but the unique fact that the sky had 'fallen' on the
country which they conquered, seems to stand out as the most awe
inspiring oath they could give expression to.

The Great Zodiac of Glastonbury[1]

ROSS NICHOLS

A System Six Thousand Years Old

Perhaps the most intriguing addition to the mythical lore of England in the present century is the apparent revelation, by aerial survey and by patient identification of local names with Celtic-Arthurian myth, of a ten-mile-wide Zodiac in North Somerset, outlined by 'rhines' or dykes, ancient paths and earthworks, and taking advantage of all available natural features such as rivers. The startling implications of such a complex topographical structure at the very early date claimed, 2700 BC, have led to considerable scepticism; indeed informed archaeological opinion has hardly yet pronounced upon the matter.

The latest antiquarian opinion on the origin of the Zodiac is that it evolved in Babylonia from incidents in the life-cycle of the hero Gilgamesh, himself superimposed upon some still earlier seasonal hero figure. Robert Graves in *The White Goddess* opines that originally it was based on a thirteen-month lunar calendar of trees. The Zodiac may be speculatively dated from a time and place when its quarterings coincided with appropriate festivals in some region; when, that is, at the Shepherd's Festival of the Spring Equinox the sun rose in the Twins, and at the summer solstice in the Virgin (Ishtar, the love and mother goddess); when the Archer coincided with the Autumn Equinox, the hunter's season of Nergal; and when the time of most rain, the winter solstice, occurred with the rising of the Fish. Gilgamesh kills a bull, has love passages with the goddess and adventures with scorpion-men, while his deluge story links with the Water-Carrier. That is, the original Zodiac was in use at least in the early third millenium BC, for about 3800 BC already the Bull was ousting the Twins from the Spring Equinox house. According to archaeologists the Egyptians took over the signs with alterations, perhaps 2000–1600 BC; it may be held, however, that both drew the Zodiac from the same source, which the occultist may believe was the lost continent of Atlantis. At any rate the Egyptian is the later by our records, and the precession of the Equinoxes had disarranged their original seasonal scheme; Leo replaced Virgo and Aquarius Pisces. These dates mean that to estimate a Zodiac as being earlier than 2000

[1] Originally published in *The Occult Observer*, vol. 1, 1949/50.

BC is now by no means an archaeological improbability. But in 1800 BC the Bull itself was displaced by Aries the Ram, and the Zodiac rearranged for Gilgamesh as a Shepherd King to lead the year; just as the Greeks later gave the Zodiac story the parallel shape of the Argonauts' voyage for the Golden Fleece (ram). Now the equinoctial line of the Glastonbury Zodiac indicates a time when the sun is just over half-way between Aries and Taurus; it may be dated with some certainty, for the base line of the central triangle at Butleigh, to whose centre points the finger of the Archer figure, is an equinoctial line of 2700 BC.

Some archaeological evidence exists of colonization in Britain by a people of Sumerian affinities near about the alleged date of the Zodiac. The Sumerian creatures at the quarterings of the year are the Bull, the Lion, Man (Sagittarius) and Bird (Phoenix), as on the standard of Sargon II of Assyria: Sargon, whose ships are supposed to have reached the tin mines 'beyond the Western sea'. The name Sumer may indeed be that 'Summerland' of Somerset whence in the sixth Welsh Triad the patriarch Hu Gadarn is said to have conducted the Cymry to Wales. Further, the ecliptic, or line of the sun's course through the Zodiac figures — 'the furrow of the heavens', as it was poetically called — is found to correspond with the way travelled by the Arthurian knights in quest of the Graal, the signs answering to their adventures.

The First Mighty Labour of Britain

Briefly, then, an equinoctial lay-out appears to link Babylon, Egypt — whose temples after a certain date are equinoctial in their orientation — and Glastonbury. The common link and origin of these will be suggested a little later. The apparent form of the Glastonbury creatures is a representation of the constellation shapes themselves as seen directly in the sky above, not a mere ring of Zodiac signs. That is, they form a reversed map of the heavens in effigy: 'as above, so below':

> Heaven above, Heaven below:
> Stars above, stars below:
> All that is over, under shall show.
> Happy thou who the riddle readest.

They formed in fact at once a true Caer Sidi, or castle of the gods, and a Caer Arianrhod, or temple of the heavens. Such a hidden great work was written of repeatedly by Welsh bards as the first 'mighty labour of the land of Britain', the second being Stonehenge. Hints of a mysterious land of hidden giants or arcane knowledge in the West of Britain are strewn freely over early British poetic literature.

The thesis is, then, that in the sub-historic period when the marshy sea-land of North Somerset with its hill-islands was being drained and tracks and defence works established, a deliberate large-scale design was carried out whereby a Sumerian Zodiac pattern of considerable astronomical accuracy was created on an enormous scale, several of the figures being over three miles long, utilizing some natural outlines, such as the windings of the Parret and Bure Rivers and the shapes of the Polden hills, marking the rest by trackways, the lines of the 'rhines', and perhaps by plantations, and signalizing significant points by earthworks.

For the information concerning these alleged outlines, and indeed for the publicizing of the whole thesis, recourse must be had to the writings of Mrs K. E. Maltwood, who for years has brooded over the Glastonbury shapes and synthesized miscellaneous lore bearing on them. The material for this and the following articles will therefore largely be drawn from the Maltwood *oeuvre*.[2].

On an ordnance survey map the area may be identified by describing a circle of five miles radius centred on the hamlet of Butleigh. Near the centre of this circle of ten miles lies to the south-east Barton St David, coinciding with the body of the mystic dove or goose. To the north, the former Island of Glastonbury (Avalon) forms the shape of the phoenix, at the beak of whose reversed head is the blood-red Chalice or Challis 'Blood' Spring. To the west, the village of Street is similarly largely coincidental with the head and forepart of the ram or lamb. Southward, Somerton, the ancient capital of Wessex, and Charlton Mandeville fall mainly within a fore-paw and the rump of the lion; while Keinton Mandeville is on the verge of the corn-baby-sheaf of the Earth Mother, Virgo.

The Origins of Druidic Beliefs

It is inevitable to those interested in the British mystical tradition to enquire what bearing this apparently new discovery has upon the already-known early beliefs in this country commonly associated with the term Druidism. However uncertain we may be of much of its teaching, some of it seems by now to be well established by comparative study of texts and by recent archaeology. The latter has been especially enlightening on origins. Instead of being forced to look eastward to Egypt and elsewhere for the origins of various elements, it now appears that we can reasonably attribute the core of both Egyptian and the proto-Druidic religions to a common origin in North Africa.

[2] *A Guide to Glastonbury's Temple of the Stars*: 'Air View Supplement' to this: *The Enchantments of Britain*, by K. E. Maltwood, FRSA. Other works used are: Lewis Spence, *The Mysteries of Britain*; Sir John Rhys, *Hibbert Lectures*, 1866; Lady Charlotte Guest, *The Mabinogion*; poems of Taliesin, the Barddas and Welsh Triads and *The High History of the Holy Graal passim*; Robert Graves, *The White Goddess*; Geoffrey of Monmouth, *History of the Kings of Britain*; *The Observations of Bell*, *the Epic of Gilgamesh* and *The Babylonian Legend of the Creation*, from the British Museum; Plutarch, *passim*; Nennius, *Historia Brittonum*; E. A. Wallis Budge, *Amulets and Superstitions*; Mme. Blavatsky, *Secret Doctrine*, and Dr. Layard, *The Lady of the Hare*.

The Neolithic long-barrow men who traded, settled and built along the north-west of the British Isles on the way to the Baltic, were definitely African in origin. There, as in Spain, they left prolific evidences of their cult of the dead. The date tentatively given for their arrival has been 2000 BC, the middle Minoan period; but it may well have been earlier. In any case the late Palaeolithic culture upon which they impinged also has most definite traces of the cult of the dead. As early as 1400 BC Aurignacian burials proved this — aeons earlier than Egypt. Megalithic remains associated with these Old Stone Age peoples show that the common origin of this belief was somewhere in North Africa, and that it then spread eastward to crystallize later as the cult of Osiris in Egypt, and northwards via the abundant remains in Spain to Brittany and Britain. Osiris appears about 3400 BC at Abydos in the First Dynasty. It may well be therefore that, if the cult of the Cabiri or 'Twins' was indeed the North African cult whence Osiris came, a similar cult may have spread northward with the great stone monuments to the dead as far as Britain long before the archaeologists' date of 2000 BC.

In Britain there followed invading waves of the 'roundheaded' or Celtic peoples, traders coming via Central Europe. They enriched culture on the physical side, but seem to have taken over these Iberian religious ideas completely. Thus the cult of Bealteine or Beltane, at one time universal in Britain and with traces of survival to the present day in Ireland and Scotland at least, is identical here and in Morocco.

Waves of further invasions and wars from Ligurian and East-Germanic peoples swept the European continent, but seem mostly to have checked at the Channel. Thus it was that in Britain there seems to have developed a more systematic and unhindered religion based on the cult of the dead, even as eastwards in Egypt the peculiarly static conditions of civilization enabled that extraordinary continuity of Pharaohs and Osiris-figures through the centuries.

Britain, when the curtain rises, a little fitfully, on history proper, was known to Caesar as the origin and training-place of the cult of Druidism; a statement that other evidence confirms. Roman and Greek notices of Druidism are unanimous in their strong assertion of its cult of the dead. Druidism obscured itself in the period of the Saxon invasions, although it is from the fifth century that the historic Arthur comes. It evidently revived later.

Our task here, however, is to relate Druidism to the Glastonbury Zodiac, which is perhaps best done by first giving a brief outline of Druidic mythology, then seeing what parts of the Zodiac are referrable to it.

The Osiris of the West

The core of the layout of this, as of every Zodiac, is the ecliptic line, and the very centre of the Druidic arcane teaching was modelled on 'furrow of the heavens'. Man rose with the sun from Annwn, the abyss of creative force, parallel with the Egyptian Nu, through which nightly Osiris passes; it seems in various aspects to be chaos, hell, or even a magical land. Any psycho-analyst would at once recognize it as an archetype of the Jungian *id*, the 'seething cauldron' of the unconscious. Man traverses earth or Abred, the sphere of human life and visible creative matter, performing perhaps the twelve tests of the sun-hero, and at death sinks in the west into Gwynvyd, the place of the tested and purified spirits. The highest or innermost of these spheres or concentric circles of creation, is the abode of the Divine, Ceugant.

Into the initial place of chaos and suffering, which also seems to be death — perhaps of the unperfected spirits — the hero-god who is the sun has gone before man, exploring the secrets of death and emerging with them to instruct him. But man must also undergo his hallowing experience, and in initiatory rites must follow the sun-hero, whom in Britain appears earliest as Hu Gadarn, the patriarch of the Welsh Race, but earlier was the supreme God; he whose attributes seem largely to be taken over by Arthur, with his mystical suffering and occlusion, his 'round table' of the Zodiac, the vigil of the initiate and the earnest promise of his coming again. The three queens of Arthur are the three seasons of his mate the earth.

Beneath the supreme Hu are the god-agents of creation, the male force Celi or Coel, and the cauldron goddess Keridwen, the pair being imaged as a white bull and cow — a very ancient image associated with India. Celi, 'the Hidden One', seems to have been the mistletoe god with his white pearl-berries of insemination; one remembers the mistletoe sacrament of the legendary Druidic rites. He lingers most clearly as a name perhaps in the Cole dynasty of Colchester. Keridwen is the English Demeter or Ceres, the 'goddess of various seeds', the White goddess of Mr Robert Graves and prototype of many goddesses who were probably local figures — Ana, Dana or Donu, Brigantia or Brigid, even Ma-Gog, the wife of Gog or Ogmios. Hers is the cauldron of the world's womb and of initiation, bringing forth Taliesin the sun and summer, and Afagddu the night and winter — the principle of pairs of opposites, one might say. Taliesin eventually becomes surrogate for Hu, perhaps when Arthur became a more underworld and fertility figure; he sits in the golden chair of the wheel of the heavens.

Solemn processes of initiation and revelation centred about Keridwen with her cauldron, as about the earth-mother Demeter and Eleusis. Three heavenly drops had been stolen from heaven or Ceugant, and to obtain inspiration the mystic descent into Annwn must be made, where they were to be found in the Cauldron of Inspiration, which eventually identifies with Annwn itself and with Keridwen. In more modern language, and robbing it of its mystic

significance, this would seem to mean, putting it baldly, that the poet
or prophet must descend into the unconscious *id* to obtain his true
'flow'.

The Boat of Millions of Years

Let us return to the point of divergence between the eastern and the
northern cults of the dead. The cult of the Cabiri, 'twins' and lords of
the dead, appears as before-mentioned to be the North African origin
of both the Egyptian Osiris-cult and the proto-Druidism of the Iberian
traders. It is surely significant that the zodiac originated at the very
period (*c*.4500 BC) when the Twins began the year at the Spring
Equinox. It becomes far more than coincidence when we find that the
deepest and most complex symbols of the Glastonbury scheme lie
unquestionably at this sign.

The final and deepest mysteries of this arcane system are lodged in
the Gemini group of figures. Within this area lies the Boat of Millions
of Years, the mystic origin of the alphabet, the regulating pointers of
time, the secret name of God. Inadequate these accounts of the zodiac
figures must necessarily be in a brief space; but the implications and
overtones of mythical meaning in the symbolisms clustering here
almost defy brief summary.

A strange-looking boat, her stern built a mile high, perhaps with a
sail, her prow lower, with the stub of a mast, extends over three miles
long and resolves itself into an outline as of an Egyptian type of ship
of the IVth Dynasty. Above is a very plainly-modelled kneeling figure
with an immense bowed head, holding up one arm in a square over it,
the effect being that of a child or dwarf-shaped giant. To the south, a
griffon shape emerges from the lion with long down-stretched paw
and beaked head over the apparent prow. At this child the rampant
lion sign appears to be gazing eagerly; the griffon, the little dog and,
from the north, the bull, also look towards him. A huge earthwork,
Dundon Hill Camp, forms the large ear of the head; at the mouth is a
tithe barn. The rest of the outline is mainly roads.

The Orion stars fall completely within the child-dwarf. He sits on the
constellation Lepus the Hare, called by Arabs the Giant's Chair. Into
the clenched fist of the upheld arm fall the Gemini stars. Upon the
ship's mainmast fall the thirteen stars of Eriganus, the River of the
Sky. If one continues the lines of the masts, they converge upon the
apex which touches the sign of the goose-dove; the mainmast line
passes on the way through two first magnitude stars. Aldebaran, the
then equinox star, and Capella in Auriga, patron star of Babylon,
where it marked the year's beginning. Now the former sign of Gemini
was two stars above a ship; and this sign saved the good ship Argo.

The names of sun gods, Lugh and Hu, are quite thickly strewn in the
neighbourhood, as e.g. Lugshorn and Huish. Dundon may be the
Dûn or fort of Dôn or Donwy, a Welsh underworld god, originally a

Jehovah, who in Eire is the ancestor of the Tuatha dé Danaan. Hu Gadarn of the Welsh poems is the previously noted British patriarch; a Noah who taught the Welsh ploughing, then with his oxen evicted a monster from Llyn Llion, causing it to burst out in a flood which he and his wife alone survived,his wife being a cow-goddess of seeds. Hu appears also to be an old Channel Islands deity of waters, Hon. Such Noah figures and sun worship were linked; Osiris the sun-god enters the ark of the crescent moon, Huan of Babylon is deity of the great deep — and Huanis the alternative name of the hero of Welsh myth, Llew Llaw Gyffes, the Lion of the Steady Hand, who is again a sun-god identified with Lugh and mourned at Lughnasadh or Lammas-tide.

Osiris's soul was believed to rest in Orion, who was identified by the Egyptians with a long-eared ass-god, Set, who was brought from the desert by the Shepherd Kings and who later became a Cretan hunter. This long-eared god may link with the huge ear of Dundon. Hu may also be Uruanna the Phoenician sun-god; and the Arthurian Logrin is fairly surely a form of Orion.

The Three Pillars of God's Name

The dwarf-giant of Dundon, then, seems first to be a flood-hero-sun resting upon a crescent-moon ark; the sun and the moon together form the Twins. Secondly and mainly, however, the figure is the child of the sun hero. Osiris as the child sun-disc Horus or Heru was sitting in the Boat of Millions of Years when he was stung by Scorpio (the opposing Zodiac sign). The boat stopped, and Thoth the scribe-god descended uttering the word which heaven, earth and hades must obey; whereupon some of Ra's fluid of life entered Horus and he came to life, just as the arrow of Sagittarius the sun-hero, who appears to be aiming in the giant-dwarf's direction, may be entering him. We have to look hereabouts therefore for a magical word. Now the Chaldean teacher-god Hoa, who seems the same as Huan of Babylon, had as emblem the arrow-head wedge, the unit of cuneiform writing, hence appears to be god of the alphabet. (The actual cuneiform invention was adopted by Babylon from the Sumerians.) And the Welsh Barddas record that Hu Gadarn beheld three pillars of light on which were inscribed all sciences, and that this giant first made a letter which was the form of God's name; 'the letters of the Holy Name are called the three columns of truth'. Three pillars therefore, presumably converging in cuneiform or arrow shape, form at once the name of God and record all knowledge.

Does anything supply such a broad-arrow sign hereabouts? The converging lines from the masts, so obviously meant to intersect at an exact point, suggest compasses. Bisecting their angle, a line falls precisely through the mouth of the dwarf-giant and continues into his thigh. This must surely be intentional; and if so, then we have the broad arrow of three lines, rays or pillars. The passing of the centre line of God's name through the mouth is a clear symbolism for its utterance by Hu.

Further, the line cuts the thigh precisely where falls the brilliant star Rigel; which looks like the origin of the wounded thighs of resurrection gods like Adonis or Mithra or the Graal King. 'Upon the wound they lay the spear and the frost from his flesh so cold it draweth . . . as crystals of glass to the spear doth hold, as ice to the iron it clingeth, and none looseth it from the blade.' Again, it is the secret name from the giant's mouth that falls on the thigh, and there is a queer tradition of names written or hidden on thighs: 'he hath on his thigh a name written, King of Kings and Lord of Lords'. Jewish legend has it that Jesus obtained from the innermost Jerusalem temple the secret name of Jehovah, and cutting open his thigh hid in it the transcribed Word.

The two lines of the compass triangle converge, as noted, at the acute angle of a triangle below the goosedove. Within this dove fall the stars of the Plough, and the revolutions of these have always been the timepiece of the sky. The secret name therefore radiates from the sign of Time, the central mystery of the universe. The centre line is that ray of creation which is dropped into the cosmic deep in the Book of Dayzan.

Compasses and surveying-line associate themselves with the square, and the dwarf-giant's arm is held up in an unmistakable square, a mason's square. Hu is obviously meant for the measurer or architect of the sky, as was the Chaldean Hur, twin of the setting sun.

Again, since we have an enormous archer-father at Sagittarius and an earth-goddess mother at Virgo, this is evidently the child of the trinity. So that if Sagittarius is Arthur, the child must be his son Lohot; as we have seen, he is probably the parallel Heru, son of Osiris. The land round here seems peculiarly Arthurian, being red. The giant-child and the countryside around are of red marl; the name Redlands occurs twice, and Red Lake is to his south and outlines the ship. Arthur's chief tournaments were at Red Land, according to the 'High History'. To the present day a fair is held on the red-earth Fair Field. Red is well established as the primitive colour of the dead and of immortality. In the 'High History' Sir Percival hears a bell and sees a ship that sails in below the manor on the shore, bearing the Graal; and just above the Somerset ship, in the bull's dewlap, is a bell-like shape. And, if the Virgo-figure is the earth goddess Keridwen, her child may be Little Gwion the wine-god, or even Taliesin the sun-god.

This great Egyptian-shape ship itself, again, is likely to be not merely the Ark but also Argo, since that constellation falls within its form. Legendarily, Argo was the first ship built, and also the vessel of the Argonauts; but the story of Ulysses is much later than this effigy, if his date is the twelfth or thirteenth century BC. Perhaps it was not Solomon but Sol the sun who built this ship whose masts converge on a sun position, which carries the Graal in the 'High History' but is manifestly, as we have seen, the former carrier-moon and twin of the sun or son of the sun. To the Druidically minded, too, the Ship of Glass comes to mind, the moon-shaped vessel from which it seems was drunk the draught of initiation or inspiration.

Is it, again, coincidence that the other chief Druidic myth-figures that we can reasonably identify with these zodiac signs lay at the other quarterings of the year in the fifth millenium BC? At that period, as we have seen, the Archer was at the Autumn Equinox; and the colossal archer figure of Glastonbury is without much doubt the figure of the sun-father-god, who to the Druids was Hu or Hesus, corresponding to Osiris in Egypt and later identified with Arthur. At the Summer Solstice was then the Virgin; and there is not much doubt that the Somerset Virgo is indeed a vegetarian goddess of the type of Kiridwen or Ceres. Now Hu and Kiridwen we have noted as perhaps the most powerful figures of the Druidic pantheon. Let us therefore take these two in detail.

The Celtic Sagittarius who is Arthur

The Hesus-figure is above Capricorn, to the south, and in close contact with the creature; he forms the year-hero of the zodiac, Sagittarius, mounted on his horse and wearing a Phrygian cap. His right leg is in fact behind Capricorn's head, and the 'horn of plenty' might be considered to be nourishing and supporting the hero, just as Gilgamesh was nourished by the goat Enkidu and Zeus by the goat's horn: 'in the horn Cornucopia was found all that could be desired of flowers and fruit.'

This fire sign, who is, besides Osiris and Arthur, at once Centaur, Herakles, Adonis, Assur, perhaps Gilgamesh himself and a dozen other identifications, covers, together with his horse, a colossal area whose overall length is more than 7,500 yards. The constellation Lyra, which has been called Arthur's harp, falls upon the figure's neck. At the place of his beard is Balsborough or Boltonsborough; the sun's head obviously being the golden ball. Where he straddles the horse the fork of his buttocks is marked by Breech Lane, whilst Canter's Green, surely a riding name, runs up his thigh. The finger of his hand points to Butleigh, centre of the system, formerly known as 'the most holy grave' and a favoured burial ground amongst the local inhabitants. The hero's arms are outstretched, but one is half bent, as drawing a bow; his eye looks along the Equinox line stretching between Aldares and the star Aldebaran; he forms a cross, he is in a sense crucified on the Winter Solstice. The inner meaning of crucifixion in the pre-Christian period seems to have been connected with mystery initiation. The initiated adept, says Madame Blavatsky, was tied on a cross in deep sleep, and at a certain time the beams of the rising sun struck him and he was re-born.

If Arthur's is the sun-father shape, the almost equally large form of the earth-sign Virgo, holding out a wheat-sheaf or Kern-doll towards the centre of the system, corresponds as the Earth-Mother, Keridwen. Her form lies partly on Wheathill, and though the definition of the shape by the Cary River and Rag Lane is not perhaps wholly convincing, the hill of Wimble Toot ('teat of an auger'), lying where her breast should be, strengthens the probability, whilst the outline of the corn-baby by the roads and fields around Keinton Mandeville is most definite. Cadbury Castle may be held to guard these lands from one side, Castle Cary, whence is the best view, from another. The Cam flows from Cadbury towards them with Queen Camel beside it, a name perhaps recalling the God Camulus, or the Carmelites, who were most devoted to the cult of the Virgin. The Kern itself lies exactly across the path of the old ecliptic; and the Virgo star of 20 September falls just on its centre.

Here, then, is the stellar explanation of virgin birth; for the Virgo constellation descending slowly with the season after September, the sun of the Winter Solstice seems as though in the arms of Virgo at the heliacal rising; 'he is as a child nursed by a chaste virgin,' says the Abbé Chauve-Bertrand. Thus from the bosom of the Virgin is born the small sun who is to be the year-hero.

Within the Kern area is the church of St Mary Magdalen, a frequent surrogate of goddesses. September is both the reaping month of the Corn Goddess and the month of the Virgin Mary's birthday.

Here, clearly, is the great mother goddess, the proto-Keridwen, the earth of eternal virginity and fertility, the basis for a western cult of Robert Graves's 'white goddess'; capricious, witchlike with her beaked nose and chin and Phrygian cap, bountiful, being all things to all men. She is Demeter the barley goddess, Danu or Ana the Danaan goddess of plenty in Munster, Nana, mother of Attis and Hermes, or a dozen other forms. In the Arthurian saga she seems to correspond with Percival's sister, the damsel Dindrain.

What of the fourth quarter of the then year, Pisces, in mid-winter? This is not so obvious.

Three miles up a tributary of the Severn, a river which was traditionally haunted by the Salmon of Knowledge, lies the salmon-shaped fish round Wearyall Hill, some 1,500 yards long. It coincides with the sign Pisces and this corresponds with the King Fisherman of the 'High History'. Part of the elevation is known as Fisher's Hill, in local legend the burial place of a giant sacred salmon.

This fish is pre-eminently the wisdom fish of Celtic lore; it fed upon the red hazel nuts (or, alternatively, the berries of the sacred rowan-tree) which were the food of the gods or the dead, and so obtained its red spots. Upon this hill landed St Joseph of Arimathea carrying the blood of the new god 'beyond the ocean to the isles called the Britannic Isles' (Eusebius of Caesarea, AD 260–340); and he represented that religion whose earliest symbol was the fish. About this time in the precession of the equinoxes the sun was passing into the sign Pisces. It was in Chaldea that the fish was a sun symbol indicating the resurrection both of sun and man; whilst in Babylon Dagon the fish-god was probably the same as the sacred man-fish Oannes of Chaldea (Greek *ioannes* = John; cf. John the Baptist — another link with water). Oannes was the god who instructed in wisdom and the arts; the wise salmon of the Celts, therefore, had a respectable ancestry. In the light of the twelve zodiac signs, Joseph's twelve companions and the gift to him of twelve hides of land, 'confirmed after the heathen manner', take on a different aspect. Had Joseph come to lay the sacred blood on the ancient altar of the Fish? And has the planting of the holy thorn any connection with the inserting of a peg, an early calendar custom?

Keridwen's Initiate in the Skin Coracle

More immediately to our purpose, Keridwen's connection with water and its purifying rites is undoubted. One of Gwidion's transform-ations, representing one of the initiation rites of the Druidic training system, is into a fish, when he is pursued by an otter, and this represents some baptismal lustration. Again, the reborn initiate was found in the weir in a skin bag, and this is now held to mean that he or she was floated in a skin coracle into the tides of Caernarvon Bay, where its course was held to indicate the divine will or the state of adeptship of the coracle's occupant. When we add to this the general dream symbolism of water as the womb and maternity, and the clearly maternal connotations of Keridwen's cauldron of rebirth, we may fairly conclude, since this at the beginnings of the zodiac was the mid-winter sign, that it was placed intentionally opposite to Keridwen's mid-summer and signified in fact the rebirth of the year and of the human soul at once.

This perhaps is as far as we can go. It seems indeed likely that the rest of the Druidic pantheon was elaborated at a period much subsequent to this zodiac, perhaps in the period of recession from the Romans, or in the Dark Ages. All one can expect reasonably to find is a group of the largest proto-figures; and these — the cult of the dead in the Cabiri-Twins, the sun-father god who is lord also of the dead, and the Great Mother in some form — we have in fact found, and surely at key points of the zodiac. If Arthur's three queens may be the other three-quarters of the zodiac beside his own autumnal one — a reasonable supposition, since they were definitely the three seasons of his bride the earth — there is no real trace of it here; nor can we identify Keridwen's very early egg of creation with any star feature. At this distance of time indeed it is surprising to be able to identify so much.

The remainder of the most significant details of this zodiac appear to be referable largely to the Sumerian origins already indicated.

Such is the case set forth by Mrs Maltwood, with certain amplifications. If it is a mere imaginative linking of apparent shapes such as the eye makes for itself in gazing at a detailed map, such as we have all made for ourselves gazing into a coal fire, the coincidences of names and traditions in their turn need explaining. Her books have been published some years; but no one of archaeological authority has pronounced, nor apparently even taken the trouble to examine the material upon which this thesis is based. Many wild and unsound theories have been propagated purporting to be based on Glastonbury; and it seems that this zodiac has been classed with them as meriting merely the scorn of serious archaeologists, who are mostly hardworked along their own lines and have learnt to avoid speculative propositions as time-wasters. He who would pronounce usefully upon this matter, moreover, would need considerable qualifications besides archaeology, for it involves sub-history and astronomy and the near-eastern cultures, as a minimum equipment, not to speak of myth in many forms.

11

Somerset's Pre-historic Zodiac Circle[1]

A. R. HEAVER

From time immemorial it has been known that modelled in the hills and landscape near Glastonbury in Somerset there existed a prehistoric zodiac circle. It was not, however, until aerial photography became perfected commercially in the thirties of the twentieth century that the layout of this vast solar calendar with its giant earth-effigies became plainly revealed for all to see. Indeed, it is only when viewed from the air that this enormous circle, ten miles wide in diameter and thirty miles in circumference, can be observed comprehensively in full completeness.

Ordinarily, a chart of the zodiac portrays twelve signs in a circle all facing towards the centre. One of the unique features of this ancient zodiac is that the heads of the effigies all face westwards whilst their bodies remain revolving around the central point upon which they appear to pivot. Although known popularly as a zodiac circle it could be described more accurately as being a circle of constellations rather than one of signs. As in the list compiled by Ptolemy, Scorpio expanded to include Libra is portrayed as a single sign whilst two extra constellations, Hercules and Orion, are included thus making thirteen constellation-signs in all.

An examination of the evidence available indicates that astronomer-architects from Sumeria gave their name to Somerset. Some five thousand years ago they came to design and construct these enormous effigies, portraying them in permanent form so that their symbolism might be preserved in perpetuity for posterity. Archeological experts and scholarly investigators claim that neither Stonehenge nor the Great Pyramid of Gizeh rival in wonder the achievement of these colossal earthworks forming as they do a panorama of the celestial plan and design to represent the dome of the starry firmament of the heavens inverted upon earth.

Nothing is haphazard about the conception revealed in the building of this model since complex geometrical patterns not only correspond to their celestial counterparts but include the position of certain fixed stars in such a way that the accuracy of positions indicated can be confirmed by making cross-check bearings from one to the other.

Thus the line of the Ecliptic is clearly defined running from Antares (marked by the hamlet of Stone) to Aldebaran (marked by Hurst Drove) properly located in the constellations of Scorpio and Taurus, respectively.

The centre of this circle is not at Glastonbury but at Butleigh, which on that account became known most appropriately, locally, as 'the enclosure of the Sun'. Glastonbury Tor falls in the constellation of Aquarius and Keinton Mandeville, where this article was written, coincides with the constellation of Virgo. In this symbolism, the effigy figure of the Virgin is depicted holding aloft a wheatsheaf in her hand, the sheaf of wheat having been designed to measure precisely to scale the exact width of the path taken by the solar orb during its annual course along the ecliptic circle.

As far back as 1934, K. E. Maltwood, author of *A Guide to Glastonbury's Temple of the Stars* was complaining: 'Astrologers of today still use the Signs but ignore the Constellations which is where the Stars really are.' If a Phillip's Planisphere is placed back to back with a composite map made of the area covered by the Somerset Zodiac, it is possible with a pin to prick through the fixed stars and find that they fall in the correct positions of their corresponding effigy constellations.

Surprise is often expressed that the existence of this amazing pre-historic construction is not more widely known or acclaimed. Incredulity also is felt as to how it could have survived intact for so long. The Druids, however, venerated it as being in their estimation the first of what they called 'the mighty works of Britain', Stonehenge being revered as being the second of these mighty works. Later, the Celts held the Circle in equal veneration until the time when the whole area came under the direct jurisdiction of Ecclesiastical authorities. By the time that King Henry VIII destroyed the monasteries, the land extending throughout the district had been held by the learned monks of Glastonbury Abbey for so many centuries that the tradition of preserving ancient landmarks, earthworks and waterways, remained secure and unimpaired.

In 1947, a local farmer asked if he could explain why it was that certain strips of land of unusual awkward shape were bounded by hedges to form a peculiar pattern, replied: 'It is all beyond memory but will never be altered' a comment which testifies to the extraordinary tenacity of loyalty to local traditions still in evidence to this day in Somerset.

Some of the outstanding features of these giant effigies are known to local inhabitants by names which have no apparent relationship to the Zodiac. Thus one of the marks of identification in the Sign of Virgo is called 'Wimbles Toot', the word 'toot' meaning 'teat'. This landmark, visible as a tumulus in a field is scheduled as an Ancient Monument, so that the preservation of its position is preserved intact despite the obvious inconvenience of its location to the farmer owning the field in which it stands.

Similarly, the horn of Capricorn is known locally as 'Pontter's Ball'. On asking the vicar of a church a mile away to direct me to its precise location, he confessed that he had never heard of it. Subsequently, when successful in locating this mound it was found to be of formidable construction, ⅜ of a mile long and rising to 21 feet above the ground. The northern-most tip of this mound terminates close to a main road but its existence is concealed from passing traffic by a cottage and some trees. However, a metal plaque by the roadside, erected by the local authorities, testifies to its authenticity as an ancient earthwork of historic interest and importance. Apart from its significance as part of the symbolism of the Zodiac Circle, this massive earthwork is said to have served a practical purpose as a landing stage for ships unloading cargoes at Glastonbury en route to the seaport at Pylle in days when the sea-moors were navigable for a considerable distance into the interior of the Somerset countryside.

Writing in *Country Life*, just after World War II, Harold Steel, who had seen these gigantic effigies from the air, claimed to have calculated the possibility of such artificial constructions having assumed their symmetrical form by chance, to be ten million to one. Roads, paths, together with dykes and the natural course of rivers, have been all utilised in delineating these outlines. Where else in the world would it be possible to discover the constellations of the starry heavens laid out upon the earth in such an astounding fashion?

PART IV
THE WIDENING CIRCLE

The Widening Circle

Legends attach themselves to Glastonbury in much the same way as iron filings to a magnet. First the Grail, then Arthur, and, more recently, the Zodiac. Alongside this astonishingly rich body of material, and interpenetrating it at many levels, are the stories of Glastonbury's many saints. Among those who are believed to have visited there are SS Brigit and Patrick of Ireland, St David of Wales, St Columba of Scotland, St Dunstan, and various other, less familiar figures. How much credence one may give to these accounts is hard to say. Certainly, Glastonbury was a very significant foundation of the Church, and it is more than likely that if it already had the reputation of being the earliest Christian church in the island, such luminaries as those listed above might well have visited.

St Brigit has an especially well-attested connection with Glastonbury. Her shrine at Beckery was well known during the Middle Ages, and at this time a larger chapel was built on or near the spot where the original shrine had stood. At some point it fell into disuse and was almost forgotten until Philip Rahtz excavated the site in 1967–8. Sadly, but perhaps inevitably, it now lies buried forever beneath a sewage-processing plant.

In the next section some of the legends of the Saints are explored, along with the idea of the church at Glastonbury being the first such Christian foundation in Britain. 'The Ancient Church in Britain' by R. W. Morgan, is part of a book that attempts to trace the evolution of 'British Christianity' as opposed to 'Papal Christianity'; while Armine le Strange Campbell traces some of the material relating to the Saints. 'Christ in Cornwall' deals in depth with the subject of the persistent traditions of Jesus' visit to Britain and to Glastonbury in particular.

Finally comes the first of several selections from the writings of Frederick Bligh Bond, of whom more will be said in the final section of this book. His account of the apocryphal legends of Glastonbury is fairly straightforward, and contains no account of the psychic investigation which underlined his work at the Abbey (see Part V); what it does offer is a much needed summary of the many layers of myth and belief surrounding Glastonbury.

12

The Ancient Church of Britain[1]

R. W. MORGAN

Two cardinal reasons, we have seen, each of national weight and extent, inclined the British mind to accept Christianity — the first, its identity in many important points with Druidism; the second, its uncompromising antagonism to the whole system of the Roman state mythology. The Roman persecution of both religions identified them still further in the popular mind. Nowhere, then, in Asia, Africa, or Europe, could the apostles find richer or a better-prepared soil for the Gospel. If we add that Britain was the only country in these ages where the Christian could profess and practise his religion free from persecution, we reasonably and antecedently conclude that a strong Christian current must have set in from both Jerusalem and Rome to this island from the first or pentecostal days of the Church. We have already propounded the evidence for the missions of Joseph of Arimathea, Simon Zelotes, and Aristobulus. We now present the reader with a chain of attestations concurring in this very early apostolic evangelization. We shall, as in the prior instances, ask for no dogmatic verdict, satisfied with the fact that all the written and circumstantial evidence we possess, or can at this lapse of time hope to collect, point to the presence of St Paul in Britain.

We shall better estimate the force of the following testimonies if we keep steadily in mind the fact that the great British Church which Augustine found AD 596 established in Britain and Ireland, was essentially Eastern, proclaiming by every usage in which she differed from Rome her direct and independent birth from Jerusalem and the apostles themselves in the first throes of Christianity. It is, indeed, an absurdity to go about explaining the existence of such a Church, abounding in all the characteristics of an ancient institution, deeply fixed in the native mind and soil, in any other way than by a frank acceptance of its apostolic origin. Every other attempt at solution fails us. How came these archbishoprics, bishoprics, dioceses, Christian colleges, parochial churches and endowments, royal Christian houses, genealogies of saints, immense and opulent monasteries, a whole nation of believers, to be in Britain? How came they, on their

---

[1] Originally published in R. W. Morgan, *St Paul in Britain* (London, Covenant Publishing, 1938).

first meeting with the missionary of the Bishop of Rome, to proclaim with one voice, 'We have nothing to do with Rome; we know nothing of the Bishop of Rome in his new character of the Pope; we are the British Church, the Archbishop of which is accountable to God alone, having no superior on earth.'[2] This is one of those tremendous facts which rise before us like a huge mountain in the plain of history. Rome found here a Church older than herself, ramifications of which struck into the very heart of the Continent, the missionary triumphs of which in Italy itself in the life of Augustine were greater than his own among the British Saxons; for Columba and his associates from the primitive colleges in Ireland were the evangelizers of the barbarian conquerors, the Lombards, of Northern Italy. The Gallican Church was entirely one with the British in this opposition to Roman assumptions. The archbishops of Treves were, as we learn from the Tungrensian Chronicles, always supplied from Britain. Treves and Rheims became the headquarters of Gallic liberties, and here rose, under Hincmar, as powerful a resistance as in Britain to Italian supremacy. The Briton could never understand why, because Rome professed certain truths, she should arrogate spiritual despotism over all who held the same. He does not appear to have troubled himself about her errors and corruptions; these he regarded as her own matters, with which, as not belonging to him, he did not interfere. Cadvan, Prince of Wales, expresses himself thus to the Abbot of Bangor: 'All men may hold the same truths, yet no man thereby be drawn into slavery to another. If the Cymry believed all that Rome believes, that would be as strong reason for Rome obeying us as for us to obey Rome. It suffices for us that we obey the truth. If other men obey the truth, are they therefore to become subject to us? Then were the truth of Christ made slavery unto men, and not freedom.'

The soldier who interrogated Augustine at the oak of Conference seems, in like manner, to treat the question between them as one quite apart from doctrine.

[2] The continental Churches admitted, for the most part, a Primacy when they rejected the Supremacy of the Bishop of Rome. The British Church admitted neither; it knew nothing of the Bishop of Rome, except on an equality with any of its own British bishops, or any other bishop in the Christian Church. The further we go back into British history, the clearer shines forth in all our laws the entire independence of the British crown, Church, and people, of all foreign authority. All our great legal authorities concur on this point. 'The ancient British Church,' writes Blackstone, vol. iv. p. 105, 'by whomsoever planted, was a stranger to the Bishop of Rome and all his pretended authorities.' 'The Britons told Augustine,' writes Bacon, *Government of England*, 'they would not be subject to him, nor let him pervert the ancient laws of their Church. This was their resolution, and they were as good as their word, for they maintained the liberty of their Church five hundred years after his time, and were the last of all the Churches of Europe that gave up their power to the Roman Beast, and in the person of Henry VIII, that came of their blood by Owen Tudor, the first that took that power away again.'

'Does Rome possess all the truth?'

'All.'

'And you say we do — our usages only differ. Now of two men, if both have all their limbs and senses complete, both are equal. Because the Romans have noses and we have noses, must we either cut off our noses to be Romans? must all who have noses be subject to the Romans? Why, then, should all who hold the faith be subject to Rome because she holds the faith?'

This rough, broad reasoning allowed almost identity in doctrine and practices to be maintained by any Christian with Rome, or any other Church, without in the most remote degree admitting any claim Rome might advance on the ground of such identity. The Briton thus had his festivals, processions, floral decorations, antiphonal choirs, cathedrals — an immense deal in common with Rome — but he had had them for centuries before Papal Rome was ever heard of. And he would have ridiculed the notion that he was to give up a good thing because Rome also had it, as he scorned the idea that a community in such things constituted the shadow of a title on the part of Rome to his allegiance. His position, in fact, was a very strong one — thoroughly Catholic, thoroughly anti-fanatical, and at the same time thoroughly anti-papal: and he knew its strength, resting on historical monuments which could neither be ignored nor destroyed: around him rose hoary cathedrals, churches, abbeys, colleges, 'imperishable stone of witness' that his Church was the primitive apostolical Church of Britain – that the Papacy, with all its claims, was a novelty, an intrusion, an invention, a fable; that there never was a time when the eyes of the Christian pilgrim did not rest on this island on vast evidences bespeaking a Church subject to no other Church on earth, built on its own apostolic foundations, and recognising the apostolic Scriptures alone for its rule of faith.[3]

The general conclusion arrived at by the writers who have previously investigated this final part of our question may be given in the words of Capellus: 'I scarcely know of one author, from the times of the Fathers downwards, who does not maintain that St Paul, after his liberation, preached in every country in Western Europe, Britain

---

[3] Bede's testimony as to the pure scriptural character of the teaching of the British Church is full and explicit, and he contrasts, with feelings of shame and reluctance, the apostolic lives of the British missionaries with those of his own Papal Church. Of Columba he writes, 'He taught only what was contained in the prophetic, evangelic, and apostolic writings, all works of piety and charity being at the same time diligently observed' — Lib. iii. c. 41. Of Aidan: 'All who resorted to him applied themselves either to reading the Scriptures or to learning Psalms' — Lib. iii. c. 5. Of Adamnan: 'He was most admirably versed in the knowledge of the Scriptures' — Lib. iii. c. 15. How entirely the British Church rejected human authority in matters of faith may be collected from the saying of Columba. 'Except what has been declared by the Law, the prophets, the evangelists, and apostles, a profound silence ought to be observed by all others on the subject of the Trinity.' Lib. iii. c. 4.

included.'[4] 'Of Paul's journey to Britain,' writes Bishop Burgess, 'we have as satisfactory proof as any historical question can demand.'[5] The same view is substantially maintained by Baronius, the Centuriators of Magdeburg, Alford or Griffith, next to Baronius the most erudite of the Roman Catholic historians; Archbishops Parker and Usher, Stillingfleet, Camden, Gibson, Cave, Nelson, Allix, & c.

Let us preface the *catena authoritatum* on this point with a few general testimonies from widely different quarters.

'The cradle of the ancient British Church was a royal one, herein being distinguished from all other Churches: for it proceeded from the daughter of the British king, Caractacus, Claudia Rufina, a royal virgin, the same who was afterwards the wife of Aulus Rufus Pudens, the Roman senator, and the mother of a family of saints and martyrs.'[6]

'We have abundant evidence that this Britain of ours received the Faith, and that from the disciples of Christ Himself, soon after the crucifixion of Christ.'[7]

'Britain in the reign of Constantine had become the seat of a flourishing and extensive Church.'[8]

'Our forefathers, you will bear in mind, were not generally converted, as many would fain represent, by Roman missionaries. The heralds of salvation who planted Christianity in most parts of England were trained in British schools of theology, and were firmly attached to those national usages which had descended to them from the most venerable antiquity.'[9]

'The Christian religion began in Britain within fifty years of Christ's ascension.'[10]

'Britain, partly through Joseph of Arimathaea, partly through Fugatus and Damianus, was of all kingdoms the first that received the Gospel.'[11]

---

[4] *Hist. of the Apostles.*

[5] *Independence of the British Church.*

[6] Moncaeus Atrebas, the learned Gallican divine, *In Syntagma*, p. 38.

[7] Sir Henry Spelman's *Concilia*, fol., p. 1.

[8] Soames' *Anglo-Saxon Church*, Introd., p. 29.

[9] Soames' Bampton Lectures, pp. 112–257. This statement is so true, that sixty-three years after the landing of Augustine, that is, AD 660, when all the Heptarchy, except Sussex, had been converted, Wini, Bishop of Winchester, was the only bishop of the Romish communion in Britain, and he had purchased his first bishopric of London from Wulfhere, King of Mercia: all the rest were British. And the cause is patent: Maelwyn or Patrick, the apostle of Ireland, Ninian, the apostle of the southern Picts, Aidan of the Northumbrians, Paul Hên his successor, Columba of the Scotch, Finan of the East Angles, Cad or Chad of the Mercians, were all native Britons, educated in the native colleges. The Romish succession had died down to one prelate, and Saxon Christianity was kept alive or refounded by British Christians. The succession of Augustine in Canterbury and Rochester expired in Damianus, AD 666.

[10] Robert Parsons the Jesuit's *Three Conversions of England*, vol. i. p. 26.

[11] Polydore, *Vergil*, lib. ii.

'We can have no doubt that Christianity had taken root and flourished in Britain in the middle of the second century.'[12]

'It is perfectly certain, that before St Paul had come to Rome Aristobulus was absent in Britain, and it is confessed by all that Claudia was a British lady.'[13]

'The faith which was adopted by the nation of the Britons in the year of our Lord 165, was preserved inviolate, and in the enjoyment of peace, to the time of the Emperor Diocletian.'[14]

Let us now trace our way back from the time of Venerable Bede, AD 740, step by step, to the apostolic era and the apostles themselves.

In the seventh century we have a galaxy of Christian bishops in England, Wales, Ireland and Scotland, whose names alone would make a considerable catalogue.

In the year AD 596 we have the Augustine mission landing in Kent, followed by three conferences with the bishops of the British Church. In AD 600, Venantius Fortunatus, in his Christian Hymns, speaks of Britain as having been evangelized by St Paul.[15]

In AD 542, Gildas writes: 'We certainly know that Christ, The True Sun, afforded His light, the knowledge of His precepts, to our island in the last year of the reign of Tiberius Caesar.'[16]

In AD 500–40, we have various productions of Christian bards, such as Talièsin and Aneurin, emanating from the courts of the Christian sovereigns of Britain — one of the latter, 'The Crowned Babe' (i.e. Christ), interesting as the earliest European specimen of any length, of rhyme in poetry: it is composed in the ancient British tongue.

In AD 400–50, we have the Pelagian heresy originated by Morgan, Abbot of Bangor, being in truth nothing else than a revival of Druidism, and of the old Druidic ideas with regard to the nature and free will of man. The beauty of Morgan's or Pelagius' Latin compositions, his extensive learning and reproachless life, spread the heresy everywhere, and Europe was in danger of relapsing into its old faith. The heresy was suppressed in Britain by the two visitations and zealous preaching of St Germanus or Garmon, Gallic Bishop of Auxerre, and Lupus, brother of Vincentius Lirinensis. We are indebted to Pelagianism for the most valuable part of the productions of St Augustine of Hippo, its opposer — the Coryphaeus of theological authors.[17]

---

[12] Cardwell's (Camden Prof.) *Ancient History*, p. 18. 1837.

[13] Alford's *Regia Fides*, vol. i. p. 19.

[14] Bede, lib. i. c. 4.

[15] 'Transit et oceanum vel qua facit insula portum. Quasque Britannus habet terras atque ultima Thule.'

[16] *De Excidio Britanniae*, p. 25.

[17] Pelagius was born the same day as his opponent, Augustine of Hippo, Nov. 13, AD 354. Vortigern or Gwrtheyrn, the British king, on being excommunicated by Vodin, Archbishop of London, for his incestuous connection with his own daughter, became

In the year AD 408 this Augustine asks, 'How many churches are there not erected in the British isles which lie in the ocean?'[18] And about the same time Arnobius writes: 'So swiftly runs the word of God that though in several thousand years God was not known, except among the Jews, now, within the space of a few years, His word is concealed neither from the Indians in the East nor from the Britons in the West.'[19]

Theodoretus in AD 435 testifies: 'Paul, liberated from his first captivity at Rome, preached the Gospel to the Britons and others in the West. Our fishermen and publicans not only persuaded the Romans and their tributaries to acknowledge the Crucified and His laws, but the Britons also and the Cimbri (Cymry).'[20]

To the same purport in this commentary on 2 Timothy 4: 16: 'When Paul was sent by Festus on his appeal to Rome, he travelled, after being acquitted, into Spain, and thence extended his excursions into other countries, and to the islands surrounded by the sea.'

More express testimony to Paul's preaching in Britain could not be delivered, nor from a more unexceptionable quarter. Theodoret was Bishop of Cyropolis, attended both the General Councils of Ephesus (AD 431) against the Nestorians, and of Chalcedon, AD 451, consisting of 600 bishops. As an excellent interpreter of Scripture, and a writer of ecclesiastical history, he deservedly ranks high.

Chrysostom, Patriarch of Constantinople, supplies (AD 402) cumulative evidence of the existence of pure British Christianity. 'The British Isles,' he writes, 'which are beyond the sea, and which lie in the ocean, have received the virtue of the Word. Churches are there

---

a Pelagian, and invited the Pagan Saxons rather against his own Christian subjects than against the Picts. He soon abandoned Pelagianism for the open Paganism of his young wife Ronixa (Rowena), the daughter of Hengist. It is memorable that Pelagius, when Abbot of Bangor, on receiving an admonition from the bishops of Gaul and Italy — the Bishop of Rome included — on the latitudinarian nature of his principles, returned it with the observation: 'Sola in Britanniâ Ecclesia Britannica judex.' He was deposed next year by a synod at Winchester, resigned Bangor, and went abroad to Rome, Africa, Jerusalem, and died finally in his native land. Of all heretics he was the largest-minded, the most learned, and the most elegant. The caution of one of his opponents — 'Speak not to Pelagius, or he will convert you,' is a very high compliment to the fascination of the man and his address. But the rapid progress of his tenets is attributable also to his commanding eloquence in the British language, of which he was a perfect master — it is, indeed, to this fact that Prosper attributes his success in Britain:

'Dogma quod antiqui satiatum felle Draconis
Pestifer vomuit coluber sermone Britanno.'

Carmina, lib. ii.

[18] Opera, fol., Paris Edit., p. 676.
[19] Arnobius, *Ad Psalm* cxlvii.
[20] Theodoret, *De Civ. Graec.* Off., lib. ix. Nicephorus seems to have followed Theodoretus (Niceph., lib. ii. c. 40;) and Eusebius Pamphilus, lib. iv — ἐπί τας καλονμενας βρετάννιλας νησούς

founded and altars erected. Though thou shouldst go to the ocean, to the British Isles, there thou shouldst hear all men everywhere discoursing matters out of the Scriptures, with another voice, indeed, but not another faith, with a different tongue but the same judgment.'[21]

'From India to Britain,' writes St Jerome (AD 378), 'all nations resound with the death and resurrection of Christ.'[22]

In AD 320, Eusebius, Bishop of Caesarea, speaks of apostolic missions to Britain as matter of notoriety: 'The apostles passed beyond the ocean to the isles called the Britannic Isles.'[23]

The first part of the fourth century is the era of Constantine the Great and his mother Helena. Gibbon, with that perversity which beset him as a mania in dealing with the leading facts of Christianity, strives to persuade himself that Constantine and Helen were not Britons, but natives of some obscure village in the East;[24] his sole support for such a supposition being the fragment of an anonymous author, appended to Ammianus Marcellinus. 'The man must be mad,' states Baronius, 'who, in the face of universal antiquity, refuses to believe that Constantine and his mother were Britons, born in Britain.'[25] Archbishop Usher delivers a catalogue of twenty continental authorities in the affirmative — not one to the contrary. The Panegyrics of the Emperors, the genealogy of his own family, as recited by one of his descendants, Constantine Palaeologus, native records and traditions, all the circumstances of his career, demonstrate Constantine a Briton, bred in the strongest British ideas. 'It is well known,' states Sozomen, 'the great Constantine received his Christian education in Britain.'[26] 'Helen was unquestionably a British princess,' writes Melancthon.[27] 'Christ,' declares Pope Urban in his

[21] Chrysostomi, *Orat.* Ὁ θεὺς Χριστὺς

[22] Jerome, *In Isaiam*, c. liv.; also, *Epistol.*, xiii. *Paulinum*.

[23] Eusebius, *De Demonstratione Evangelii*, lib. iii.

[24] Naissus. Colchester, the birthplace of Helen of the Cross, has, from time immemorial, borne the cross with three crowns for its arms.

[25] Baronius, *ad ann.* 306: 'Non nisi extremae dementiae hominis.' Until the reign of Constantine the Roman Christians had no other church than the Titulus to worship in: 'Ante Constantini imperium templa Romae non habuerint Christiani,' observes Bale (*Scriptores Britan.*, p. 17.) The Pope, it is well known, claims the sovereignty of the States of the Church by right of the decree of the British Emperor Constantine making them over in free gift to the Bishop of Rome. That this decree was a forgery no one doubts; it was, however, confirmed by Pepin. By the papal Church's own shewing, it is infinitely more indebted to the ancient British Church and sovereigns than they ever were to it. Without the benefactions of the Claudian family and Constantine, it would never have risen above the character given it by Pius the First, the brother of Hermas Pastor — 'Pauper Senatus Christi'. For its earthly aggrandisement it is mainly indebted to ancient British liberality.

[26] Sozomen, *Eccles. Hist.*, lib. i. c. v. So Eumenius, in his Panegyric on Constantius to Constantine: 'He begot thee in the very flower of his age.' — *Pan.* 9.

[27] *Epistola*, p. 189.

Brief, *Britannia*, 'shewed to Constantine the Briton the victory of the cross for his sceptre.' 'Constantine,' writes Polydore Vergil, 'born in Britain, of a British mother, proclaimed Emperor in Britain beyond doubt, made his natal soil a participator in his glory.'[28] Constantine was all this and more — by his mother's side he was the heir and representative of the royal Christian dynasty of Britain, as a glance at the table below will serve to shew.

The policy of Constantine, in carrying out which for twenty years with admirable wisdom and inflexible purpose he was supported by armies levied for the most part of his native British dominions, consisted in extending to the whole Roman world the system of constitutional Christianity which had long been established in Britain. But his religious sympathies, as well as those of his mother, were wholly Eastern, not Roman. They were those of the British Church. They revolved around Jerusalem, and the Holy Land, and not Rome. Constantine made but two brief visits, during his long reign, to the Italian capital. Helen spent all her declining years in restoring the churches and sacred sites of Palestine. The objects of Constantine's life are well explained by him in one of his edicts: 'We call God to witness, the Saviour of all men, that in assuming the government we are influenced solely by these two considerations — the uniting of the empire in one faith, and the restoration of peace to a world rent to pieces by the insanity of religious persecution.' Regarded in his threefold character of general, statesman, and legislator, the British founder of secular Christendom may justly be considered the greatest of the Roman emperors. The British Church was represented during his reign by native bishops at the Councils of Arles, AD 308, and Nice, AD 325.[29]

In AD 300 the Diocletian persecution raged in Britain, but was stopped in one year by Constantius Chlorus, continuing to ravage the rest of the empire for eighteen years. We have elsewhere given a list of the British martyrs who perished in it. We cannot doubt that we stand, during these centuries, in the midst of a Church as broad and thoroughly national as the present Protestant establishment; indeed, in one chief respect more so, for the present national Church of England is not that of the people of Scotland, Wales, or Ireland, whereas the ancient British Church embraced all these populations in its fold. Their very names indicate the broader national character of the ancient and primitive Church, one being the British Church, or Church of Britain, the other the Church of England.

Continuing to trace the British Church back, we find Origen, AD 230, alluding thus to its existence: 'The divine goodness of our Lord

[28] *Historia Brit.*, p. 381.

[29] The archbishopric of York was founded, at the request of Helen, by Constantius the Emperor, AD 290. Its second archbishop, Socrates, was martyred in the Diocletian persecution.

ROYAL CHRISTIAN DYNASTY OF ANCIENT BRITAIN

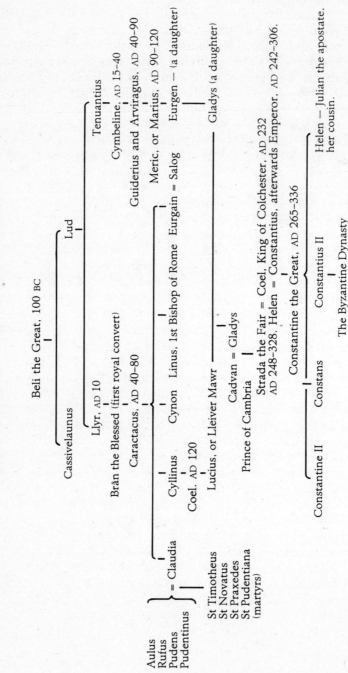

and Saviour is equally diffused among the Britons, the Africans, and other nations of the world.'[30]

In AD 230, however, Britain had been re-incorporated in the Roman empire. What was the case in AD 192-8, in the reign of Commodus, when it proclaimed its independence, and the British legions elected Albinus Caesar? Was the Church confined to the Roman province then insurgent, or were the stubborn British tribes — the Cymri, the Caledonii, the Picts, whom no efforts of peace or war could succeed in bringing to acknowledge the right of a foreigner to plant hostile foot in Britain — within its pale? Tertullian, who flourished during the war of Commodus in Britain, which Dion Cassius terms 'the most dangerous in which the empire during his time had been engaged', says expressly 'that the regions in Britain which the Roman arms had failed to penetrate professed Christianity for their religion.' 'The extremities of Spain, the various parts of Gaul, the regions of Britain which have never been penetrated by the Roman arms, have received the religion of Christ.'[31] We have seen that the British Church had, long before Tertullian's age, founded the Churches of Gaul, Lorraine, and Switzerland, and that its missionaries had made their way into Pannonia. Coming nearer Rome itself, we find that in Tertullian's own age a missionary of the British Church founded, AD 170, the Church of Tarentum. This was St Cadval, after whom the cathedral at Tarento is still named.[32] Not only, therefore, did the British Church, AD 170, embrace Roman and independent Britain, but it had struck its roots in France, Switzerland, Germany, and the extremities of Italy.

We now come to AD 120-50, within the era of the disciples of the apostles. It is certain from St Paul's own letters to the Romans and to Timothy, that he was on the most intimate and affectionate terms with the mother of Rufus Pudens, with Pudens himself, with Claudia his wife, and Linus. The children of Claudia and Pudens were instructed in the faith by St Paul himself. The eldest was baptized Timotheus, after Timothy, Bishop of Ephesus, the Apostle's 'beloved son in Christ', The four, Timotheus, Novatus, Praxedes, Pudentiana, with their father Pudens, sealed at different times their faith with their blood in Rome, and were, with Linus, the first Britons who were added to the glorious army of martyrs. And, Pudens excepted, they were not only martyrs, but royal martyrs; not only royal martyrs, but martyrs of the most patriotic and heroic blood in Britain. Let us confirm these statements by the evidences of primitive antiquity.

The reader will recollect the 'natal day' of a martyr is the day of his martyrdom.

---

[30] Origen, *In Psalm* cxlix.

[31] Tertullian, *Def. Fidei*, p. 179.

[32] MS Vellum of the Church of Tarentum; Catalogue of Saints in the Vatican, published AD 1641; Moronus, *De Ecclesia Tarentina*.

Pudens suffered AD 96, Linus AD 90; Pudentiana suffered on the anniversary of her father's martyrdom, in the third persecution, AD 107; Novatus in the fifth persecution, AD 139, when his brother Timotheus was absent in Britain, baptizing his nephew, King Lucius.[33] Shortly after his return from Britain, and in extreme old age, about his ninetieth year, Timotheus suffered with his fellow-soldier Marcus in the same city of Rome, 'drunk with the blood of the martyrs of Jesus'. Praxedes, the surviving sister, received her crown within the same year. Claudia alone died a natural death, in Samnium, before any of her children, AD 97, surviving Pudens one year. They were all interred by the side of St Paul in the Via Ostiensis.

May 17. Natal day of the blessed Pudens, father of Praxedes and Pudentiana. He was clothed with baptism by the apostles, and watched and kept his robe pure and without wrinkle to the crown of a blameless life.[34]

November 26. Natal day of St Linus, Bishop of Rome.[35]

May 17. Natal day of St Pudentiana, the virgin, of the most illustrious descent, daughter of Pudens, and disciple of the holy apostle St Paul.[36]

June 20. Natal day of St Novatus, son of the blessed Pudens, brother of St Timotheus the elder, and the virgins of Christ Pudentiana and Praxedes. All these were instructed in the faith by the apostles.

August 22. Natal day of St Timotheus, son of St Pudens, in the Via Ostiensis.[37]

September 21. Natal day of St Praxedes, virgin of Christ, in Rome.[38]

Have we, again, any direct contemporary evidence that Linus, the first bishop of Rome, was the son of Caractacus, and brother of Claudia Britannica? Putting aside, for a moment, British genealogies and tradition, does any contemporary of St Paul and Linus, in Rome itself, assert the fact? Undoubtedly. Clemens Romanus, who is mentioned by St Paul, states in his epistle, the genuineness of which has never been questioned, that Linus was the brother of Claudia — 'Sanctissimus Linus, frater Claudiae.'[39] Clemens succeeded Cletus

---

[33] All authors concur in this fact, though all do not see how naturally it followed the relationship between the royal house of Britain and its branch settled in Rome.

[34] Martyr. Romana, ad diem Maii 17. To the same effect the Martyrologies of Ado, Usuard, and Esquilinus.

[35] Martyr, Rom., ad diem; Martyrologies of Ado; Greek Menologies; Usuard, & c.

[36] Martyr. Rom., ad diem; Ado, & c.

[37] Martyr. Rom., Ado, Asuard, Greek Menol.

[38] Martyr. Rom., Ado, & c.

[39] In the Oxford edition of Junius, published AD 1633, 'The son of Claudia'. *Apostolici Patres*, lib. vii. c. 47; *Apostolici Constitutiones*, c. 46. The Apostolic Constitutions may or may not be what their present title infers; but no scholar who peruses the opinions *pro et contra*, collected by Iltigius (*De Patribus Apostolicis*), Buddaeus (*Isagoge in Theologiam*), and Baratier (*De Successione Primorum Episcoporum*), will assign them a later date than AD 150. The mention of Linus in them runs thus:

within twelve years of the death of Linus, as third bishop of Rome. He had also been associated with the British missionary Mansuetus, in evangelizing Illyria. His sources of information are, therefore, unquestionable. St Paul lived, according to all evidence, whenever he was at Rome, whether in custody at large (*libera custodiã*) or free, in the bosom of the Claudian family. There is no dispute that Claudia herself was purely British, and whether Linus was her son or brother, the British character of the family, and the close, the domestic ties of affection between such family and St Paul, are equally manifest. The relationship is, in many important regards, more intimate between St Paul and the British mind — that mind being the leading, because the royal, influence in Britain — in the domestic circle and family worship of the Claudian palace at Rome, than when he addressed the British people themselves in Britain.

But Clemens Romanus not only proves to us that the family which the Apostle thus honoured with his constant residence and instruction was British, that the first bishop appointed by him over the Church at Rome was of this British family, but that St. Paul himself preached in Britain, for no other intperpretation can be assigned his words, - επὶ τὸ τέρμα τῆς Δυσέως — 'the extremity of the West'. 'Paul, after he had been to the extremity of the West, underwent his martyrdom before the rulers of mankind; and thus delivered from this world, went to his holy place.'[40]

It may be suggested that Linus, the first bishop of Rome, was, however, some other than the brother of Claudia, mentioned by St Paul. Not so; for if the above authorities permitted a doubt to remain, the evidence of Irenaeus as to their identity is conclusive. 'The apostles,' writes Irenaeus., AD 180, 'having founded and built up the Church at Rome, committed the ministry of its supervision to Linus. This is the Linus mentioned by Paul in his Epistles to Timothy.'[41]

'Concerning those bishops who have been ordained in our lifetime, we make known to you that they are these: Of Antioch, Eudius, ordained by me, Peter; of the Church of Rome, Linus, the (son) of Claudia, was first ordained by me, Peter.' Lib. i. c. 46. In the original, Αίνος μὲν ὁλ Καυδίας πρῶτγος ἱπὸ Παίλου Analogy requires υἱός to be supplied, but the relationship might have been so well known as to render ἀδελφὺς superfluous.

[40] Clement. Rom., *Epistola ad Corinthios*, c. 5. The passage *in extenso* runs thus: 'To leave the examples of antiquity, and to come to the most recent, let us take the noble examples of our own times. Let us place before our eyes the good apostles. Peter, through unjust odium, underwent not one or two, but many sufferings; and having undergone his martyrdom, he went to the place of glory to which he was entitled. Paul, also, having seven times worn chains, and been hunted and stoned, received the prize of such endurance. For he was the herald of the Gospel in the West as well as in the East, and enjoyed the illustrious reputation of the faith in teaching the whole world to be righteous. And after he had been to the extremity of the West, he suffered martyrdom before the sovereigns of mankind; and thus delivered from this world, he went to his holy place, the most brilliant example of stedfastness that we possess.'

[41] Irenaei Opera, lib. iii. c. 1. Irenaeus was born in Asia, became a disciple of

We are not aware we should be stating anything improbable if we regarded St Paul's domiciliation at the house of Pudens, or his being ministered to immediately before his martyrdom by Pudens, Claudia, and Linus, as additional presumptive evidence of his sojourn in Britain. At any rate, we observe that all the sympathies with which he was surrounded, after his arrival at Rome, in the Claudian family, all the influences of that family in their native country, would lead him to Britain in preference to any other land of the West. This was the great isle of the Gentiles, the centre and source of their religion, and, through his royal converts, a 'mighty door and an effectual' for its conversion was opened to him.

Caractacus meanwhile continued to reside at Aber Gweryd, now St Donat's Major (Llan Ddunwyd), in Glamorganshire, where he had built a palace, *more Romano*. Everything invited Paul to Britain, to follow the bishop he had already commissioned for the work of the Gospel therein, and to be the guest of the royal parent of Claudia. Considering the combination of circumstances which now favoured the execution of his long-cherished design of visiting the West of Europe, we should regard it much more extraordinary if the Apostle had not come to Britain than we do his coming here. When to this circumstantial evidence we add the written testimonies we have adduced of Eusebius, Theodoret, Clemens, and others, that he positively did preach in Britain, we see fair reason for concurring in Bishop Burgess's conclusion, though the bishop had but a part of the evidence we have collected before him, 'That we possess as substantial evidence, as any historical fact can require, of St Paul's journey to Britain.'[42]

There are six years of St Paul's life to be accounted for, between his liberation from his first imprisonment and his martyrdom at Aquae Salviae in the Ostian Road, near Rome. Part certainly, the greater part perhaps, of this period, was spent in Britain — in Siluria or Cambria, beyond the bounds of the Roman empire; and hence the silence of the Greek and Latin writers upon it.

Has any portion of his doctrine or teaching in Britain come down to us? Any such would be sure to be transmitted in a British form, and

Polycarp, Bishop of Smyrna, afterwards a presbyter of Lyons, whence he was sent as a delegate to the Asiatic Churches. He succeeded Photinus in the bishopric, and suffered under Severus.

[42] The ancient MS in Merton College, Oxford, which purports to contain a series of letters between St Paul and Seneca, has more than one allusion to St Paul's residence in Siluria.

Had the large collection of British archives and MSS deposited at Verulam as late as AD 860, descended to our times, invaluable light would have been thrown on this as on many other subjects of native interest. Amongst these works were the poems and Hymns of Claudia. Vide Matthew of Westminster, William of Malmesbury, *Life of Eadmer*.

most probably in that triadic form in which the Druids, the religious teachers of Britain, delivered their teaching. Now we find in the ancient British language certain triads which have never been known otherwise than as 'the Triads of Paul the Apostle'. They are not found *totidem verbis*, either whole or fragmentally, in his epistles, but the morality inculcated is, of course, quite in unison with the rest of his Gospel preaching.

Triads of Paul the Apostle

'There are three sorts of men: The man of God, who renders good for evil; the man of men, who renders good for good and evil for evil; and the man of the devil, who renders evil for good.

'Three kinds of men are the delights of God: the meek; the lovers of peace; the lovers of mercy.

'There are three marks of the children of God: Gentle deportment; a pure conscience; patient suffering of injuries.

'There are three chief duties demanded by God: Justice to every man; love; humility.

'In three places will be found the most of God: Where He is mostly sought; where He is mostly loved; where there is least of self.

'There are three things following faith in God: A conscience at peace; union with heaven; what is necessary for life.

'Three ways a Christian punishes an enemy: By forgiving him; by not divulging his wickedness; by doing him all the good in his power.

'The three chief considerations of a Christian: Lest he should displease God; lest he should be a stumbling-block to man; lest his love to all that is good should wax cold.

'The three luxuries of a Christian feast: What God has prepared; what can be obtained with justice to all; what love to all may venture to use.

'Three persons have the claims and privileges of brother and sisters: The widow; the orphan; the strangers.'[43]

The evangelical simplicity of these precepts, contrasting so forcibly with monkish and medieval inventions and superstitions, favours the traditional acceptance of their Pauline origin. Their preservation is due to the Cor of Ilid.

The foundation of the great abbey of Bangor Iscoed is assigned by tradition to St Paul. Its discipline and doctrine were certainly known as 'the Rule of Paul' (*Pauli Regula*), and over each of the four gates was engraved his precept, 'If a man will not work, neither let him eat.' Its abbots regarded themselves as his successors; they were always men of the highest grade in society, and generally of the blood royal. Bede and other authors state the number of monks in it at 2,100. The

---

[43] Ancient British Triads; Triads of Paul the Apostle. *Barddas:* Iolo Morgannwg.

scholars amounted to many thousands. Pelagius was its twentieth abbot. St Hilary and St Benedict term it 'Mater ominum monasteriorum', the mother of all monasteries. The first Egyptian monastery was founded by Pachomius, AD 360.

By the conversion of the British dynasty in its various members, a very important class of prophecies were fulfilled. Isaiah especially abounds in predictions that the infant Church should have the kings and queens of the Gentiles for its nursing-fathers and nursing-mothers. In the infant or cradle days of the Christian Church there were no Gentile kings or queens, except the British, converted to Christianity. Isaiah again pointedly refers to the 'isles afar off' as supplying these kings, and it is to the 'brightness of the rising of the Church' they are represented as coming. 'The isles of the Gentiles afar off', and their glory, their kings and queens, ministering to the Church in its infancy, forms indeed a most striking portion of the evangelical predictions. In none other than the British royal family could they be fulfilled, for no other royalties in such days, nor long after, were to be found within the pale of the church. The expressions, also, 'the ends of the earth', 'the uttermost parts of the earth', 'the isles afar off', used by Isaiah, are precisely those which the Roman authors also used to designate Britain. These prophecies must have experienced realization — 'for the Scriptures must needs be fulfilled' — in the precise times to which they definitely refer. And the historical evidence we have adduced, proves that in these early kings and queens of our island — 'the far-off island of the Gentiles' — they were literally and to a tittle substantiated. Brân, or Brennus, Caractacus, Linus, Cyllinus, Claudia, Eurgain, were members of even then perhaps the oldest Gentile sovereignty in the world. This sovereignty was that of the great Gentile isle: to these various members of it were sent those disciples that escaped from the first persecution of the infant Church at Jerusalem; some of these members were converted within five years of the Crucifixion; they came literally to the brightness of the rising of the Church, when the glory of Christ and of the Pentecostal descent was yet resting upon it; they become its nursing-fathers and nursing mothers, both at Rome, through the Claudian family, and in Britain, through the elder reigning branch. In the next century the same Silurian family established Christianity, under Lucius, as the national religion, and in the commencement of the fourth century its direct heir in blood and succession, Constantine the Great, made such Christianity the religion of the whole Roman world, his mother Helen being at the same time the benefactress of all the Eastern Churches, especially that 'which is the mother of us all' — Jerusalem. From the captivity of Caractacus and the life of St Paul in the family of his daughter Claudia at Rome, to the turning of the Roman empire into Christendom, the history of the royal dynasty of Britain in connection with the Church of Christ is indeed one long, continuous, and exact verification of Scriptural prophecy.[44]

Against the British Church itself no charge of heretical doctrine has at any time been advanced though the heresiarch, the very prince of heretics — Pelagius, was nursed in her bosom. Bede's reluctant testimony is, on this point, decisive. Whilst the Christian Churches in Asia, Africa, and on the continent of Europe were overrun with false doctrines, the British Church grew up and covered with its shade the whole nation, untroubled for the space of four centuries by any root of bitterness. It is reasonable to infer that the foundations of such a Church were very deeply and faithfully laid by the hands of wise master-builders. According to the foundation rose the superstructure, resting on these four pillars — St Paul, Simon Zelotes, Joseph, Aristobulus. Its great evangelist in the second century, St Timotheus, the baptizer of his nephew King Lucius and of his nobility at Winchester, has also received the faith from the mouth of Paul himself. This unanimity of faith in the founders impressed itself on the Church they founded, which 'continued in the things it had learned and been assured of, knowing from whom it had learned them.'

Having thus first surveyed the religions of the ancient world at the birth of Christianity, and next traced the introduction of the latter, and its progress in Britain, a bird's-eye view will shew us the following Churches, making up the Catholic Church sixty-six years after the Incarnation: In Palestine — Jerusalem, Samaria, Caesarea, Lydda; in Assyria — Babylon; in Syria — Antioch, Damascus; in Asia-Minor — Antioch of Pisidia, Iconium, Lystra, Ephesus, Smyrna, Sardis, Thyatira, Pergamos, Philadelphia, Caesarea in Cappadocia; Laodicea, Colosse, Galatia; in Greece — Athens, Corinth, Thessalonica, Beraea, Philippi, Crete; in Egypt, Alexandria; in Italy, Rome; in Gaul, Lyons; in Britain — Cor Avàlon (Glastonbury), Cor Salog (Old Sarum), Cor Ilid (Llan Ilid) in Siluria.

The force of the testimony for St Paul's residence in Britain may be more clearly estimated by comparing it with that for St Peter's at Rome. The earliest testimony in favour of the latter is that of Irenaeus,

---

[44] A few of these prophecies we subjoin:
'It is a light thing that thou shouldest be My servant to raise up the tribes of Jacob, and to restore the outcasts of Israel: I will also give thee for a light to the Gentiles, that thou mayest be My salvation unto the ends of the earth. Kings shall see and arise; princes also shall worship. Behold they shall come from the north and from the west. Kings shall be thy nursing-fathers and queens thy nursing-mothers. Arise, shine, for thy light is come, and the glory of the Lord is risen upon thee. The Gentiles shall come to thy light, and kings to the brightness of thy rising. Thy sons shall come from far, and thy daughters shall be nursed at thy side. The sons of strangers shall build up thy walls, and kings shall minister unto thee. Thou shalt suck the milk of the Gentiles, and shalt suck the breast of kings. I will set My sign among them, and send them that escape of them unto the nations, unto the isles afar off, and they shall declare My glory unto the Gentiles. They shall inherit the land for ever, the branch of My planting' — Isaiah xlix., lx., lxvi.

bishop of Lyons, AD 180,[45] prior to which we find no indication in the Scriptures or ecclesiastical authors that St Peter ever visited or ever intended to visit Rome, which, as a Gentile Church over which St Paul in the most pointed manner claimed jurisdiction,[46] was certainly not within the province of the apostle of the circumcision. Britain, on the contrary, was within Paul's province, placed already, as Ephesus and Crete had been, by Paul himself under one of his bishops, Aristobulus. If we are to concede that St Peter founded the Roman Church in person, much more are we compelled by infinitely stronger evidence to acknowledge that St Paul in person founded the British Church.[47]

Of St Paul's life after quitting Britain no particulars have descended to us. After visiting Asia we find him in the last scene of his life returned to the bosom of the British royal family at Rome. In his farewell charge to Timothy he sends him the greetings of Pudens, Linus, and Claudia. These, with that of Eubulus, the cousin of Claudia, are the only names of the brethren mentioned by him; these ministered to him on the eve of his martyrdom, these attended him when he was on the block of the state lictor at Aquae Salviae, a little out of Rome and these consigned his remains with their own hands to the Pudentinian family tomb on the Ostian Road. Like his Divine Master, 'he made his grave with the rich in his death.' Linus, Claudia and Pudens and their four children, when God in His appointed time called them to receive the same crown of the Cross, were buried by his side: the other royal converts, Brân, Caractacus, Cyllinus, and Eurgain died peaceably in Britain, and were interred in the Cor of Ilid

---

[45] Irenaei Opera, lib. iii. c. 1: 'Matthew published his Gospel among the Hebrews in his own language while Peter and Paul were engaged in evangelizing and founding the Christian Church at Rome.'

[46] 'My apostleship for obedience to the faith among all nations, among whom are ye also . . . that I might have some fruit among you also, as among other Gentiles' — Rom. i. 5. 13.

[47] If we desired to strengthen from Roman Catholic evidence the apostolical foundations of the British Church, or to insist that it can with equal justice, at least, as the Roman Church, claim St Peter amongst its founders, it would not be difficult to adduce the affirmative evidence of Roman Catholic authorities upon the point. Cornelius à Lapide, in answering the question 'How came St Paul not to salute St Peter in his Epistle to the Romans', states, 'Peter, banished with the rest of the Jews from Rome by the edict of Claudius, was absent in Britain.' (*Cornelius a Lapide, in Argumentum Epistolae St Pauli ad Romanos*, c. xvi.) Eusebius Pamphilus, if we can credit the quotation of him by a very untrustworthy author, Simeon Metaphrastes, states St Peter to have been in Britain as well as Rome — (*Metaphrastes ad 29 Junii*). The vision to which St Peter refers, 2 Pet. 14, 'Knowing that shortly I must put off this my tabernacle, even as our Lord Jesus Christ hath shewed me', is said to have appeared to him in Britain on the spot where once stood the British Church of Lambedr (St Peter), and now stands the Abbey of St Peter's Westminister. Lambeth may be a corruption of Lambedr. But this question lies between Roman Catholic authors and their own Church, which will scarcely put the seal of its infallibility on a position that places the British Church on its own special appropriated Rock.

in Siluria. All — kings, heroes, apostles, martyrs, saints — were united in the kingdom of light, in the joy of their Lord.[48]

[48] Bede was a very earnest adherent of the novel papal Church, introduced AD 596, by Augustine into Britain, but the honesty and simplicity of his character has rendered his history in many respects a very inconvenient and obnoxious record to the said Church. What became of the remains of St Peter and St Paul? At Rome they still pretend to exhibit them, but Bede — and it must be remembered he is a canonized saint in the Roman calendar — expressly states that the remains of the bodies of the apostles Peter and Paul, the martyrs St Lawrence, St John, St Gregory, and St Pancras, were, at the solicitation of King Oswy to Pope Vitalian, removed from Rome to England, and deposited at Canterbury AD 656, Pope Vitalian's letter to Oswy being extant — (*Bedae Hist.*, lib. iii. c. 29). Their remains, then, if any, repose in British soil.

13

'The Saints in Glastonbury'[1]

A. LE STRANGE CAMPBELL

The Coming of St Patrick

Glastonbury of old time was a tranquil and peaceful valley far from the haunts of men. On a glorious spring morning it is an unforgettable sight. The beeches stand in their first fresh beauty of powdered green, the grass at their feet golden with their silken bud-sheaths. There is a sense of pulsing life animating the unfolding leaves as they shake themselves out as a butterfly from its chrysalis, and the profound silence all around is intensified by the almost inarticulate sound of the growth of plants and the murmur of myriads of tiny insects.

> From sky to sod
> The world's unfolding blossom smells of God.

This is the site of the first Christian church in our land, surrounded with the cells of the laura nestling in leafy glades and sheltered by hills on three sides. The discovery within the last decade of the remains of a mud and wattle hut beneath the Edgar chapel but a stone's throw from the place where the primitive oratory stood, brings the life of the early hermits very vividly before us. It suggests the beautiful couplet of an ancient poet which may appropriately be addressed to the cell in that peaceful solitude which is filled with God:

> Tu mihi curarum requies, tu nocte vel atra Lumen, et in solis tu mihi turba locis.[2]

(O cell, sweet rest amid the sorrows of this world, in blackest night thou dost illumine me with light, and in thy solitude I find companionship.)

In those days the sea, now fourteen miles away, rippled up to the foot of the Tor, and the hills, today surrounded with orchards and pasture, then rose from the water and marshy land which bordered the Bristol Channel.

Here, then, the Solitaries settled, and surely this were paradise enough for a poor hermit. He walked with Christ beneath the apple trees whose delicate blossom tossed like rose-coloured foam into the azure dome of heaven, while the clear brooklets babbled and sparkled

[1] From *The Glories of Glastonbury* (Sheed & Ward, 1926).
[2] Tibullus.

at their feet in the sunshine, and the birds sang so sweetly among the branches. He held familiar intercourse with Our Lady and the saints in the grey dawn, the grass still spangled with innumerable glistening dew-drops. The sea-girt island was his enclosure, the broad woods his cloister, the wide world the object of his apostolate of prayer.

And in the silence of that place may we not see in the sunset glow at Vespertime, the shy furry inhabitants of the coppice creep out from the brushwood to join in the praise of their Creator, and do homage to Christ's saints who, by their union with God, had recovered original innocence, and thus regained the sovereignty over the animal world which is the right of the head of creation. What countless prayers and tears cried to heaven for the conversion of the pagan 'barbarians' from that little oratory where the sanctuary lamp was first lighted in England. With what fervour the Holy Sacrifice was offered day by day for the salvation of the souls for whom Christ died.

To this place, about a hundred years after the death of St Joseph of Arimathea, the two missionaries Phaganus and Deruvianus, were sent by Pope Eleutherius at the request of King Lucius in AD 179. They journeyed through Surrey and not only restored the wattle church, but also built the church of St Michael on the Tor and a monastery where a small community was established.

It is said that about three hundred years later, after many generations had passed away, there came hither an aged and venerable man of ninety years. He had journeyed from Ireland, the land which, by his labours, his prayers and his miracles, he had so marvellously won to God. This was St Patrick who now joined himself to the Solitaries of Avalon, and giving them a Rule, he became their first Abbot. He continued to guide and govern them for thirty years, until, at the age of 120, he passed, in AD 464, to the bliss of heaven.

Figure 9: 'Artist's impression of The Church of Wattles'

His burial-place was believed to be at the right side of the altar, and many Irish pilgrims and scholars visited his shrine, leaving behind them traces of the culture and learning for which they were renowned.

His disciple, St Benignus, who succeeded him, had been an early follower of St Patrick, to whose feet he clung while yet a tiny child, and from whom he could not be parted without tears; wherefore he changed his name to Benignus (kind one) from his former name of Beon. He laboured long in Ireland, but followed his master to Avalon, and built a hermit's cell at Ferramere, where he lived and died.

Some centuries later, during the reign of William II (1087–1100), his relics were wrapped in finest linen and borne with great solemnity to the barge which was rowed to the landing-place by a monk and a secular, in a radiant glory of supernatural light. There it was met by Abbot Thurstan, preceded by a great procession of monks bearing torches and tapers, and singing-boys, nobles and peasants, who came to do honour to the Irish saint. At the place where the church of St Benignus now stands the panegyric was preached, and many wonderful miracles were wrought when the relics were there exposed to the veneration of the faithful. They were then laid to rest beside those of his master.

Omnes sancti Monachi et Eremitae Glasconiae.
Orate pro nobis.

The Irish Martyrs

The Sanctuary already famous as the shrine of the relic of the holy Blood, the burial place of St Joseph of Arimathea and the home of a band of men who went forth ablaze with the love of God to evangelize the pagan world now become yet more renowned as the tomb of St Patrick.

It was probably in the seventh century that a company of Irish pilgrims left Ireland to make the long and difficult journey to Rome, facing undaunted the perils of the sea and all manner of discomfort that they might pray at the tombs of the holy Apostles. In their love of St Patrick they purposed on their return to visit his shrine also.

But the fierce pagans of the neighbourhood, fell on them and they gained the martyrs' palm in the village of Shapwick. Thus these pilgrims to the Eternal City ended their pilgrimage of this earthly life almost within sight of the 'Second Rome', whence they were translated to the City of God Eternal in Heaven.

No details have come down to us but we know that soon after, the great and good King Ina, so famous for his long and prosperous reign of thirty seven years, carried their relics to the new Saxon Abbey which he had built in AD 708.

We may easily picture the scene; the solemn procession from the shore amid the chanting of the monks, the perfume of incense mingling with the scent of flowers, the gay banners floating in the sunshine, the rich copes of the priests and the gorgeous apparel of the King, and the sense of triumph and joy in the hearts of those who preceded the relics of the glorious athletes who had given their lives for the faith. Then we seem to see the great King himself. He is bearing, perhaps, that precious reliquary, with its yet more precious treasure within, to the church, the little Saxon church among the beeches on the walls of which the holy oils had yet scarcely dried.

St David, Patron of Wales

Saint David of Menevia was probably born about the year AD 500 and lived to a very great age. It is said that he came with seven bishops to consecrate the little church at Inyswytryn (the Glassy Isle), as the Britons named Avalon, but he learned in a vision that it had already been dedicated to Blessed Mary by our Lord Himself; and he therefore resolved to build another church under the dedication of Our Lady on the site where the Galilee stands today.

He brought with him great treasures with which to adorn it; among these was a magnificent altar-stone of sapphire, gilded, and studded with precious stones, which had been the gift of the Patriarch of Jerusalem. This was the famous 'great sapphire' which, hidden for a while at the approach of the Danes, escaped the ravages of the pagans, and was one of the glories of Glastonbury for over a thousand years until it was stolen by those thieves who respected neither the beauty of the jewel in situ, nor the antiquity of its history, nor the rights of its owners, nor even the fact that, consecrated with chrism, it had served as the altar-stone for so many centuries.

For the sacrilegious hands of Henry VIII, through his agents, Pollard, Tregonwell and Peire, seized 'a super-altar garnished with silver-gilt and part gold, called the Great Sapphire of Glastonbury', and sent it to the Royal Treasurer on 2 May 1539, together with '493 ounces of parcel gilt and silver plate', and many other treasures taken from the monasteries in the west country.

Fearful lest the precise site of the wattle church should be lost by any additions made to it, St David set up a pillar the base of which, measuring 7 feet in diameter and uncovered in 1921, may be seen at Glastonbury at the present time. A brass plate, lost about the middle of the seventeenth century, was fixed to it upon which was engraved a short account of the coming of St Joseph of Arimathea, the dedication of his church by our Lord, the vision of St David, his addition to the church, and his gift of the great sapphire. And it goes on:

> And lest the site or size of the earlier church should come to be forgotten by reason of such additions, this pillar is erected on a line extended southward through the two eastern angles of the said church and cutting off from it the chancel aforesaid. And its length was 60 feet westward from that line; its width 26 feet; the distance of the centre of this pillar from the middle point between the said angles 48 feet.

The relics of St David were brought in the tenth century to Glastonbury by Edgar the Peaceable, who did so much to beautify the abbey in which he, too, was laid to rest, not far from the holy patron of Wales.

St Bridget in 'Little Ireland'

About half a mile almost due west of the Church of Our Lady was a low lying island among the reeds and marshes where St Bridget of Ireland is said to have spent many years in solitary prayer and penance. It is two-thirds of a mile long, and a few hundred yards across. In ancient and medieval times it lay there surrounded by water and was called the isle of Beckery or 'little Ireland'. At the extreme western end of the island there is an ancient ford over the river Brue, and there was probably another ford or a bridge in a direct line from there which would have connected the isle with Glastonbury near the church of St Benignus.

Beckery was given to the Abbey by Kenwald about AD 640. John of Glastonbury[3] tells us that St Bridget came to Glastonbury about AD 488; that she spent some years in an island named Beckery, where, already in her day, there stood a chapel dedicated to St Mary Magdalen. On her return to Ireland shortly before her death she left her wallet, her rosary and her weaving tools at Beckery and they were carefully preserved and reverenced as relics, in memory of the sweetness and holiness of her life. The chapel was afterwards dedicated in her honour. The Abbey furnished it with half a pound of wax at Easter, doubtless for the paschal candle. The fields around are called 'Brides' to this day, while in 'Beckery Mill' the name again survives. In Ireland she made her cell under a large oak-tree and hence the place was called Kil-dara, 'the Church of the Oak', and afterwards Kildare, where, in the words of the old chronicler, 'the holy virgin, St Bridget, in 517, departed to the Lord'.[4]

The foundations of the chapel were explored in 1887–8. They were found upon the highest point of the island in a field called Chamberlain's Hill, whence a beautiful view could be obtained over the waters of the mere to the Bristol Channel. In other directions the landscape would be bounded by the Polden ridge, the Tor, Weary-all hill and the more distant Mendips.

The foundations of two chapels were discovered, one within the other. The newer chapel was quadrangular, carefully and solidly built of the lias stone of the district. Decorated tiles, wood, slates, and other building materials were found. It is possible that this was the chapel built by Abbot John of Glastonbury, about 1275.[5]

[3] Hearne's edn., p. 68.
[4] Roger of Wendover, *Chron.*
[5] Adam of Domerham.

Figure 10: 'St Bridget and her Cow' from a carving on the Tower of St Michael on Glastonbury Tor

Within this building were uncovered the foundations of a very small and early church, the nave of which was only 14 feet by 11 feet: they were of very massive work, probably of Saxon origin. The remains of six skeletons were found all lying with the head to the west, and these appear to have been buried before the building of the older church, thus taking us back to a very early period.

About twenty feet to the north-east of the chapel are the foundations of a quadrangular dwelling house shewing a hearth, and with a small porch on the north-east corner.[6]

These foundations, probably older than any of the existing ruins of the Abbey, are now covered up and overgrown with grass, but though no traces of the convent of St Peter on Wirral are to be found, we here have the site of the cell of the Irish saint, and of the 'Chapel Adventurous' where King Arthur beheld his marvellous vision.[7]

[6] John Morland, *Som. Arch. Soc.*, Vol. 35 (1899).
[7] See 'King Arthur's Vision of the Grail', pp. 55–63.

14
Christ in Cornwall?[1]
A. H. LEWIS

I. LEGENDS AND HISTORY

A talented authoress has lately published a booklet, in which she sets out to disprove most of the holy legends of Glastonbury and Cornwall, and in particular that of the visit of Our Lord to this land. She has entitled it *Glastonbury, Truth and Fiction*. The title alone shows the prejudiced attitude of the writer and her fellow-sceptics. Since when has legend or oral tradition become identified with fiction? Or truth confined to facts attested by documents of unimpeachable reliability? The utmost that the writer has proved is that many of these holy legends have not the documentary support which she and her kind require in order that they should be classified as 'truth', or at any rate be removed from the realm of 'fiction'. I wonder in which category the writer would place the following, to mention only three generally accepted traditions:

The martyrdom of most of the Apostles. The episcopacy of St Peter at Rome. The residence of St John at Ephesus.

If documentary proof is the only requisite of truth, and *all* legend is fiction, then surely these, too are fiction.

The view taken by the present writer has always been that legends often, perhaps generally, contain a germ of truth, and that the probable degree of truth can be fairly gauged by such considerations as the source of origin; the localities where the legends had vogue; the likelihood or otherwise of the influence of careless legend-mongers; and finally the result of applying to the legends the acid test of history and archaeology.

I claim that the legendary visit of Our Lord to Britain, and to Cornwall in particular, comes through all these tests remarkably unscathed, leaving all reasonable people with the conviction that it *may* have been, and many of us who have given years of study to the subject, the growing faith that it is probably true.

I shall presently record the various versions of the legend, mostly in the very words in which they were given me by my informants, the majority of whom are simple folk with no pretention to much 'book-learning'. It will be seen at once that it is almost exclusively associated

[1] Privately printed pamphlet (1948).

in Cornwall with the tin trade, in the mining districts and the adjacent ports from which British tin was exported before and during the first century AD. It is *not* usually found in parts where monastic influence was most pronounced. Even at Glastonbury the legend perpetuated and embellished by the monks of the middle ages was about Joseph of Arimathea, rather than about Our Lord, as the holy visitor.

You have to go to Priddy by the old lead mines of the Mendips, or to Pilton, the reputed port from which much of the lead was shipped, to hear the local traditions of the visit of Christ or the Christ Child. In Cornwall it is found at such widely separated places as Marazion and Ding Dong in Penwith, St Day and Falmouth in Carnmarth, St Just-in-Roseland, and Lammana (Looe Island) in Wivelshire. These are all either tin districts or adjacent havens. Only Lammana can claim definite association with any of the big monastic houses[2] and, what is to me most striking, St Michael's Mount, while expressly mentioned in the tinners' version of the legend, did not itself perpetuate it through the monastery, whose claim to pilgrimage was based on supposed apparitions of the Archangel.

It will be seen, too, that this holy legend is given in the simplest of language, without any of the 'artistic detail' so dear to legend-mongers, but so damaging to the value and credibility of many of their stories. The legend of the Holy Visit itself is not found in the elaborate romances of the Arthurian cycle, though there is indirect support for it in the claim of the greatest knights of the Round Table to descent from Joseph of Arimathea, who is, as we shall see, closely associated with the legend, and who provides an important clue to its credibility.

As regards the test of history and archaeology, I do not propose here to give more than passing reference to the early documents which tend to prove the existence of the legend at the time they were written (see Appendices); but I claim with assurance that there is not one word in the Gospel narrative which in any way disproves it. The argument from silence leaves me cold. The omission of direct or indirect reference is of little value, in view of the fact that there is, as I imagine, only one alternative lengend with regard to the eighteen years of Our Lord's boyhood and early manhood, viz., that he spend all his time at Nazareth as a carpenter, and there is certainly no more support for this belief in the story of the Evangelists. On the contrary, I consider that the account of his visit to Nazareth during the ministry fits in far better with the possibility of a prolonged absence, for he appears in the Synagogue as at least a comparative stranger. Even if he had made Nazareth his home for all those eighteen years, there would still have been plenty of *time* for a visit to Britain if the *opportunity* were there. We shall see that Joseph, the traditional tin merchant, and supposed uncle, provides a simple and quite convincing 'opportunity'.

[2] Lammana was a tiny priory of Glastonbury before the Conquest. For its history see my *Ab Antiquo*.

It has often been objected that such an adventure would have shown itself in his parables and discourses. If there is little or no reference to travel abroad, there is equally little to carpentry and Nazareth; and, as I pointed out in *The Child Christ at Lammana*, those of us who have lived abroad know that most people are not much interested in hearing about our lives there. Our Lord spoke about the things in which his hearers were interested and which he used to point the moral of his teaching.

It has again been objected that such a voyage as this legend suggests would be impossible for an ordinary Hebrew child or man. I do not know the real grounds of this objection, unless it means that it *seems* difficult to us. You have only to study the writings of Diodorus Siculus to see how accessible was Western Britain to the merchants, or the Acts and Pauline Epistles to see that travel by land or sea, presented no great difficulties to the Apostle and his friends.

Archaeology is showing us more and more the absurdity of the old idea that the Britons in the time of Christ were wild painted savages. The finds in the Lake villages of Meare and Glastonbury show a remarkable degree of culture and art, and so do the excavations now going on in the old 'Castles' of Cornwall. It is more than possible that the Phoenician and Hebrew traders had many friends in these islands of a culture little (if any) inferior to their own.[3]

II. The Legend as Traced

Some sceptics are quite incorrigible. They would even deny the existence of the legend at all. While anyone who really seeks can find abundant evidence that it was a household tradition at Priddy in the last generation that Christ came there, and while it is certain that there is an age-old proverb in parts of the Mendips 'As sure as Our Lord was at Priddy'; yet a dignitary of Wells lately suggested that the 'legend of Priddy' was invented quite recently by a schoolmistress, to afford a plot for a children's play! Miss Hamilton Thompson was bold enough to assert in the booklet already referred to that two references to ancient writings which she could not trace were, in her opinion, 'deliberate fabrications'.

Before I proceed to show that the legend did actually exist in Cornwall, and still survives in parts, I throw out a word of warning to casual searchers. It is no use tackling all and sundry with a bald question 'Did you ever hear . . .?' The probability is that you would get a negative answer in almost every case. The Cornish folk are not fond of talking about their old legends and traditions to us

---

[3] On St Martin's Scilly, I have recently found much pottery of the Bronze age (c. 1000 BC), which has decoration of high artistic merit together with an exceptionally beautiful blue bead, which must have been made in Egypt or Phoenicia, and been imported to Scilly by traders from the Mediterranean.

'foreigners'. They are very sensitive to ridicule, and ridicule has, alas, nearly killed the Holy Legend. Once suggest that a tradition is 'rubbish', and no oyster can ever be closer than the Cornish man or woman. For the same reason, the younger generation has not often heard of it, because the parents have feared that their sophisticated children would laugh at them.

In the course of some six years of rather intensive searching, I have gathered the following, which, in all cases of direct information, I give as nearly as I can in the actual words spoken. In no single case has the theme been enlarged on or 'dressed up'.

(1) **St Just-in-Roseland**. My original informant here is the late Rector, the Revd J. V. Hammond, who has often told me that a number of the older people still say that 'Christ came to St Just.' He quoted one man of middle age as saying, 'Of course we know Christ came to St Just.' I proceeded to verify this for myself, and in this case found confirmation much easier to obtain than had been the case round Looe. I have had it confirmed by past inhabitants of St Just that it was a common tradition of their childhood that Christ came there. One variant version was that 'Joseph of Arimathea and Our Lord came in a boat, and anchored in St Just Creek.' I know a man in Falmouth who, as a boy, used to go frequently to St Just, to visit the farmers in their homes, when acting as a local preacher. He tells me that the older folk often talked about it, and in particular records how as a boy he used to sit with the farmers on the beach below the Church, waiting for the tide to bring barges of manure. He tells how, 'as often as not', the conversation would come round to the Holy Legend, and he says that 'it was as much as your life was worth' to express any doubt about Christ coming to St Just. The period of which he is speaking cannot be more than forty years ago. He tells me also of a certain flat stone, with curious but unintelligible markings on it, which they used to point out as 'the stone on which Christ stepped' when he landed. I hold no brief at all for this part of the story, but I think I know which stone it is, and where it stands today.

(2) **Falmouth**. This is, of course, a comparatively modern town, and I should not expect to find much material here, but I have procured the following, which I value as highly as any in my collection.

A man of about 75 who used to live near the Strand (the oldest part of Falmouth, by the old village of Smithick) said his father always used to say that 'Joseph of Arimathea landed at the Strand, crossed the stream, and went up Smithick-hill.' This could hardly have been invented by a modern schoolmistress, as there are few living who even know of the stream which used to flow over the site of the Moor today.

A dear old lady, but very illiterate, who recently died at the age of over 80, came out with this, when I was talking about the song 'Joseph was a tin-man',[4] 'Of course, we know Our Saviour preached to the miners. He was very fond of the miners.'

Last, but far from least, a marvellous old saint, who has just found rest from long and painful cancer, said once in the dreamy voice with which she brought out all her bright 'gems': 'Folks say that Jesus passed by here, and blessed these parts.'

(3) **Mining District of St Day, Redruth, etc.** A well-known Falmothian, who was brought up near Chacewater, says he often heard the old people, when he was a boy, say that 'Joseph of Arimathea and the Child Christ worked (sic) at Greeg Brawse.' This is a very ancient tin mine between Chacewater and St Day.

Another exceptionally well-informed person tells me that at St Day the miners always used to say that Christ came to the mines. I always suspect that this was also the original tradition about Gwennap Pit, but if so it has been obliterated by the recent connection with John Wesley. It may well have been one of the reasons why Wesley chose it as his open-air chapel.

The son of a prominent business man in Penryn says that, as a boy, he was somewhere between Cowlands Creek and Come-to-Good, when a village woman, in the course of conversation, said something like this: 'Some people say that Our Lord came to these parts, but I don't know if it be true or not.' These places are between the ancient tin-streaming district of Carnon Downs, and the creeks of the Fal river, from which the tin would be shipped.

Several informants from Redruth have said they had heard something about the legend, and one in particular knew the song 'Joseph was a tin-man' very well.

(4) **Marazion and Penwith District.** Canon Jennings, in his *Madron, Morvah and Penzance*, refers with confidence to the existence, at any rate in the past, of the tradition that Christ came to Mount's Bay, and suggests this legend as a possible basis for the name 'Penzance' (Holy Headland).

A very prominent Falmouth lady, who lived in her childhood in Penwith, says she was always told that Christ visited Ding Dong mine, which is reputed to be one of the oldest in Cornwall.

(5) **Looe, Talland, and Polperro.** Several informants had memories, albeit sometimes faint, of the Holy Legend. One in particular gave it as follows: 'My grandmother often used to say that Joseph of Arimathea and Our Lord landed at Looe Island.' Another told how her mother would say to her father 'You must go and get your hair cut, or folks will say it is Joseph of Arimathea come back!' Others said that scoffers of Looe would point to the arms of East Looe, which show a boat, with two figures, and say 'There is your Joseph of

---

[4] An old song, once well-known among mining people in Cornwall.

Arimathea.' While the remark seems to have been made in jest, yet it must have reflected a story actually told and believed by others. The arms in question have no connection at all with the Legend, but that does not affect the implication of the words. One illustration will show the difficulty of collecting material. An old man who had lived all his life at Port Looe (the old Lammana), used to deny stoutly that he had ever heard about the tradition. I persisted, because this was the very land mentioned as the scene of the landing. At last I was able to confront him with evidence that his late wife had often spoken of it. A final question elicited the following, 'Oh yes, I've eared 'er talk of it.' Another old man who was born on Looe Island was as close as can be. He would say he never talked of anything he did not believe, or believe anything he did not see, etc., but he talked vaguely of 'all kinds of stories'. He remembered an old inscription on stone, now alas, lost. His wife, now nearly a centenarian, who came from Porthallow, spoke mysteriously of a piece of cloth which, they said, 'was part of the cloth in which Our Saviour's body was buried', and of other 'relics' of the sepulchre. These might have been 'relics' from the old Chapel of Lammana, and, whether genuine or not, would then reflect an old Arimathean tradition, in line with that of Glastonbury, the parent Community.[5]

At Talland, a late incumbent, according to his sister, often used to talk with conviction of Our Lord having come to Cornwall, and a family who later inhabited the Vicarage said that, in their childhood they had often heard the story.

Polperro seemed to contain few memories of the legend, but one woman said she had always heard that Our Lord came to Cornwall, 'and why not?'

(6) **Elsewhere**. In Somerset I have definitely traced the legend at Priddy, in other parts of the Mendips, and at Pilton, where Our Lord and Joseph are said to have landed in the old harbour. At Glastonbury we saw that it was chiefly concerned with Joseph in popular memory, but the holier version undoubtedly existed once. In ancient Gaul Dr Taylor in his *Coming of the Saints* tells how he has traced the stories of Joseph in Morlaix, Limoges, and the Rhone Valley. Anatole le Braz, in *Au Pays des Pardons* records the beautiful and traditional Breton legend, in equally beautiful language, that St Anne was a 'duchesse' of

---

[5] In reply to Mr Painter of Glastonbury and Miss Twycross of Menheniot, both of whom would discount the existence of the tradition at Looe, Mrs A. Jeffery of the latter place, in a letter written to *The Cornish Times* (21 May, 1948) says: 'An aged Looe couple kept alive for 70 years the lovely Island story, but were reluctant to speak of it for fear of ridicule.' Mrs Jeffery, whom I quoted in my *The Child Christ at Lammana*, told me her grandmother spoke of 'The Child Jesus and his uncle landing on Looe Island.' She was undoubtedly one of the aged couple to whom she now refers. I wish sceptics would realize that they are the *last* people to whom the old folks of Cornwall would disclose their treasured memories.

'Cornuaille', and was visited there by Our Lord before her death (see Appendix 7). Whether the original legend referred to the present Cornuaille in Brittany, or to the old home of the Breton Colonists in our own Cornwall is really immaterial. If Christ could come as far as Brittany, he could quite well have come on here, and these legends of France, along the old tin-trade route, form a definite connecting link in a story which is entirely woven round the tin trade.

Since issuing the second edition, I have now traced the story at the following additional places. A Welsh woman told me she had been told by her school-teacher that Christ came to *Caerleon*. The vicar of Glastonbury tells me that Our Lord is said to have walked along the *Pilgrims' Way* to Winchester, which was very likely the old tin-trade route. A lady has recorded the existence of the tradition of Our Lord landing at Hordle, near *Bournemouth*. I have myself traced a tradition, albeit faint, that Christ came with Joseph on one of his trading voyages to Merchants' Point on *Tresco* in Scilly, which is said to have been so-named from the Phoenician traders. Perhaps the most interesting is a statement by Mr E. V. Duff, Count of the Holy Roman Empire (per the vicar of Glastonbury), that among the Maronite Christians of the Lebanon district of Northern Galilee 'there lingers a tradition that Our Lord as a youth came to Britain as a shipwright aboard a trading ship of Tyre, and that he wintered on the shores of the *West of England*, owing to bad weather.' We note the close proximity of these tribesmen to Tyre, and their probable racial connection with the Phoenicians.

In view of the above, it is not at all surprising to find strong trace of the legend among the traditions of the miners and tin workers. The late Mr H. Jenner, FSA, Chief Bard of Cornwall, and a great authority on all things Cornish, was much impressed by this. He wrote twice at least to the *Western Morning News* about it, and contributed a masterly article about St Joseph of Arimathea to *Pax*, the organ of the Benedictines, in 1916, in which he points out the difficulty of finding an 'adequate reason' why Joseph should be singled out in tradition as the Apostle of Britain, 'unless it happened to be the literal and actual truth'.[6] He then goes on to tell how a certain 'invocation' among tin workers, who say quietly to themselves 'Joseph was in the tin trade', may afford some ground for the legend. He quotes Mr Bailie Hamilton, through Mr Hallam (a master at Harrow), as having heard from the foreman of these workers the following explanation of the invocation. 'One of these [traditions of metal workers] is that St Joseph of Arimathea, the rich man of the Gospels, made his money in the tin trade between Phoenicia and Cornwall. We have also a story that he made several voyages to Britain in his own ships, and that on one occasion he brought with him the Child Christ and his Mother as passengers, and landed them at St Michael's Mount in Cornwall.'

[6] *Pax*, (Summer 1916), 135.

While many have told me that they have heard of this 'invocation', and I have been positively assured by one informant that it is still used by some workers in tin, I should rather doubt whether the modern tinners who use it are aware of all its original import, as given above.

I have already referred to the old song beginning 'Joseph was a tin man'. It is known to many, but, unfortunately, I have so far failed to find anyone who can remember the rest. One informant said it went on 'And the miners loved him well.' Beyond that it still remains a blank, apart from one woman who was sure it was about 'his coming in a Ship'.

It will be noted that the tinners' tradition, as given through Mr Jenner, included the Blessed Virgin Mary. Even this is not so impossible as appears at first sight, at least if we feel that there is any basis at all for the Breton tradition given above.[7]

III. The Tin Trade With Britain

We have abundant evidence that the tin trade with Britain was flourishing long before the Christian era. Posidonius[8] quoted by Diodorus Siculus (v. 21, 22, 31), comments on the friendliness and good manners of the people of Damnonia (Devon and Cornwall), because of their intercourse with the traders. Britain was the principal, and, at times, almost the only place where tin was obtainable for the ancients. The Phoenicians came here for it, and it is practically certain that among the traders would be found Hebrews as well, for this race has always known where and how to find profitable trade. There are names in Cornwall suggestive of Hebrew origin, or at least of a Hebrew tradition, notably Marazion and its counterpart Market Jew-street, in Penzance. A considerable part of Cornish folklore deals with 'Jews' Houses' and the 'Knockers', who were said to be the spirits of Jewish miners. If, as we are told in the Gospels, Joseph of Arimathea was an exceptionally wealthy man, he might well have made his fortune in tin. The fact that the Evangelists, who all mention him, have so little to say about him, surely suggests that he may have been a trader whose visits to his 'homeland' were intermittent and short.

Among other things which we learn from Posidonius are details about some of the trading posts round the coast, the way in which the tin was brought there by the natives in ingots, and the route taken by the traders to the Mediterranean. This was over the Channel to Morlaix, or some adjacent port in Brittany, and thence across Gaul to the Rhone estuary at Marseilles and Narbonne. In Britain, he speaks of a certain 'Ictis', a sort of high-water island, as a great trading post. He speaks as though this sort of place (an island at high water) was a

[7] This subject is dealt with fully in the Glastonbury Supplement, Part 2.

[8] *Circa* 80 BC. There seems to be divided opinion among experts as to whether Diodorus was quoting from Posidonius in this passage, or whether it was from his own experience. Diodorus wrote shortly before the Christian era.

common feature in the trade, and any one, or all, of the following suit his description quite well: Looe Island, St Michael's Mount, or the one-time 'islands' round Glastonbury. Ptolemy and others speak of Voliba as a chief port of Britain, and this has been identified by many with the Fal estuary, which is *the* chief natural harbour of Britain. It is directly opposite Morlaix, and a rock off the adjacent coast is pointed out as the nearest land to Brittany. The inference that the present Falmouth was the port from which the tin was shipped across the channel is too obvious to need elaboration. It was in Falmouth harbour that the only identifiable ingot of tin of the period was dredged up, and Falmouth and St Just-in-Roseland are, as we have seen, two of the places where the name of Joseph is mentioned in legend. On the other side of the channel, the tin trade route is traced across Gaul by Limoges and the Rhone Valley.It is at least suggestive that the name of Joseph is found in local tradition at all these places I have mentioned, and, as far as I am aware nowhere else except in the mining districts of North-West Spain. The Rhone Valley legends, while dealing principally with the reputed settlement there of Martha, Mary and Lazarus, mention Joseph as their 'companion' in emigration, but distinctly suggest that he moves on elsewhere. Where should that be, except to his eventual legendary home at Glastonbury?

The lead mines near Priddy in the Mendips were certainly in existence before the Romans began to exploit them about AD 50, and the need for this metal would account for Joseph's connection with Glastonbury and the district. If I were to venture to reconstruct a trading voyage of the tin merchants from materials available, I should say that it probably began at Tyre or Joppa, that the merchants disembarked at Narbonne, that they travelled overland from thence to Morlaix, re-embarked for the crossing of the Channel to the Fal, and, after calling at various trading places along the Cornish coast, proceeded to their terminus in the Severn estuary.

In connection with Joseph, we must remember that he was almost certainly a decurion in the Roman Empire. 'Nobilis decurio' is St Jerome's translation in the Vulgate of St Mark's 'honourable counsellor' (AV), and I believe he meant what the Latin words mean, *not* a member of the Jewish Sanhedrim, but a member of a provincial Roman Senate. We hear of decurions in charge of mining districts[9], which is very striking. It is interesting to see how this title has been misunderstood, not only by most modern biblical commentators, but also by the Arthurian romancers, who, thinking it was a purely military term, call Joseph 'that noble soldier of Pilate'. Hence King Arthur and his nearest of kin boast of their reputed ancestor, not as the wealthy trader that he was, but as the founder and paragon of

[9] Dr Davey Biggs, *Ictis and Avalon*. See pp. 34–49 of the present volume.

chivalry, and, according to John Hardyng (*c.* 1450), the original bearer of the 'arms of St George'[10]

IV. The Holy Visit — When and Why?

When I wrote *The Child Christ at Lammana*, I was going on one aspect of the legend only, that which I traced at Looe, and that which is enshrined in the tinners' tradition, viz., that our Lord came as a Child with Joseph of Arimathea. It will be noticed, however, that in other versions, notably those at Priddy and St Just, I find no suggestion at all that they are about a child. I am indebted to the Revd C. C. Dobson (*Did our Lord Visit Britain?*) for the suggestion which I now accept, that Christ *first* visited our shores as a Child and that he later sojourned here for a longer or shorter time as a Man.[11] If this sounds too bold and fantastic an idea, I ask you to bear in mind the following points: (1) If, as legend suggests, and as the story of the Entombment surely confirms, Joseph was an uncle or some older relative of the Blessed Virgin, he might well have brought the Holy Child to Britain, and given him his first introduction to Glastonbury and the Lake villages then existing near there. Archaeology, as I have said, pictures the villagers as possessing a high degree of culture, and living a simple, quiet life of fishing and husbandry. The growing Child would naturally fall in with any chance of seeing the greater world — all the more if he realized it then as the world he came to save. Later, when he was grown up, he would surely look for a peaceful retreat in which to prepare for his life's work. Is it so remarkable that he would remember the Vale of Avalon, and find it there? The most cursory study of Josephus and contemporary writers must convince us that, whatever we may think of the suitability or otherwise of Avalon, it could not have been more unsuitable for quiet preparation than Galilee, whose claim to notoriety at that time appears to have been that it was the breeding-ground of sedition and lawlessness. With his 'uncle's' frequent trading voyages, there would be no difficulty whatever about transport there and back.

(2) His chief friends and acquaintances there would be in the Lake villages, and archaeology distinctly concludes that the one at Glastonbury did not survive till the Roman occupation, and that the one at Meare did not outlive that occupation for long. Small wonder then that such a faint memory should survive of that holy visit. But it did survive more by the mines of Priddy, which continued to be worked without a break for long after the Romans came to Bath. It probably survived also in the deep veneration felt for that building

---

[10] And thus this armes, by Josephes' creation, Full long afore Sainct George was generate, Were worshipt heir, of mykell elder date.'

(Ed'n H. Ellis 1812 Cap. 48).

[11] For Our Lord's supposed residence here. See Glastonbury Supplement — Part I.

which men *may* have believed to have been constructed by the very hands of the Carpenter of Nazareth.[12]

(3) Some friendly critics have raised the question of language, if Christ were living in a foreign land, but I cannot really see that difficulty. He came from Galilee, where the population was very mixed, and where probably most people had some knowledge of Greek and other languages. And I cannot imagine that he would have found greater difficulty in making friends with folk of another tongue than many people find today, who go and settle in foreign parts, with no preliminary knowledge at all of the language.

V.   Indirect Support for the Legend

Some indirect support for the legend, which will weigh heavier or lighter, according to the prejudices of the reader, is afforded by the following:-

(1) **Place Names**. In Cornwall we have Penzance ('Holy Headland'), Marazion (suggesting Hebrew connection), Jesus Well, opposite Padstow (an unique well-dedication, I believe), St Saviour's Chapel, Polruan (a dedication dating from the thirteenth century), Essa, at Saltash and Polruan (which might suggest the Holy Name in Hebrew) and the so-called Aesop's Bed, a rock near Talland, which certainly has nothing to do with the fabler, and might, with some probability, be also a corruption of the Hebrew 'Yesu'.[13]

In Somerset there is Christon, near Cheddar, on the old route from the lead mine of Priddy to Uphill, another reputed port of the old merchants.

(2) **The Wattle Church, called in Saxon time 'the Ealde Chirche'**. I have mentioned the reverence in which it was held from the earliest times of which we have any record. William of Malmesbury, by no means a credulous writer,[14] speaks of it with reverential awe, and, in describing some curious stones on the floor, says, 'If I were to suppose that they concealed a holy secret, I should do no harm to religion.' And he is our only historian of repute who *saw the Ealde Chirche* before the fire in 1184. He also quotes, with no apparent misgivings, the story of St David's vision, with its supposed message from our Lord about the old church, 'I have dedicated it long ago to my mother.' It is, indeed, hard to find any justification for such language and such reverence, unless we seek for a supposed origin far holier than its

[12] The Wattle Church at Glastonbury.

[13] Pronounced locally 'Essa's Bed', or by obvious corruption, 'Acc-o'- spades'.

[14] At the end of *The Child Christ at Lammana* I expressed the opinion that William of Malmesbury rejected the story of the coming of Joseph to Glastonbury. I now think that the word 'rejected' was much too forcible, but he was certainly inclined to be suspicious of legends as a whole. He undoubtedly knew of the tradition and referred to it.

building by an early disciple. The dedication to the Blessed Virgin certainly dates back before the conquest, when, as the present vicar of Glastonbury points out in his *St Joseph of Arimathea at Glastonbury*, such dedications were probably unknown (6th edition p. 43).

(3) **The Holy Cemetery**. This was held in a reverence as great as, if not greater than that accorded to the Wattle Church. I have shown in the Glastonbury Supplement that this may be due to the belief that the Blessed Virgin had been laid to rest here. It is interesting also to note that in the *Nova Legenda* and other medieval stories events are frequently dated from the Assumption, even when the Year of Our Lord is given as well. At the same time, if this supposition be rejected, the reverence in which it was held suggests some holier connection than the burial place of Joseph of Arimathea and subsequent saints. It was, apart from the old Church, the holiest part of the Holy Land of Britain.

(4) **Folklore and Folk Songs**. I can see the smile of sceptics, when I include these. But they often contain a germ of truth, and more often reflect old legends and traditions. At Looe I traced a pretty bit of folklore in connection with the Giant's Hedge. According to this version, from a centenarian of Looe, 'The piskies of Cornwall heard that a little boy and his uncle had landed at Looe Island, and they were so anxious to protect them, that they went to the giants, and got them to build a hedge.' Note the entire absence of names, and yet the obvious reference to our holy legend.

Of songs and so-called carols, popular now or once in Cornwall, I mention

'Joseph was a Tin-man'
'I saw Three Ships'
'Jerusalem'.

The second of these is most obscure, and has been sadly corrupted in later nursery versions. In the oldest form I can trace, the three ships bring, among others, 'Joseph and his fair ladye'. Of course, this might mean Joseph of Nazareth, but in view of the fact that the rhyme is about ships, I think it is quite probable that it first referred to the holy legend, and that 'his fair ladye' was originally 'our fair Ladye'. Blake's 'Jerusalem' is still a prime favourite, with its haunting and challenging question, never yet answered in the affirmative *or negative*:

Did the countenance divine
Shine forth upon these clouded hills?'[15]

[15] It has been suggested that Blake was simply drawing on his fancy when he wrote these words. How are we then going to explain that in 1773, when he was 16, he did a drawing entitled 'Joseph of Arimathea among the rocks of Albion'? I am told that one branch of Blake's family lived in or near Glastonbury.

VI. Light From Ancient Documents

Critics of all times have harped on the everlasting theme that the legends 'have no documentary support', at any rate before the thirteenth century. If by this they mean cast-iron proof, of course they have not. I never expect to find such.

We are dealing with a time which falls within the darkest period of the 'dark ages' of history. Take the years AD 8 to 25. Search the writings of the Evangelists, Josephus, the Roman historians, and Gibbon, and apart from the defeat of Varus and his legions in Germany in AD 9, you find next to nothing recorded. Josephus is never so short and uninformative as during this period, when, apparently, he was short of any reliable source of information. Of our old 'historians' in Britain, Gildas and Nennius are fragmentary to a degree, and never attempt to show how and when Christianity was first introduced into Britain. The Anglo-Saxon Chronicle, as its name suggests, deals principally with the Anglo-Saxons, and the compilers were probably woefully ignorant (as St Augustine was) of the early history of Celtic Christianity. Our own Celtic saints are little more than names, around which, as the late Canon Doble showed, reverence has woven beautiful and totally incredible legends. But, as Canon Doble again insisted, they were real men and women, who lived saintly lives in the districts where their names are commemorated. The reason we know so little about them is the same reason why we know so little of Glastonbury and Cornwall in the first centuries of the Christian era. They lie in almost impenetrable darkness.

I have collected and transcribed in the various Appendices all the pertinent ancient documents which, in my opinion, tend to confirm the truth of the Holy Legend. Meanwhile I append the Supplement dealing with the holiest traditions of Glastonbury itself. After that I leave the documents to face the scrutiny of experts and await the final verdict of History on the possibility, likelihood, or truth of the wonderful story I believe in and tell.

Glastonbury
The Holy Land of Britain

In this Supplement to *Christ in Cornwall?* I return to the spot whence I started on 'The Quest'. It had its origin in a short reference to the Holy Legend of Our Lord's visit to Britain in an early edition of Revd Lionel Lewis' *St Joseph of Arimathea at Glastonbury*. At Talland I traced the beautiful story of the visit of 'A little boy and his uncle' (The Child Christ and Joseph) to Lammana (Looe Island in Talland parish). This was the subject of my first booklet *The Child Christ at Lammana*. At Falmouth I traced a more definite and rather different version of the Holy Visit. Here it was rather of a grown man (The Saviour) visiting, with or without Joseph, most of the old mining districts of Cornwall.

This part of the Quest is dealt with in *Christ in Cornwall?* I have since traced the wonder story in places further afield, but still connected with early trade in metals. I always thought it should be found on the Welsh side of the Severn estuary, and I now hear definitely from a woman of Welsh extraction that she was told by her teacher at school that 'it was said that Our Lord came to Caerleon'. Caerleon can trace its history as an important centre for trade before the time of the Romans and the later times of King Arthur. Now, in the Isles of Scilly, I hear that Merchants' Point on Tresco is said to be so named because the Phoenicians came here to barter for tin brought over from the mainland by the Britons. Some add the belief that Joseph of Arimathea also came, and there is a faint but quite definite memory that Our Lord's name was also mentioned. This is referred to in my *St Martin's, St Helen's and Tean*, with comments on the possibility of Scilly as a place of trade or barter.

But Glastonbury, Priddy and the Mendips have always been the focal point of it all. Here, on the 'holyest erth of England' I have looked for, and I believe I have found, the culmination of the whole story. Here it is the legend, *not* of a visit, either by a Child or a Man, but of a retreat for the Saviour of the world during the hidden years of early manhood. And, hardly less wonderful, of another hidden retreat, the final home and grave of his blessed Mother.

Wild as these ideas may seem, I beg you to suspend judgement while I unfold the grounds on which the growing conviction has been forced on me that they are both true, and that the dear anonymous writer whom I quote on the cover had all this in mind when he called, and rightly called, Glastonbury 'the holyest erth' in our beloved land.

To begin with, we must rid ourselves of all prejudices and preconceptions. I have dealt with some of these as regards Our Lord in *Christ in Cornwall?* I would add a word about travel and emigration among Hebrew men *and women*. I said before that the story of Our Lady coming here was harder to conceive, but that it could not be discounted altogether in view of the tinners' tradition. As regards women, we know that there was a large and early settlement of Hebrew folk in the Rhone valley, whither the Bethany family is said in local legend to have migrated en masse after Our Lord's Ascension; and Priscilla, a Jewess, is known from the story of the Acts to have travelled, apparently without much difficulty, between Rome, Ephesus, and Corinth.

Again, in considering the credibility of one legend, we must weigh it against that of alternative ones. With regard to Our Lord, the alternative is a permanent residence at Nazareth. I can conceive of no place less suitable in those turbulent times in which to prepare for his life's work. The same applies with still greater force to the idea of Jerusalem or Ephesus as a final home of rest for Our Lady of Sorrows. Both these alternatives are purely legendary, and if they are more generally accepted, there are very palpable flaws. Our Lord's visit to Nazareth at the beginning of his ministry does *not* fit in with the story of a village carpenter who has only been away for a few weeks or months. The chief flaw in the case of the Blessed Virgin is the site of her grave. The place now pointed out to pilgrims near Jerusalem was *never mentioned* by St Jerome, who, in the fourth century, explored and described all the holy places of Judaea. Her alternative residence at Ephesus is faced with the glaring omission of all reference to her by St Paul in his Epistles and by St Luke in the Acts.

Having thus cleared the ground, let us see what clues have led me to the conclusions outlined above. I have acknowledged my debt to Revd C.C. Dobson for the suggestion that Our Lord came to Britain *twice* at least, first as a child or youth, on a visit with Joseph, and secondly as a man, to reside for some years at or near Glastonbury. The two fit in quite well. The first visit would introduce him to the peace and, as I believe, the friendly atmosphere of Avalon and the Lake villages of the neighbourhood. In seeking a retreat in preparation for his work, what more likely than that he should choose this spot?

While of course I can produce no documentary evidence in any way *proving* this surmise, it is confirmed in my own mind by the following passages from authors of the twelfth century and earlier. These passages suggest that the writers were conversant with, and did not altogether discredit, ancient traditions which attributed a mysterious and holy origin to the spiritual Church in Britain, and to the material Wattle Church at Glastonbury in particular. In this Supplement I use the conclusions I have formed *without comment*, and translations which I claim to have justified in the said Appendices.

(1) The old wattle Church of Glastonbury was held in a veneration which far transcended that which would be accorded to an early Christian sanctuary, even if it were supposed to have been erected by or in the time of the Apostles. William of Malmesbury, who has never been accused of being a credulous legend-monger, in describing the holy fane *as he saw it*, mentions in particular some strange stones in the pavement, and suggests that they concealed a holy secret. The same writer records a traditional vision of St David, where Our Lord appeared and told the saint that he had *already dedicated the building of his Mother*.

He also quotes a far older unknown historian, quoted, as he says, already by St Augustine, as saying that the *'Ealde Chirche' was built by no human art*.

(2) While no writer can be quoted as saying explicitly either that Our Lord lived there, or that he built the Wattle Church, yet Gildas in the sixth century said that the *'true Sun' first shed his beams on these islands at the height of Tiberius' reign* (AD 14–37).

(3) In the great Register of Glastonbury of the Middle Ages occur

two titles, 'Domus Dei', and 'Secretum Domini', which bear the obvious meaning of '*The House or home of God*' and '*The Secret or retreat of the Lord*'. No special pleading or sophistry will ever make me believe that they had such mundane meanings as Domesday Survey and the Abbot's private note-book.

Fireside stories of the Holy visit still linger at Glastonbury, and far more so at Priddy in the Mendips. Why the tradition was not *more* emphasized at Glastonbury has always puzzled me.[1] That it existed is beyond doubt, but the monks of the Middle Ages appear to have elaborated the cult of Our Lady and St Joseph, almost to the exclusion of the holier tradition of Our Lord. Perhaps even then there were doubters, as today, who would say 'Oh! That is going a bit too far.' But what of that stone in the South wall of the Lady Chapel, with the two mysterious and isolated names 'IESUS–MARIA'? No explanation. A monk called Edward Stourton wrote about them in the abbacy of Adam de Sodbury (1312–34), but his work, alas, is lost. Is it too fantastic a flight of fancy to picture the Old Church, 'Built by no human art', but by the human hands of the Son of God, and inscribed with those names by him, in dedication, as he told St David later, to his own Blessed Mother? I know they were carved in stone in the twelfth century. But they *may* have reproduced what an earlier generation remembered carved in the rough woodwork of the original building.[2] And, while they did not blazon it in their writings, may not the monks of later years have deliberately enshrined the Holy Tradition in their name 'Domus Dei'? The 'Secret of the Lord' too had, perchance, a more momentous import than they even knew. It was not only his retreat, but his deliberate secret as well. Has the time at last arrived foretold by the old bard Melchinus in the dim ages of Glastonbury's story, when 'long ere the day of Judgment all will be open and plain to the world'?

At Priddy the precious tradition of Christ's visit remained as a treasured belief to within living memory, and modern scepticism has failed to destroy it entirely today. The comings of Christ there have

---

[1] A lady who tells me that her ancestors lived in Somerset, and some time near Glastonbury, but who would rather remain anonymous, says in a letter to me: 'My family (on both sides) have lived in Somerset for many generations, and have always believed that when Joseph of Arimathea came to trade in tin, he brought the boy Jesus with him to 'the Summerland' to continue his education on the Isle of Avalon, and that after the Crucifixion Joseph of Arimathea, Mary, and other disciples lived, and died, there.' She says also that she was brought up by her grandmother, who 'never questioned' these legends. As my correspondent can hardly be less than middle-aged, and as she says that her grandmother had been told the Story by *her* grandmother, we have here no mean link in the long chain of oral tradition round Glastonbury.

[2] I am inclined to accept Mr Bligh Bond's idea that the *original* building was a circular hut, which was enclosed in a rectangular church of wood at a somewhat later date.

always sounded to me more like the visits of a teacher. It was a schoolmaster of recent years who used to recall his pupils to their task with the admonition 'Suppose you saw Jesus coming up the hill now?' surely a memory of far-off days when the children gathered to watch for the coming of the beloved Teacher up the long coulee to the crest of Mendip.

The other amazing conclusion I have reached is that Our Lady lived and died at Glastonbury. Again, first consider the alternatives, which all presume that she lived all her latter life with the 'Beloved disciple'. All that has biblical support is that Our Lord entrusted her to St John from the Cross, and that 'from that hour that disciple took her to his own (home)'. It nowhere says that she was expected to or actually did live with him all the rest of her life. Indeed, an early tradition of the fourteenth century, recorded by Capgrave in the *Nova Legenda Angliae*, says explicitly that while the blessed John was labouring at Ephesus, he handed her over to the care of Joseph as her 'bridesman' ('paranymphus'), and that Joseph was present at her Assumption. So another legend had come into existence before the fourteenth century, showing that there was no *universal* belief in the Church *then* that she lived all the rest of her life with St John. To return to the New Testament story, she is curiously missing in St John's own account of Easter morning, and our last reference shows her after the Ascension living with all the Apostles and the other women in Jerusalem.

As regards the alternative *places* where she is supposed to have lived, Jerusalem was a scene of incessant turmoil, with revolts against the Romans alternating with persecutions of the Christians; Ephesus lacks any confirmation either from local legend or New Testament writings; Mount Carmel is only mentioned in legend as, perhaps, a temporary refuge; and Nazareth was the place which had rejected and tried to kill her Blessed Son.

As to her death, we have a most fanciful story in the *Transitus Mariae*, telling how all the Apostles came at divine bidding to be present at her passing. This story is not, I believe, taken seriously by any branch of the Church today. The story of the Assumption is generally located in or near Jerusalem, but St Jerome's silence makes such a tradition sadly lacking in a firm foundation. All the alternative legends of Our Lady's later life are purely legendary, unsubstantiated, and, in my opinion, unlikely.

The main basis of my 'amazing' surmise lies in striking phrases in old documents more than in folk memories and oral tradition. We shall see that such oral tradition did exist in 1502, and I have traced a dim echo of it in living memory. After I had just returned from Glastonbury, a lady said to me 'Did you ever hear that Our Lady came to England and died here?' I was amazed. I had just returned from the spot outside the walls of the Lady Chapel at Glastonbury, where the surmise had first caught and stunned me, but I had said no word of it to her. I then asked where she had heard it, and she said she had been at school in Alexandria with Nuns who were all connected with the old aristocracy of France, and 'it might have been they' who told her. A Roman Catholic friend of mine has just pointed out how remarkable it would be for Nuns of the French aristocracy to attribute such a story to England rather than to France, if it were pure invention.

Outside the Lady Chapel at Glastonbury I had been pondering over two passages which I had often read, but perhaps had never sufficiently studied. One day as I sat looking at the 'IESUS—MARIA' stone it all came back, and staggered me by the implication. First there was the passage from the old bard Melchinus, where he speaks of the early disciples building the Wattle Church *over* ('super') *the powerful, adorable virgin*. The present vicar of Glastonbury said afterwards that he believed I was the first person who had dared to translate the simple Latin word literally. Why not? It is at least a simpler translation than Dean Armitage Robinson's 'for the adoring of a powerful virgin'. What Melchinus said, rightly or wrongly, was that the Ealde Chirche was built over the grave of the Blessed Virgin.

For my other passage, we must jump perhaps 900 years, and we find that, while oral tradition on this subject is practically defunct now, it was not so when the anonymous bard of 1502 wrote of the coming of Joseph of 'Armathia' to Britain.

> Now here how Joseph came into englande;
> But at that tyme it was called brytayne.
> Than xv yere with our lady, as I understande,
> Ioseph wayted styll, to serve hyr he was fayne.

The meaning is obvious, and though he does not expressly say that she died here, he goes on to quote from 'the boke' about what happened after 'hyr assumpcyon'. And note that the story of her residence with Joseph is from oral tradition ('as I understande'), and not from 'the boke'.

I now proceed to reconstruct the story as I see it. St John took Our Lady away from the cross 'at that very hour', that she might be spared the horror of the three hours of darkness. She lived with him, or under his charge, for a comparatively short while. He then transferred his trust to Joseph, who, after seeing the Bethany family safe in the Rhone valley, brought the Blessed Virgin to Avalon. This was to be *her* secret refuge, beside the little building which her Blessed Son had built and already bequeathed to her. Here she died, probabably about AD 48. Here they buried her, and here the 'first neophytes of Catholic law'[3] erected the Vetusta Ecclesia *over* her resting place. Joseph now went to join St Philip in France. Commissioned, and perhaps ordained by him,

---

[3] See Appendix 2. The Latin phrase for those who founded the old 'Church' is 'primi neophytae', which would hardly be used of any missionaries *after* the first century AD.

he returned about AD 63 with his band of twelve hermits to take up their abode around the same sacred spot.

This reconstruction would solve some puzzling problems. On Weary-all hill is a stone placed by John Clark (1801-9) with the inscription 'J.A. ANO.D.xxxi.' The Vatican MS (see Appendix 2) dated Joseph's coming as AD 35. The dates are near enough for rough chronology. Either would allow approximately for 15 years here with Our Lady, and then for time with St Philip before his final return to Avalon. In the claim for precedence put forward by the British Church in the fifteenth century councils, the date of Joseph's coming is given as 'immediately after the passion'. ('statim post passionem'). It also fits in with the very ancient dedication of the Church to the Blessed Virgin, perhaps the earliest on record; the strange, haunting Breton Legend of St Anne's original connection with Britain or Brittany; and most notably with the two following references, with which I close;

(1) Why is England called 'Our Lady's Dowry'? All our Roman Catholic friends know of the title, and pray for us under it. It was assuredly her dowry, if it had been bestowed on her as her final home by her Son. And Joseph was then indeed her 'bridesman' who was to conduct her to her inheritance.

(2) Lastly, I return to the subject of reverence. We noted this in connection with the Wattle Church. It is perhaps even more striking with regard to the Holy Cemetery. William of Malmesbury (*Gesta Regum*, i, 2) tells how acts of irreverence, seemingly trivial, met dire retribution, how the Holy Cemetery was the haunt of countless pilgrims, and how large numbers of holy men and women craved to be buried here, and here 'especially chose to await the day of resurrection *under the protection of the Mother of GOD*'.[4]

Appendices
1. Gildas (AD 560-600)

De Excidio, Section VI (ex MS Cod. Cantab. Ed. Gale).

'Verus ille Sol, non de firmamento temporali, sed de summaetiam coelorum arce tempora cuncta excedente, universo orbi praefulgidum sui coruscum ostendens; tempore, 'ut scimus, summo Tiberii Caesaris . . . radios suos primum indulget.'

'He the true Sun . . . revealing his excellent brightness to the whole world, . . . first bestows his rays (on this island), as we know, at the height of the reign of Tiberius Caesar.'

The translation of 'tempore summo' may be disputed. In any case Gildas says it was *during* the reign of Tiberius, who died AD 37. That he referred to Britain is defined in earlier words ('glaciali frigore insulae'), a truly Roman estimate of our climate.

I claim that it is more likely that Gildas meant that Christ came here himself than that some disciples reached our shores before AD 37. The traditional

---

[4] *Deipara*. A common medieval title of Our Lady.

date of the arrival of Joseph of Arimathea *with his twelve companions* is AD 63. My own surmise of an earlier visit with the Blessed Virgin could only be at the extreme end of Tiberius' reign, when the emperor had retired into semi-insane obscurity. I cannot believe that Gildas would have used the words 'tempore summo' of such a period.

2. The 'Ancient British Historian'

William of Malmesbury, who plainly says he is shy of the legendary, is yet constrained to write thus:

After referring to the twelve disciples, said to have been sent to Britain by St Philip and St James, he goes on: 'Hoc autem ita se habere tum ex carta Beati Patricii, tum ex scriptis seniorum cognoscimus. Quorum unus Britonum Historiographus, prout apud Sanctum Edmundum, itemque apud Sanctum Augustinum Anglorum Apostolum vidimus, ita exorsus est.' (Gale's transcript. *Historiae Britannicae*, 292–3.) He goes on to quote, approximately, the words given below, from the *Vita Sancti Dunstani*.

William distinctly says here that this passage had already been quoted by St Edmund and St Augustine. This at least shows its great antiquity. I cannot actually trace St Augustine's reference, but I would note a certain mysterious Vatican MS, mentioned by Cardinal Baronius as his authority for an assertion that Joseph of Arimathea was a companion of St Philip, Lazarus, etc., in their flight to Gaul in AD 35, and later preached in Britain. Baronius' actual words in the margin are 'ex manuscripta Historia Angl. quae habetur in Bibl. Vaticana' (Lansdown MS, 255.f.364. British Museum). Baronius was librarian of the Vatican.

Now we turn to the *Vita Sancti Dunstani*. Bishop Stubbs, (*Memorials of St Dunstan*, 1874), gives the following version of the passage by the anonymous writer called Saxon Priest 'B', which he says is probably the oldest and most accurate. He thinks the writer was perhaps a contemporary of St Dunstan.

TEXT

Quem [St Dunstan], pii parentes sacri baptismatis undis renatum Dunstanum vocaverunt. Crevit itaque puer et effectus est tam Deo quam hominibus carus, Erat autem quaedam regalis in confinio ejusdem praefati viri [King Athelstan] insula, antiquo vicinorum vocabulo Glastonia nuncupata, latis locorum dimensa sinibus, piscosis aquis stagneisque circumducta fluminibus, et plurimis humanae indigentiae apta usibus, atque sacris, quod maximum est, Dei dicata muneribus. In ea siquidem ipsius loca [sic] primi catholicae legis neophitae antiquam Deo dictante repperunt aecclesiam, nulla hominum arte[1] constructam, immo humano saluti coelitus paratam; quam postmodum Ipse coelorum fabricator multis miraculorum gestis multisque misteriorum virtutibus[2] hanc[3] Sibi sanctaeque genetrici Suae[4] Mariae consecratam fore demonstravit. Huic etiam aliud addiderunt opere[5] lapideo[6] oratorium quod Christo ejusque Sancto Petro Apostolo dedicaverunt.

FOOTNOTES (Stubbs'):
(1) *arte*) ut ferunt, ins. B. in marg.
(2) *misteriorum virtutibus*) virtutum misteriis. B.
(3) *hanc*) om. B.
(4) *(Suae)* Dei. B.

(5) *opere*) operes. A.

(6) *lapideo*) lapideos. A.

The important footnote is (1), which shows that the version accepted by Bishop Stubbs did not have the words 'ut ferunt' in the text, and that 'B' only had it in the margin. William of Malmesbury includes it in the text. This gradual insertion of 'so they say' is a very interesting commentary on the growth of scepticism. Note also the sudden and abrupt change from the account of St Dunstan's boyhood to this amazing story of the 'ealde chirche'. The writer is clearly copying an older MS.

FREE TRANSLATION

'Now there was a certain royal island within the confines of the realm of Athelstan, called in the old language of the vicinity Glastonia, embracing broad tracts of country, surrounded by waters abounding in fish, and river-beds rich in lead; adapted to the satisfaction of every human need. Also, best of all, consecrated by the gifts of God himself. Indeed, when they came into these parts, the first neophytes of catholic law, under the guidance of God, found a Church, constructed by no human art, but actually prepared divinely for the salvation of man. Which Church the Creator of Heaven himself, by many miraculous acts and mysterious virtues, showed was to be consecrated to himself and to Mary his Mother.'

3. 'Domus Dei' — 'Secretum Domini'

I have seen the names 'Domus Dei' and 'Secretum Domini' applied to Glastonbury by several writers, and have done my best to trace their origin. Ussher, in his *Britannicarum Ecclesiarum Antiquitates* gives the following footnote to the word 'Domesday', '*Domus Dei*; in magno Glastoniensis Monasterii Registro, quod *Secretum Domini* vocatur: fol. 249b.'

Certain authorities at the Bodleian Library tell me there is no doubt that 'Secretum Domini' is an abbreviation of 'Registrum Secretum Domini Abbatis', and it is certainly true that one such register of the time of Walter de Monyton (Abbot 1341–74) was called 'Secretum Abbatis' (MS Bodl. Wood. empt. 1). But there were earlier registers. Dr Oliver mentions an 'Original Survey of the Property of Glastonbury Abbey' in the time of Abbot Adam de Sodbury (1308–1326), and Ussher may have got his 'Secretum Domini' from one of these.

With the utmost deference to the experience of the Bodleian librarians on the subject of the ways of monastic scribes, I do find it very hard to believe that the 'Private Register of the Lord Abbot' was shortened by them to the most ambiguous form of 'The Secret of the Lord'. Is it not at least equally possible that the original 'Great Register' of Glastonbury was called, with no intentional ambiguity, the 'Secretum Domini', and that later Abbots, not understanding its original purport, altered it to 'Secretum Domini Abbatis', and later again quietly dropped the 'Domini'?

The problem of the words 'Domus Dei' is still more obscure. On fol. 249b, (the same reference as Ussher's above), of the 'Secretum Abbatis' is the following:

'Terra sancte Marie Glastonie sicut continetur in libro scaccarii Londoniensis qui dicitur domus dei quem componi fecit rex Willelmus primus subacto sibi et pacificato regno Anglie.'

On the face of it, this certainly seems to give 'Domus Dei' as a fourteenth-century name for Domesday, and Stuart Moore, quoted by Dove in *Domesday Studies*, says that, 'according to the compiler of the Red Book of the Exchequer', it was called 'Domus Dei', or 'the Roll of Winchester'. But is this 'liber scaccarii' identical with the Domesday Survey? The usual title of the latter is 'Liber Judicialis vel Censualis Angliae'. A book of laws and customs, now lost, existed in the time of King Alfred, called 'Dombok', and 'Liber Judicialis' is a remarkably close rendering of the old Saxon word.

Here again, the experts, though with less certainty, would attribute the name 'Domus Dei' to careless monastic scribes, trying to put into Latin the vulgar names 'Dome-book', 'Domesday-book', or 'Domesday'. They may have been poor latinists, but were they really as poor as all this? 'Domus Dei' has such an obvious meaning, even for the poorest Latin scholar, and it is a very different meaning to either 'Dom-bok', 'Domesday', or 'Doomsday'.

Others again have apparently given up the attempt to derive 'Domus Dei' from 'Domesday', and have attributed this name to the supposed circumstance of its having been kept in some room or chapel, which was called 'Domus Dei'. But they do not even seem sure whether this was at Winchester or Westminster. It looks very much like a surmise, and nothing more. Was any room or chapel ever called 'Domus Dei'? The cathedrals themselves would of course have the right to the name, but so would the humblest 'House of God'. You might as well call the Survey a 'Church', and be done with it! The explanation sounds forced and unreal.

Once again, I humbly put forward my suggestion. It is that the name 'Domesday' may well have been the vulgar name for the Survey, based on the Saxon 'Dom-bok'. But that 'Domus Dei' must have a different explanation, in which case the vulgar 'Domesday' might equally well be a corruption of this. Something, some place, or the whole realm, may have been known as 'domus Dei', the 'Home of God'. And those to whom it was thus known may well have been the old monks of Glastonbury in whose registers the name has been preserved. In other words, I suggest that they regarded either Glastonbury itself, or the whole of Britain, as in some sense 'God's Home'. Through them the name might easily become transferred to the Survey of the Conqueror, and have been copied by others, who perhaps never understood its original sacred import.

This may sound fantastic to some readers. I wonder if it is more so than any of the other explanations of the name 'Domesday' which are put forward by more learned students.

Nor do I see that my theory about 'Secretum Domini' is seriously affected by the fact, which I acknowledge above, that the folio reference given by Ussher from what he calls 'Secretum Domini' is the same apparently as that in 'Secretum Abbatis' at the Bodleian. It is clear that these registers were recopied and brought up to date from time to time, but a great part of them would probably be a verbatim transcript, and therefore have the same folio reference. The same words might well be on the same page, both in the known 'Secretum Abbatis', and in Ussher's 'Secretum Domini'.

Since the above was written I have found confirmation of my concluding argument in Adam de Domerham (*c*. 1300). Trin. Coll. Camb. MS R.5.33. fol 131a. Adam de Domerham here quotes a document called 'Secretum domini', and gives the identical passage as that in the Bodleian 'Secretum abbatis', *with the same folio number* (249b). There can be little doubt that this

is the document which Ussher quotes from, and note that the date of this
is certainly older than the 'Secretum abbatis' (1341-74).

Since the second edition was issued, the controversy over the meanings of
these two phrases were resumed in the columns of the *Somerset County Herald*,
and in the issue of 19 April 1947, under No. 4264, Abbot Horne quotes, with
apparent approval, the comments of Dom Aelred Watkin. I give the exact
words of the latter's pertinent summary in each case. (1) *Secretum Domini*.
'On account of the fact that it was copied out for the private use of the Lord
Abbots of Glastonbury, [it] went by the name of *Secretum Domini* — a nick-
name implying that it was set apart for the use of the Lord Abbot.'

I should like confirmation of that word 'fact'. As for the 'nick-name', I ask
any intelligent reader to judge for himself as to its suitability! (2) *Domus Dei*.
'The scribe attempting to find some Latin form for the word *Domesday*, in-
vents the somewhat ridiculous *Domus Dei*, perhaps as a rather laboured witticism.'

'Curiouser and curiouser', to quote Alice. 'Ridiculous'! 'Laboured witticism'!

Surely for the poorest Latin scholar, both nickname and witticism verge
perilously on the profane.

4. Melchinus

Melchinus or **Melkinus** (Celtic **Maelgwyn?**). He is most obscure in origin
and date. John of Glastonbury, following Glastonbury tradition, says he was
'before Merlin'. Pits (*De illustribus Britanniae scriptoribus* — 1619), describes
him as an 'Avalonian', and calls him a British bard, historian, and astronomer.
He dates him with assurance as AD 560. Leland (*c*. 1530), noted the document here quoted as a very treasured possession in the old Library of the
Abbey. He calls it 'a fragment of history written by Melchinus an Avalonian'.
Apart from tradition, the language suggests great antiquity, and, whatever
else we may call it, it does not sound in the least monastic. The passage is
quoted, apart from John of Glastonbury, in the *Nova Legenda Angliae*, and
the following translation is from the text as given by Skeat (*Joseph of Arimathie*,
p. 70-1).

'The Isle of Avalon, hungry for the burial of the natives, once adorned,
above all others in the world, by oracular circles ('sperulis vaticinantibus')
of prophecy, will for the future also be furnished with worshippers of the
Highest. Abbadare, mighty in judgement, noblest of natives, with one hundred and four knights ("milibus" for "militibus") fell asleep there. Amid
whom, Joseph of Marmor, named of "Armathia", found his perpetual rest.
And he lies inside the forked line near the southern angle of the oratory erected
there (of wattles prepared before), over ("super potentem adorandam
virginem") the powerful adorable virgin, by that circle of thirteen inhabiting
the spot. Joseph forsooth, has with him in his sepulchre two cruets, white
and silvery, filled with the blood and sweat of the prophet Jesus. When his
sepulchre shall be found, it will be seen in future years complete and undamag-
ed, and it will be open to the whole world. Thenceforth, neither dew nor
rain shall ever fail those who inhabit this most noble island. Long before the
judgement day in Josaphat, these things will be open and manifested to living people.'

I have always felt that this document, though quoted by sceptics like Dean

Armitage Robinson, has never had the consideration it deserves. The language stamps it as far earlier than the Conquest, and the phraseology as native or even Hebrew in origin.

5. St David's Vision

St David's Vision and William of Malmesbury. William of Malmesbury (twelfth century), who actually saw the old Wattle Church, is, by his own confession, very cautious in repeating unsubstantiated legends, yet he records, with no apparent suspicion, the following supposed vision of St David (*De Antiquitate*, Hearne, p. 25). The translation here is by Mr H. F. Scott-Stokes, a sceptic on Glastonbury legends:

'In what reverence the great David, Archbishop of the Menevesians, held the place is so well-known, that it needs to report of mine to elucidate it. Through him a divine miracle corroborated the antiquity and sanctity of the Church. For, thinking to consecrate it, he came with seven Bishops, of whom he was the primate, to Glastonbury. But when all was ready for the ceremony, on the night before it was to take place (as he thought), he bade sleep welcome. And having relaxed all his senses to rest, he saw the Lord Jesus standing by, and courteously inquiring why he had come. He at once explained, but the Lord recalled him from his intention by saying that he himself had long ago dedicated the Church in honour of his Mother, and the sacrament ought not to be profaned by human repetition.'

6. The Ealde Chirche

The following gives William of Malmesbury's own description of the Wattle Church, with the feelings which it inspired in him:

Gesta Regam Anglorum, I.20. 'In it the bodily relics of many saints are preserved, some of whom we shall note in due course; nor is there any space around the shrine which does not contain the ashes of the blessed. Indeed, the tesselated pavement of polished stone, yes, even the sides of the altar, and the very altar itself, both above and below, are piled with the crowded relics. In places also one may note in the pavement on either side stones carefully placed, in alternate triangles and squares, and sealed with lead; beneath which, if I believe some holy secret to be held, I am doing no harm to religion.'

7. The Breton Legend

I append in full the legend current in Brittany, connecting St Anne, the mother of the Blessed Virgin, with that land. While it is obvious that the Bretons themselves locate the scene of the legend in their own country, it is at least possible that it was transplanted from Cornwall, with many of their place names, at the time of the great migration. The district with which the legend is connected is called 'Cornuaille'. The version which I append is my own translation of an extract from Anatole le Braz' 'Sainte Anne de la Palude' in *Au Pays des Pardons*.

The writer tells how he was struck by the likeness of a poor peasant woman to the figure of St Anne, before which she had been praying.

' "Do you know," I said, "that St Anne and you look like sisters?"

"I am, like her, a grandmother," she replied, "and, like me, thank God, she is a Breton."

"St Anne — a Breton? Are you quite sure about that, my worthy woman?"

She turned her dreamy eyes on me, and answered in a pitying tone: "How easy to see that you are from the town! The townsfolk are ignorant; they despise us country folk, because we cannot read their books. But they! What would they know of their land, if we were not there to tell them? Oh yes, St Anne was a Breton. Go to the Château de Moëllien, and they will show you the room she inhabited, in the days when she was Queen of that country. For a Queen she was; nay, she was even 'Duchesse', a far more beautiful title. They blessed her in the streets, because of her goodness and her boundless pity for the humble and unhappy. Her husband, in turn, passed for a very hard man. He was jealous of his wife, and did not want her to bear children. When he discovered that she was with child, he flew into a violent passion, and drove her out like a beggar, in the middle of the night, in the depth of winter, half naked, into the icy storm. A piteous wanderer, she walked blindly on. In the bay of Tréfentec, under this dune, a barque of light rode placidly, though the sea was rough, and at the stern stood an angel in white, his wings spread out like sails. 'Embark,' said the angel, 'that we may take care of you; for the time is short.' 'Whither would you take me?' she asked, and he replied, 'The wind will direct us; the will of God is in the wind.'

"They passed along the coast of Judaea, and landed in the port of Jerusalem. Some days later Anne gave birth to a daughter, destined by God to be the Virgin. She brought her up piously, taught her her letters in a book of Psalms, and made her wise in body and spirit; meet to become the mother of Jesus. Her task ended, as she felt herself growing old, she prayed Heaven, saying, 'I am pining for my Bretons. If only, ere I die, I may see again my parish, and the beach, so sweet to my eyes, of la Palude in Plounévez Porzay!' Her prayer was answered. The barque of light returned to take her, with the same angel at the helm, only now he was robed in black, to show the saint of her widowhood, for the Seigneur de Moëllien had died meanwhile. The castle folk, gathered on the shore, received their châtelaine with transports of joy, but she immediately hushed them. 'Go,' she commanded, 'and distribute all my goods among the poor.' She was resolved to end her earthly days in penitence. Henceforth she lived *here*, under this barren dune, in one perpetual orison. The light of her eyes radiated far over the waters like a moonbeam. On stormy nights she was the saviour of the fishers. With one gesture she calmed the sea, and drove the clouds back to bed, like a flock of sheep to the fold.

"Jesus, her grandson, undertook for her sake the voyage to Basse-Bretagne. Before he was to climb Calvary, he went to ask her blessing, accompanied by the disciples Peter and John. Their parting was a bitter one. Anne wept tears of blood, and Jesus tried in vain to console her. At last he said to her, 'Think, grand-mère, of your Bretons. Speak, and in thy name I will grant them whatever they ask.'

"The saint checked her tears. 'Ah! then,' she cried, 'May a church be dedicated here to me, and as far as its steeple shall be seen, as far as its bells shall be heard, may all sickness be healed, and every soul, living or dead, find peace!' . . . There, my gentleman, is the true history of Anne of la Palude, in Plounévez Porzay. There it is, just as I had it from my mother, who had it from hers, at a time when families transmitted piously, from memory to memory, the things of the past." '

These simple words of the Breton peasant woman sum up the whole case for the credibility of oral tradition. Allowing for all possible embellishments in the course of time, the fundamental basis of the tradition dates back to those far-off ages when, in the beautiful words of the original, 'les familles se transmettaient pieusement de mémoire en mémoire les choses du passé'.

15

The Mystery of Glastonbury[1]

FREDERICK BLIGH BOND

Evidences of the Early Settlement

It will rest with the science of archaeology to prove with final certitude the date and character of the first Christian settlement. The 'Lignea Basilica' or wooden church was not the first to be erected. It was much more likely to have been the work of the two British missionaries sent over by Pope Eleutherius in the second century AD, in response to the call of King Lucius of Britain.

The first chapel was that built by Joseph of Arimathea and his companions, and the form of this chapel is described by Malmesbury as being circular. This would be quite in accord with the earliest Christian foundations known to archaeology: for example, the very primitive church excavated not many years ago at Etchmiazin, the old ecclesiastical capital of Armenia, is described as being of circular form and having around it Twelve subsidiary chapels symbolic of the XII constellations of the Zodiac — the Signs being sculptured upon them. The Church of the Holy Sepulchre in Jerusalem had the same circular form.[2] It is thought to be of Persian origin.

The tradition as to Joseph's little chapel with its wattle roof is found in Malmesbury's *Antiquities of Glaston* (see Lomax's translation). Before any excavation around the site of St Joseph's Chapel at Glaston had been undertaken, the present writer, who was then acting as Director of Excavations, had formed the opinion that a ring of circular cells around the site of Joseph's chapel might be looked for.

In 1921 the late Dean Armitage Robinson commissioned the writer to discover the true position of the monument (pillar or pyramid) erected by Saint David in the sixth century to mark the true extent of the sacred site, then in danger of being lost. This was discovered about 29 ft to the north of the Norman chapel now standing and it proved to be exactly in line with its eastern wall, thus shewing that the builders of the later chapel had faithfully adhered to the original measures of the Wooden Church. But what most strongly attracted

[1] From Frederick Bligh Bond, *The Mystery of Glastonbury* (Glastonbury Publications, 1930).
[2] It is worthy of note that the Ethiopian churches of Abyssinia are practically all of circular form.

Figure 11: 'Sketch of Glastonbury Abbey before its destruction in 1539'

attention was the discovery beneath the remnants of the monument, of a circular platform or foundation seven feet in diameter, of apparently very ancient workmanship and quite probably dating from the earliest period.

On testing the distance from this little circular 'cell' foundation to a point centrally placed within the existing Chapel, it was found to accord exactly with the dimensions of a circle already theoretically marked as that of the probable ring of cells around Joseph's first church. This conjectural circle gave correct positions — according to theory — for the two cells lying east and west on the central axis of the chapel.

St David's 'pyramid' or 'pillar' was not the only monument of this nature about the central chapel. Others are on record. Two are spoken of as having been opposite the south door of the chapel; and there were remains of these as late as the eighteenth century. In the present writer's view, all these 'pyramids' and other monuments would have been placed to mark more ancient foundations; and he therefore felt some confidence that excavation, if permitted, would reveal some proof of the form of the first Christian settlement.

Consequently he was glad when Dean Robinson, as Chairman of the Trustees of the Abbey, asked him also to ascertain, if possible, the position of the two pyramids to the south, mentioned by John of Glaston. The radius of the circle having already been proved correct in theory it became a fairly simple task to find the true position or distance of these from the centre of the Norman chapel. So he knew exactly where to dig for the first of these. The point was 32 ft south of the southern door of the chapel and a little to the west of its centre. Immediate success resulted. On removing the top soil, there appeared the remains of a heavy stone monument of rectangular form, and beneath this again, traces of what looked like a circular foundation similar to that found under St David's pillar. Alas! that the knowledge of these things — found too easily and without the usual preliminary of cutting trenches — should have proved so unwelcome to the authorities concerned. Unfortunately in this case, official repugnance to the method of discovery — which was based upon a recall of the latent memories of the past[3] — now speedily put an end to the research. Without warning, and before any measurements could be taken, the excavation was filled up on the order of an executive official. Other points where the ground had been opened were closed down in the same manner. A Norman wall found on the north side of the Lady Chapel was despoiled of its best stones, which were carried away to another part of the site. Shortly after, the whole arrangement for research, carried on over a period of fourteen years by the Somerset Archaeological Society, was brought to an end.

[3] As described in *The Gate of Remembrance* and *The Company of Avalon*.

Since 1921 nothing further has been attempted on this part of the site. The investigation of the Circle of Cells remains inconclusive. Nevertheless, the discovery of these two foundations offer fair presumptive evidence of the existence of a complete ring of cells round about the circular chapel of Joseph. The record of the several 'Pyramids' surrounding the chapel at various points also clearly indicates the intent to mark in perpetuity the true position of older landmarks rendered faint by lapse of time. This we know in the case of St David's pillar and it is obviously to be inferred in the second case, where the remains of the pyramid were right over an older foundation. To the west of the Chapel lies the little cell or chapel of Saint Dunstan. This would take the place of yet another of the XII original cells, since it lies on the central axis of the great circle (see Fig. 14). There is a hard concrete flooring here inside the four walls which has not yet been explored. A future investigation may reveal something of interest. The position marked for the cell at the extreme east — opposite St Dunstan's — would bring it just over the place in the very ancient crypt (still intact) where later the shrine of Joseph is believed to have stood. Above this, in the thirteenth century, the Galilee was built. And when the east wall of the existing Chapel of St Mary was thrown down and opened to the Galilee by an arch (now restored) the place of the Altar above ground would again correspond with a cell-position. So we have no less than four out of the twelve cell sites reasonably accounted for.

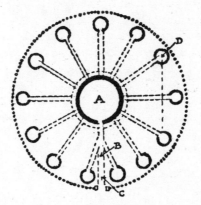

Figure 12: 'The Circular Chapel Ring of Cells'

A. St Joseph's Circular Chapel (AD 37).
B. The Forked Paths (*linea bifurcata*). Traditional burial place of Joseph.
C. Site of Arthur's grave, between the pyramids.
D. Site of one of the XII cells, marking the eastward boundary of the Vetusta Ecclesia (*see Fig. 13*).

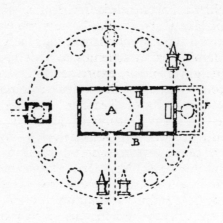

Figure 13: 'The Lignea Basilica Ring of Cells'

A. Circular Chapel.
B. The Wooden Church.
C. St Dunstan's Chapel (over cell).
D. St David's Pillar.
E. Pyramids on South.
F. Extension of later date (site of crypt).

Fig. 12 shows the circular chapel or wattle church of Joseph in the centre of the circle. In Fig. 13 the 'Lignea Basilica' replaces this and the monuments are seen on the sites of the vanished cells around.

The Symbolic Twelvefold in the Semitic and British Tradition
The shepherd people of Abramic stock who coming from Chaldea and Mesopotamia, overran the plains of Shinar and thence congregated in the land of Goshen and Nile Delta brought with them a deeply rooted symbology of a Twelvefold order. This was clearly a symbolism of an astronomical nature, probably originating in Chaldean teaching. From Egypt this people dispersed in various groups and at various times, leaving the same symbolic token in the form of monuments of Twelve Standing Stones, such as are now found all along the African shores of the Mediterranean, and throughout southern Europe. With the monuments we find also the constant tradition of Companies of Twelve. The same symbolism is traced with the Ionic Greeks and spreads northwards into the obscure Scythian regions. These peoples were nomads — never settling long in one district but constantly on the move, breaking new ground. But their final trend was eventually westward and to the north-west. Coming to these islands they brought with them not only the colonising instinct and genius, but the sublime philosophy of Druidism with much richness of tradition

gathered in their former Egyptian and Mesopotamian homes. Thus we find the Twelvefold symbolism marked with equal strength in our own megalithic monuments whilst the Bardic companies of Twelve reflect again the older teaching and symbolism of the Hebrew Scriptures. The twelvefold idea dominates all schemes of orderly control. It is the symbol of a Divine government, expressed as a simple astronomical figure — the XII constellations of the zodiac around the Sun — figured by the Twelve disciples about the Teacher. This zodiacal symbolism is found perpetuated in many features of our early churches, for the Church carries on the tradition. Our twelvefold system of measures also reflects a far older one found in Egyptian monuments and doubtless brought thence in very early days. They are apparently geometric in origin, the fruit of a mathematical science. In the case of the Lady Chapel at Glastonbury, built after the great fire of AD 1184, in precise agreement with the dimensions of the more ancient chapel (Fig. 14) we have a most perfect instance of this geometry. The measures north and south are marked in English feet. Those running east and west are the same in Royal or Babylonian cubits. They are the relative measures of the Double equilateral triangle or Vesica Piscis — the great Arcanum of the ancient guilds of Temple Builders. We can find human measures to correspond, such as the digit and the palm and the cubit of seven palms: but these are only secondary, being adjustments for popular use.

The Twelve Knights of King Arthur and the Round Table
In the great tapestry of the Glastonbury tradition the story of Arthur, the British prince and his Twelve Knights is inevitably coupled with that of Joseph of Arimathea and his Company of Twelve.[4] The Round Table of Arthur clearly reflects the form of Joseph's first settlement, just as the Twelve Knights are the symbolic counterparts of his company of fellow-missioners. Moreover, in the romantic form in which the legend comes down to us, these knights are Hebrew princes, descendants of Joseph.

We can, if we choose, derive the Round Table from the native form of Council-place, surviving still in the Welsh 'Gorsedd' or Circle of Twelve standing Stones. It does not greatly matter which view we take, as the tradition is the same. Those ecclesiastical Tribes which, in Wales and Cornwall, gave the names of their chieftains to be later perpetuated as the Patron Saints of our village churches, doubtless were ruled by similar companies of Twelve, over which the 'Saint' presided. The Table is always associated with conference upon matters of high spiritual import. In some monastic Chapter-Houses of Celtic Britain the Twelve-sided figure is found. In the Templars' churches the nave itself takes the form of a circle.

---

[4] Possibly eleven only when they reached Britain, but making Twelve with Joseph.

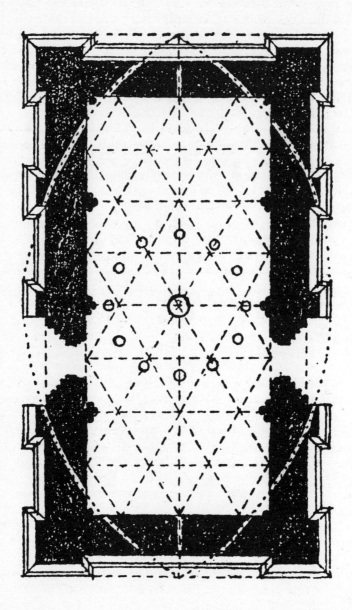

Figure 14: 'Chapel of St Mary the Virgin: Glaston'

An example of the Divine Geometry traditional in the Schools of the Temple Builders. The system here indicated is that of the Triangular Setting (á Trigono); but the alternative *Square Setting* (á Pariquadrato) is more usually found in Northern Europe.

It was quite general in the Middle Ages to figure the Signs of the Zodiac on the floor of the sanctuary, thus marking it like the 'paved work' of heaven. In England we have a fine Zodiac on the floor at Canterbury. Doubtless something of this nature was what William of Malmesbury saw on the floor of the Old Church at Glaston when he speaks of a pavement 'designedly inlaid with Squares and Triangles, as to which, if I believe some sacred enigma to be intended I do no dishonour to the cause of religion.'

Now if these legends of Arthur and the quest of the Holy Grail were merely medieval fabrications, as certain modern writers both lay and clerical would have us suppose, nothing could be more unlikely than that the heroes of these legends should be of Jewish nationality. It is, in fact, grotesquely improbable to assume such a thing. And when it is made manifest that the sources of the Romance writings are derived from chronicles many centuries older — certainly not later than the seventh century AD, we are compelled to believe that this element in the story reflects original facts in the history of our race and its reception of Christianity.

The Romances of the Grail, as they reach us from the troubadours of the thirteenth century, are full of myth and fantasy though they hold ideas and ideals which live immortally in the imagination of the race. Yet they make but little sense unless we hold the right clue to their meaning. Scholars of great learning and tireless industry have racked their imagination to interpret these legends; adopting one theory after another to account for the mythical elements they contain. There is a thread of Christian imagery running all through these tales, and side by side with this, other threads and images which are clearly pagan in origin. Which then is the parent stem, and which is the graft? Can we not understand that the advent of Christian teaching in its reaction on the poetic imagination of the native Bards would produce just such a blending of sober truth and romantic fiction? But the bedrock of the legends is something far more solid than mere fantasy. In the considered opinion of such judges as Alfred Nutt, the Grail Cycle gives us, in romantic form, with poetic appeal, the story of the conversion of Britain to Christianity, by a Hebrew mission and a group of Hebrew heroes of noble lineage. In the light of this view, all fantastic features and irrelevances subside into their proper place and we are left with a clear thread of Christian tradition confirming and vindicating that which has been immemorially held at Glaston and accepted by the English Church and nation at large.

In William of Malmesbury's day — early twelfth century — the great Library of Glastonbury Abbey held many manuscripts of vital import to our early history. From these and from others of a like kind then extant in various places such as the Abbey of Bury St Edmunds, Malmesbury drew when he became a resident member of the Abbey of Glaston. He was a man of wide learning and had been Librarian of his own monastic House at Malmesbury — another very ancient foundation. The *High History of the Holy Grail*, compiled about a century later (*c.* 1220 AD) is affirmed to have been drawn from one of these Glastonbury scrolls — an MS Book of Josephes in the Abbey Library. There are reasons for believing that this MS, and also the 'Book of Melkin' in the same library — quoted by British historians — were documents of Eastern provenance. The Jewish nomenclature of many of the Knights of Arthur and their associates is obvious in the *High History*. Yet, as its learned editor, Dr Sebastian Evans, attests in his epilogue, this 'romance' was accepted by the English as true history and as a 'wellspring of authentic knowledge.'

The Mystery of the Sangreal

The *Perceval* of Chrétien de Troyes, written at the close of the twelfth century, discloses the history of the Holy Grail. But this is not the oldest of the Christian series of Grail romances, for the *Titurel* and the *Parceval* of Wolfram von Eschenbach are German translations of older versions. The legend here is to the effect that when Christ was transfixed by the spear, there flowed from His side blood and water. Joseph of Arimathea collected the blood in the vessel from which the Saviour had eaten the last supper. This vessel was taken by Joseph to Britain, and before his death, was confided by him to the care of his nephew. According to another version the Grail is withdrawn to heaven until a race of heroes appears who are fitted to be its guardians. Again, as regards the nature of the vessel which holds the Blood of Christ, this is conceived of as a Cup or Dish and again as Blood-Jewel or Stone[5]; and in the Glastonbury tradition Joseph brings with him two little silver cruets, one containing the Blood and the other the Water (or Sweat of Christ). The form of these is preserved for us in the still existing carvings at Glastonbury and in the sixteenth century glass of the southern window of the chancel at St John's Church, Glastonbury, where we also see another Grail symbol, the five-petalled Rose of the Passion, which is now our national emblem. This beautiful symbol is constantly met with in the carved fragments from the Abbey. It was the favourite Glastonbury token of the Sangreal and is associated with the most ancient tradition of a divine fragrance emanating from the sacred fabric or permeating the holy ground, a fragrance of roses, spices, and rare incense gums which, strange to say, has been observed by quite a large number of witnesses in these latter days and has never been traced to any normal physical cause.

The question has been asked in regard to the blending of Christian and pre-Christian elements in the Grail stories: 'Which is the parent

---

[5] This being the oldest, and perhaps the most important of Grail symbols.

stem and which is the graft?' The answer to this is perhaps not difficult to discover. Revd Sabine Baring-Gould points out (p. 616 of his *Curious Myths of the Middle Ages*) that Chrétien de Troyes certainly was not the inventor of his mystic tale (the Christian version of the Grail legend), for there exists in the Red Book of Welsh romances the tale of Pheredur which is indisputably the original of Perceval. Pheredur is not a Christian. The Grail is not a sacred Christian vessel, but a relic of an older pagan rite. Peredur is mentioned in the *Annales Cambriae* which commence in AD 444. Taliesin the poet alludes to this vessel in a manner which connects it with Bardic mythology. He makes it the source of inspiration, poetic genius and wisdom, giving knowledge of futurity and of the whole treasure of human sciences.

This belongs to the mythological element in the Grail legends. And we may confirm the assurance that our early Christian instructors did what the Church has always done, namely, brought home to the people the truths of the Christian religion by adapting them to the native folklore, transforming Pagan heroes into Christian saints and modifying all the older symbolism of worship to bring it into harmony with the new teaching. Hence we shall not be surprised to find beneath the surface of the Christian legend or tradition a substratum of far more ancient ideas. The secret of success for any sort of missionary enterprise is the casting of the teaching in a form in which it can be assimilated as something familiar and readily understood. And in this sense we can readily accept the verdict of that most competent modern student (Mr Alfred Nutt) that the Grail Legends are the story of the Conversion of Britain to Christianity.

Precisely the same thing appears to have taken place in regard to another group of Grail Legends which Miss Margaret Murray has traced to an Egyptian source. It is strange to think that we have this same story of Joseph of Arimathea coming from Christian sources in the Nile Delta. The tradition, as Skeat has pointed out, is separable into two distinct versions; one, he says, 'is legendary and does not greatly transgress the bounds of probability' whilst the other 'is purely fabulous and obviously of later invention.' This 'fabulous' version appears, says Miss Murray, to be a solid block of history recording the wars between the kings of Sarras and Babylon (Evalach and Tholome). But a second part deals with Joseph and his son Josephes and this part is essentially the story of the conversion to Christianity of that part of Egypt. The third part gives the adventures of Mordrayns and Nasciens after the departure of Joseph and his little company of Christians, and ends with the reunion of all the *dramatis personae* in Britain.[6]

[6] An excellent epitome of the story is given by Miss Murray in part 1 of *Ancient Egypt* for 1916 (published by the British School of Archaeology). She has succeeded in identifying quite a number of place-names given in the Grail Legends with others in the Nile Delta from Babylon on the south up by the Rosetta branch of the Nile towards Alexandria.

In Wolfram's *Parceval* occurs a passage which distinctly shews that he gathered his story from an Arabic manuscript found in Toledo. The date would be about the middle of the seventh century. It came to England as the 'Book of Melkin' — a treasure of the Library of Glastonbury Abbey. The title 'Book of Melkin' is again Arabic, meaning 'Book of the Kings'. The Legend itself was said to have been written by Christ. In the French version, Christ writes the Lord's Prayer on stone tables. In the Coptic tradition, the Hand of Our Lord is seen engaged in some physical action such as consecration. We recall in this connection the story of St David who, intending to consecrate a church at Glastonbury, is warned by Christ in a vision that he must not do this since He Himself had already performed the act: and in token of this, He impresses the palm of St David's hand with His finger, leaving a permanent stigma as evidence of the reality of the vision. The little pilgrims' token unearthed by the writer in 1910 close by Herlewin's Norman sanctuary shews this sign of the wounded Hand.

The Sangreal as an Actual Relic of the Master

So far, we have been chiefly concerned to examine documentary history and this has been largely concerned with pre-Christian myth and legend overlaid with a veneer of early Christian history. We will now take a nearer view of the facts which go to support the belief that Glastonbury did actually hold and possess a veritable personal relic of the Master such as the various Sangreal legends depict.

Long before Christian times, even in the days of the prophets, such personal relics were held in veneration. Among those which were most prized would be some part of the body and chief of all, the blood of the one who, by his life or by his death, had merited this regard. Such relics were deemed to have the power of healing. In 2 Kings 13:21, we read of the man who was cast into the sepulchre of Elisha the prophet and who, when he was let down and touched the bones of Elisha, revived and stood up upon his feet. But the blood would have even more power, and in the days of the Roman persecutions when the arena was drenched with the blood of Christians, there was much effort to secure and preserve a little of this vital token. It was customary to hold the blood in a phial or crystal. Not many years ago there was held in a bank repository at Beyrout — and it may be there still — a sealed phial of the blood of a great prophet having an authentic history.

The Church, from earliest days, sought and prized these relics. Some have attained great notoriety. The Abbey of Fecamp possessed one. But the Chapel of the Saint Sang in Bruges can perhaps claim a definite history as a direct gift from an Eastern ruler to the Church, in the twelfth century. But it is the Glastonbury relic which in point of long continuity of history as well as extreme probability of its actual origin, stands pre-eminent and alone above all others in its virtue and power to heal all human ills. We, as Christians, believe that Joseph took down from the Cross the body of the Master, Jesus. It is no stretch of imagination to realize that he would have taken the utmost pains to secure for all time that most precious relic of all, a phial of His Blood. And this he brought to Glaston, where, by tradition, it lies buried beneath the soil — not to reappear until the time is ripe for its revelation.

PART V
THE MYSTIC WHOLE

THE MYSTIC WHOLE

In this final section we gather together the works of several visionaries who have either made Glastonbury their home, or who have contributed significantly to our understanding of what it is that makes this small piece of earth different.

Dion Fortune (the pseudonym of Violet Firth) is probably the best known esoteric writer of the twentieth century. She was the author of such classic works as *The Cosmic Doctrine* (1976), *Esoteric Orders and their Work* (1962), *The Training and Work of an Initiate* (1930), and *Sane Occultism* (1967). She also wrote a number of occult novels, including *The Sea Priestess* (1957), *Moon Magic* (1956), and *The Winged Bull* (1935), which are as brilliant as they are hard to define. The esoteric school which she founded. The Servants of the Light, is still operating today. Her collection of essays *Avalon of the Heart* was published in 1934 and has scarcely been out of print since. It is from this book that our first piece, 'Avalon and Atlantis', is taken.

No book on Glastonbury would be complete without something by Dion Fortune, and this particular piece, which develops the theory that one of the last survivors of the great continent of Atlantis, who escaped when it sank beneath the waves, came to Britain. This survivor was no less a figure than Merlin, the architect of Arthur's kingdom. Despite the cautious way in which she presents the theory, as 'one more [story] to add to the fairy fantasy woven about these ancient days of the twilight of our race', there is no doubt that the material that forms the basis of the article was received from Inner Plane sources, either by Dion Fortune herself, or by one of her psychically gifted associates.

Whether or not one accepts its premise, the idea of linking Glastonbury with Atlantis is a fascinating one. At least one contemporary writer, Marion Zimmer Bradley, has taken this up in her best-selling book *Mists of Avalon*, which, though cast in fictional form, plumbs the spirit of the mystical world of Glastonbury to great depths.

In the second piece we meet again the gifted architect Frederick Bligh Bond, who became well known and respected in the area for his archaeological activities at Glastonbury in the early 1900s. As a member of the Somerset Archaeological Society, he made several investigative digs in the grounds of the Abbey, finally discovering a hitherto unsuspected Lady Chapel. It was only later revealed that his method of working included the use of a psychic, John Alleyne, who produced, with Bond's assistance, a large amount of automatic script purporting to be from various monks who had been part of the Abbey's medieval community. Once this fact was known, Bond was ridiculed — despite the fact that his work had born fruit and been proved accurate on a number of occasions. He died in Wales, an unhappy and neglected man, in 1945.

Yet, while he was at the height of his powers, he produced a series of remarkable books, part derived from automatic script, part from careful and painstaking scholarship. His perception of Glastonbury's inner world was profound, and some of his writing still shines with an undoubted authority. The first example in this section is from the book entitled *The Company of Avalon*. It is mostly received material, from a group of Inner Plane workers who called themselves by this name. Whatever one believes of such matters, the words themselves are powerful and wise.

Next come two brief poems by a fine and much neglected American poet, Thomas Samuel Jones, (1882–1932) whose story 'Taliesin' appeared in *A Celtic Reader* (ed. John Matthews, The Aquarian Press, 1990). They present two different, yet similar, faces of Glastonbury, from the pen of a man who loved the Arthurian and Celtic mysteries deeply.

These are followed by a long extract from the novella *Avilion, or the Happy Isles* by Dinah Mulock, who under the pen name of 'Mrs Craik' was the author of a number of popular Victorian romantic novels (notably *John Halifax, Gentleman*). The work included here is an unusual one. It tells a love story that crosses the boundaries of the inner and outer worlds. It has humour and psychological grasp rare for the period in question (it was published in 1853); and it represents a side of Glastonbury that is less often seen — its mystical shadow-self, which few writers, except perhaps John Cowper Powys, have chosen to observe.

Next comes a selection from Frederick Bligh Bond's remarkable *Glastonbury Scripts*, a series of nine visionary essays and poems privately produced in the 1920s. Three are reproduced here: 'The Vision of the Holy Grail', 'The Rose Miraculous', and 'The Full Story of St Hugh of Avalon'. They are rough and unsophisticated works, but they shine with a curious light of their own. Whether one believes them to be the work of Bond's imagination, or genuine received texts, they are still well worth reading.

Finally comes William Blake's poem 'Jerusalem', now so closely associated with the town that it is better known as 'The Glastonbury Hymn'. Blake was almost certainly not thinking of the visit of Christ to Britain at all but rather to the giant Albion when he wrote of the feet that 'walked upon England's green and pleasant land' — but the analogy is still as important. Albion is the tutelary spirit of ancient Britain, a figure of great importance in the inner history of this land. No book on Glastonbury would be complete without these lines, which make a fitting coda to this varied stroll through some of the many intricate pathways that surround the Tor.

There are many other aspects of Glastonbury not discussed here for reasons of space or the general availability of the work in question. The writings of John Cowper Powys, especially his *A Glastonbury Romance*, are without peer in the annals of the place. Of a very different calibre are the Arthurian operas of Rutland Boughton, who very nearly succeeded in turning Glastonbury into an English Bayreuth in the 1930s. Though seldom, if ever, performed today, they are worthy of revival. Yet another of Glastonbury's august sons was Wellesley Tudor Pole, a mystic whose legacy to the town finds concrete form in the shape of the Chalice Well, a peaceful garden at the foot of the Tor where weary pilgrims may rest and assess the effect the magic of Glastonbury has had upon them.

No amount of reading is a substitute for visiting ancient Avalon itself, and it is hoped that this collection will inspire others to go there and discover for themselves its unique and magical spell.

Figure 15: 'The Mysteries of Glastonbury' by Chesca Potter

16

Avalon and Atlantis[1]

DION FORTUNE

When the Romans came to Britain they found savage tribes dwelling in stockaded villages in the dense forests. Roads there were none, save the perilous tracks that led through the swamps from village to village. Nevertheless, the Romans were not the first road-makers in Britain. Over the uplands went the ways of an ancient civilization which had fallen to dust and has been forgotten ages before the Romans conquered the Tin Islands.

What the Roman remains are to us, so were these ancient tracks to them. Wherever the short close turf of the chalk defied the trees there were the traces of an ancient, organized civilization upon a vast scale. Its roads, its guard-houses, its dew-ponds, and, most wonderful of all, its giant standing-stones, which to this day among the country people are called sarsen-stones. The etymologists tell us that the word sarsen is a corruption of Saracen, or stranger. Who were the strangers who erected the great stones?

History cannot tell us, for its records do not reach beyond the dawn of our civilization. But before that dawn there was the twilight of another civilization. History may ignore it; folk-lore may move in circles; nevertheless the vestiges remain. Great stones on the uplands and green ways winding across the chalk bear witness to the works of an ancient people long since fallen on sleep.

There are traditions more ancient than folk-lore, which tell of a Golden Age when the gods walked with men and taught them the arts of civilization. But even these gods themselves were not the first of created things; they had predecessors — giants whom they overcame and whose kingdoms they took by storm. These most ancient and terrible ones, gods of the rocks, were the first of created beings.

Everywhere do we find this tale of an ancient race, this myth of the gods who made the gods in the dim twilight of the dawn of ages.

But there is another story that companions it — the story of a drowned land and lost civilization. The ancient tradition of Chaldea has it, and the songs of our own Celtic tradition are full of it. For us it is the lost land of Lyonesse, whose church bells can be heard ringing out in the Atlantic beyond the stormy coast of Cornwall, where the

[1] From Dion Fortune, *Avalon of the Heart*, (The Aquarian Press, 1936).

dark figure of Merlin moves through the mists of legend — a figure that baffled even the makers of the songs that told of his power and wisdom. They knew not whence he came nor what he was.

Merlin was the guardian and teacher of two children, Arthur Pendragon, King of Britain, and Morgan le Fay, the dark Lilith of our island legend, sometimes identified with the Lady of the Lake, and reputed to be the half-sister of Arthur. Who was Merlin with his profound science, and these two children whom he taught — the fairy woman, not of mortal birth, and Arthur, whom the magician bred according to some secret science of his own, regardless of human law?

Here are many threads that have never been unravelled and pieced together. Does there exist a clue that shall reveal the significance of these ancient tales and justify their wisdom, or shall we dismiss them as idle fancies woven to pass away the long hours of darkness around the fires of the tribes of Britain? We may dismiss the tales, but we cannot dismiss the great stones on the uplands nor the ancient roads between them.

Here, then, is another story, one more to add to the fairy fantasy woven about these ancient days of the twilight of our race.

The Egyptian priests, themselves the heirs of tradition to extreme antiquity, told Plato of an even older civilization, of which their own was the descendant. They told him of a lost land to westward, drowned by the waters of the Atlantic. The ancients accepted these statements for fact unquestioningly; it remained for later ages to cast doubt upon them, and finally to reject them as such stuff as myths are made of.

But have they been finally rejected? There is a steadily increasing body of opinion which is inclined to view the mythical lost continent of the Atlantic as offering the solution of many of the problems of prehistory. The data on which the evidence is based and the conclusions drawn therefrom may be found in many books, I cannot enter upon them here, for they are not germane to my subject. Nevertheless, they indicate that I am not altogether without justification for the pattern in which I have pieced together the fragments of legend that lie buried in 'the holiest erthe in Englande'.

What is my theory, then, to add one more to the innumerable company of speculations already extant? Let us begin at the very beginning, as the children say when a story is to be told, and tell something of the tale of Lost Atlantis, and see whether it has any bearing on our own island tradition of Merlin and Arthur and the drowned land of Lyonesse.

From the centre of the Atlantic, reaching out towards what is now Central America, so the secret tradition goes, there was a great continent whereon dwelt the Root Race that succeeded the Lemurians and preceded our own. There was a great civilization, built up with the help of the gods who then dwelt among men. There was built the wonderful City of the Golden Gates, concerning which the folklore of all races has a tradition. This city, so we are told, was built upon the flanks of an extinct volcano on the sea-coast of this ancient land. Behind it was a plain stretching back to the inland mountain ranges. It was an isolated pyramidal hill, shaped like a truncated cone, with one side, the inland side, sheered off into a precipice. At its base there was a vast concourse of wattle huts in which dwelt the bearers of burdens. On the shoulder of the mountain dwelt the merchant and craftsman castes, and upon its flat top were the palaces and colleges of the sacred clan, which was divided into two branches, the military caste, and the priesthood.

This sacred clan was most carefully segregated from the rest of the population, and its breeding was carried out under the supervision of the priests. As soon as the boys of this clan were of an age to show their dispositions, those who were deemed fit were taken into the sacred colleges to be prepared for the priesthood, and those who were not suitable for this discipline were sent to the military colleges to be trained for the army. The maidens of the sacred stock were guarded with the greatest care, and were given in marriage to priests or soldiers, according to their lineage and temperament. So was the heritage of the sacred clan kept pure, and a carefully selected stock bred for the development of those rarer powers of the mind so highly esteemed among the ancients and so little understood among ourselves — the powers which enabled the Greeks and Egyptians to discover the basis of modern astronomy, and the atomic theory of chemistry, and the cellular structure of organic matter, without the aid of any of the instruments whose invention modern science has had to await for its development.

The Atlanteans, the old tradition tells us, were great navigators, ranging in trade from the Black Sea to the Pacific; they were also great colonizers, and wherever they planted their colonies they brought their priests and their altars. They were Sun-worshippers, and adored the Lord and Giver of Life in open circular temples, paved with great flagstones of marble and basalt. They themselves were of giant stature, and they possessed the knowledge of utilizing the latent force in germinating seeds as a motive power. Their architecture was of the cyclopean type — great blocks of dressed stone that no primitve man could have handled.

Now what of our own Avalon in connection with this story? Is there any possibility that in the legends of Merlin and the drowned lands of Lyonesse we are touching the history of Lost Atlantis? The Atlanteans, so Plato tells us, were great seafarers and colonizers. Is there any possibility that Avalon, with its undercurrent of pagan legend, was originally an Atlantean colony? Is it possible that Merlin was an Atlantean — a priest-initiate; and in presiding in the birth of Arthur he was carrying out the Atlantean custom of the kings bred for wisdom? In order to bring the higher consciousness of the evolved Atlantean race into the Celtic tribes of the colonized island, did Merlin, in defiance of the strict laws of the sacred clan, and in pursuit of ends of his own, cross the Atlantean stock on the Celt, and so breed Arthur? And was Morgan le Fay, the half-sister of Arthur, the witch-woman learned in all sciences, with her name derived from the Celtic word for sea, a pure-bred Atlantean, the British-born daughter of the sea-people?

Welsh legend is full of stories of drowned lands; and Lyonesse, beyond the coast of Cornwall, is a tradition of the Cornish Celts. Is it possible that these drowned lands are the Lost Atlantis? Did the Celts learn of that ancient civilization from the adventurous navigators who came to them for trade and settled among them as colonists? It is noteworthy in this respect that the peculiar combination of consonants, Tl, which occurs in the word Atlantis is very characteristic of the languages of the aborigines of Central America, and that a similar sound exists in the initial Ll of the Welsh language, which is pronounced as a gutteral click.

It is also noteworthy that the spread of the Arthurian legends corresponds with the distribution of the standing-stones of the ancient Sun-worship.

Do we owe the Green Roads of England, winding over the chalk, to this ancient race of seafarers who colonized the southern half of Britain and planted their trading-posts along the west coast of Scotland? Was it they who raised the cyclopean stones, so closely resembling those found standing today in the virgin forests of Central America?

Is the streak of psychism that runs through the Celtic race due to the Atlantean blood introduced by the daring experiments of Merlin, the Atlantean initiate who had thrown in his lot with the island peoples after his own race was sunk in the sea?

One more curious point may be referred to here, and its value and significance left to the discernment of the reader. Those who have seen the famous Glastonbury Tor about which so many legends gather, are always perplexed as to whether it is natural or artificial. Its pyramidal form, set in the centre of a great plain, is almost too good to be true — too appropriate to be the unaided work of Nature. Viewed from near at hand, a terraced track can clearly be seen winding in three tiers round the cone of the Tor, and this is indisputably the work of man. Who were they who worshipped in high places and climbed to them by a processional route?

It is well known that the ancients delighted to build their colonial cities upon the same plan as the mother city in the land of their race. Is it possible that our strange pyramidal hill, with its truncated top and its inland side as steep as earth will stand, may have been wrought to that likeness by human hands in memory of the sacred mountain of the mother continent? Here and there about the plain are rounded hills, still called islands locally — hills with no rocky skeleton, but of boulder clay, left behind by some eddy of the Severn before the silting sands had narrowed its channel. It would not be a difficult matter to take such a mound of clay, and with no other tools than picks and baskets, mould it to the desired shape.

Tradition tells that the Tor was indeed a high place of the ancient Sun-worship, and that a circle of stones like a miniature Stonehenge once stood upon its crest. These stones were overthrown when the worship of the Son supplanted that of the Sun, but so strong were the forces generated in the spot sacred to the rites of an older race that a church dedicated to St Michael had to be erected upon the spot in order to keep down the dark influences of the pagan worship. These churches to St Michael, built upon the tops of hills, which certainly could not have been for the convenience of the parishioners, are characteristic of districts where the ancient Sun-worship is known to have flourished. Legends of Arthur, standing-stones, and hill-top churches to St Michael all seem to go together.

St Michael is always represented as treading upon a serpent; he is the mighty archangel of the south in magical invocations, and to the south is assigned the element of fire. Here again we have a curious link. The Atlanteans were Sun-worshippers, and fire is the mundane symbol of the sun. Its sacred quarter is the south, just as the sacred quarter of Christianity is the east. The serpent is a symbol of two things — of wisdom and of evil. May it not be that the serpent, in its dual aspect, represents the ancient wisdom of an older race, a wisdom fallen on corruption, and therefore evil to a regenerated faith, yet, nevertheless, a mine of the profoundest knowledge?

Michael, the Christian saint, is a member of an older hierarchy; he is the mighty regent of the element of fire. Who but he should be implored to hold down the serpent of fire-worship, fallen on decadence?

There are no standing-stones left now upon the Tor; but tradition asserts that they were broken up and used in the foundations of the Abbey; and, indeed, there are stones found in the Abbey which were cut in no local rock and are of a hardness to turn the tools of the local masons. May not these be the fragments of the ancient sarsens, the Stones of the Strangers, who used for their temples the mighty boulders of an extreme hardness which occur in chalk where silicates have mingled with the sand, and which form the 'Grey Wethers' of many an upland pasture?

Whether tradition speaks true or not, there exists at the foot of the Tor the prehistoric well-head wrought of just such cyclopean blocks as were used by the builders of Stonehenge, Carnac, and the buried temples of the Mayas and Toltecs. In the well-chamber is the niche for human sacrifice, the water-sacrifice of a sea-people; and we are told that it was the love of the Atlanteans for human sacrifice and black magic of the basest kind which brought about their downfall and led to the destruction of their land. Where lost Atlantis sank there is the deepest gulf in the oceans, to this day an unplumbed abyss; and over it floats the Sargasso Sea, a vast island of sea-weed so dense that gulls alight upon its surface and ships lay their course to avoid it.

All this is speculation, not history; modern myth-making, not research. But standing alone upon the Tor, when the Lake of Wonder all but closes over it, one cannot forget the end of Lost Atlantis.

17

The Company of Avalon

FREDERICK BLIGH BOND[1]

On the Imperishable Ideal and its Translation into Mental and Material Images

It seems fitting here to introduce some of the more philosophic teaching received from the Company of Avalon from time to time, chiefly through the hand of John Alleyne. This teaching has reference to the permanence of all spiritual Ideal and the eternal capability of that Ideal to express itself first in the Mental Image, and thence by the creative faculty of Mind, in a concrete symbol on the material plane.

Spirit is always the true creative source, but there are secondary powers and agencies of spirit, pure emotional values which, influencing the minds of men and women, in their turn become the parents of Thought. Thus images of spiritual beauty are conceived in the mind, and seek to translate themselves into concrete form. Every perfect work of art thus holds in some measure an emotional value derived from a yet more inward spiritual impulse. This spiritual content gives personality or true unity of character to the work. That true unity may be expressed in infinite abundance and variety of detail, yet so long as the material symbol is a true one, the unity is there in each and every part, and can be discerned by the spiritual consciousness.

Spirit eternally seeks Self-expression in ever-varying modes, and the work of Man's spiritual evolution is the conquest by the Will of the Spirit of every grade of Matter, and in this term we include not only physical Matter, but all those intermediate forces, substances, grades of being, etheric and mental, which are external to himself in so far as they offer resistance to his spirit, and are hostile to his effort to the extent that he has not succeeded in subduing them. So it is seen that the more important field of conquest is not, as material thinkers have supposed, the exterior domain of physical Nature, but rather that other and unexplored field which, though in a sense, *within* ourselves, is yet by no means subject to the rule of our true Self: in other words, the Field of the Subconscious. The subconscious mind IS NOT OUR OWN: IT IS NOT OURSELVES, save in so far as we have penetrated it by sympathetic activity to our mind, and mastered it and brought it into

[1] Originally published by Blackwell (1924).

perfect obedience. Then it becomes an added Personality with power over the external kingdoms of Nature reciprocal to, and equivalent to, the inward kingdom ruled by the individual Spirit.

SCRIPT of the 23rd May 1918. (Following a visit to Glastonbury.)

ARGUMENT: The Ideal image of the Abbey as designed by its architect is imperishable, and may be retranslated into concrete form when the impulse is not baulked by the materialism of men. The Ideal can have a more spiritual expression, which is not necessarily translated into the concrete. The mental image may be faulty, and this happened in the case of Glastonbury Abbey, which was unstable as a building through error in conception. Jerusalem is an untranslated spiritual ideal, and both Jerusalem and Glastonbury will rise again in obedience to a periodic law of growth.

SCRIPT[2]

(J. A.) 'We who observe the Laws tell you that the Image of the Building remains always, because it is a genuine symbol of the Divine impulse which gave it birth. It is but a secondary symbol (a symbol of a symbol), but it is a link in the Divine chain, and so it ever lives in the spiritual consciousness of the men who conceived it, and therefore will again be manifested as of old, when the spiritual impulse tending to its recreation has gained sufficient force to bring this about. This impulse may come from the Idea itself, which may first move the Spirit, and then afterwards, by a more vivid and concentrated effort, begin to stimulate material conditions, moulding them into an environment suitable for the display of its influence. Thus Idea reinforced by the Spirit must raise its intensity of influence until it reaches the plain of Action, before it can complete its domination of Matter. And this force of Idea will vary in strength according to the degree of resistance met with in its destined environment.

'At this stage a difficulty may occur. In old days, the working activities of the many were controlled by the intellectual leadership of the few. In such a case as the building of this Abbey the conditions were simple, for two or three masters were alone responsible, and where they led, the rest obediently or willingly followed. Two conditions then made for success: the one the strength of the Ideal, the other the united influence and effort of a multitude obedient to the rule of the master-builders. Where the leaders control, the majority is easily led. But where they do not control, it is always possible for a small minority influenced solely by material motives, to confound and impede the work and spiritual impulse of the majority.

'Now at present there exists a spiritual majority in whom the Idea has attained a dominance so great that it is able to find a more perfect

---

[2] Paraphased for clearness, 31 August 1919.

spiritual expression than it did even in the old days, when it was more easily manifested in the material plane owing to the comparative absence of opposition. But we who have held that Ideal, and whose scheme of Beauty lives on eternally, can now see before our spirit eyes the imperfections in the former manifestation of that Ideal.

'The Ideal, though perfect, has as yet failed to gain immortal manifestation, and in like manner the subtle or ethereal manifestation failed because of its material deficiencies. Had the great Abbey been perfect in its conception, it would have been standing now. But the system under which it was built failed by reason of the defects induced by the faultiness of the ideal conception, and thus the building itself, crumbling and out of balance by reason of these defects, was doomed to failure.

'We who know tell you that had it been as perfect and as well conceived as was Westminster or Wells, it would have been standing yet.

'It was destroyed, as building, because of its imperfections. For the evil of its faultiness, the perfect parts suffered, and so that which *had not fallen* out of its own inherent ruin was taken down.

'It will be rebuilt as a manifestation of that more perfect and selfless Ideal that in itself expresses Perfection and Beauty combined with great utility in the world of men, and having been rebuilt, it shall endure. We await its coming, and so we deem it shall be again. But this end will be attained by harmonizing the ancient and pure Ideal with the spiritual forces at work in this more enlightened and complex age in which you live. We have told you that places have a spiritual significance. Here you have this in perfection, and the truly perfect changes not. The perfect principle showed itself, but the interpretation of it was not perfect. Now on this perfect foundation there is need to reconstruct a Perfection which shall endure. Thus would we have it, and would wish to see the coming thereof.

'Jerusalem, no longer a symbol of value to the spiritual progress of Man until stripped of her terrestrial values, was a symbol of the Spirit. Now, denuded of her earthly garment, as one who has passed the gates of Death, she becomes a dominating force of the Spirit.

'And so we tell you that Jerusalem shall yet be the centre of the united spiritual forces of the whole world. And when this is so, then also — and in a like degree and proportion — Glastonbury shall arise.

'Thus History repeats itself — shall repeat itself in obedience to a law of Nature which is a Law of the Spiritual: and thus shall ye see the law fulfilled in the great rebirth and growth of spiritual influence; a growth developing in the mind of man as a reaction from the greatest materialism the world has ever known; the materialism of Intellect tainted by the study of Matter and material things, unleavened by the purifying influence of the Intuitions and Emotions of the Spirit which is the greater partner in the Duality, Man.

'The influences which find response in your minds are many, and they are evolved from the interaction of a vast multitude of those who dwell on the other side, and with whom all sympathy is developed — as with you — through the Emotions which alone are Divine, but which with us are clothed with the acquired Reason and Experience of our life on Earth or on other Earths.'

Owing to the frailty of human nature and the dualness of human understanding, the spiritual Ideal for which Glastonbury stands has, as yet, never succeeded in translating itself in any measure of fulness.

There have been periodical surges of new spiritual activity in this appointed focus for the evolutionary work of establishing the Kingdom.

These have ramified over the whole West, and have diffused the Light. These impulses, having spent themselves, have faded out, and periods of apparent desolation, material destruction being the symbol, have supervened. Yet think not that the shrine and focus once divinely appointed can ever fail in the end to bring about the Desire of Nations, nor think that the good work already done is in the smallest measure really lost. It is not lost: it is obscured, but it is in the hearts of a vast multitude as a seed ready to sprout and to yield a harvest of spiritual values such as Earth has never yet witnessed. External expressions of Spirit may fade: in particular, organized religion may altogether lose its hold, becoming empty of the Spirit: but unseen, the leaven has penetrated the masses of men and women, and the leaven is working now. Look for it in those who hold no dogmatic belief, and who yet are guided by an ineradicable instinct of justice and mercy, honesty and purity: whose minds are given to the cultivation of the beautiful in all its modes, who are touched by a sympathy which extends not only to their fellow-men, but to the lesser lives in Nature and to her powers not individualized, but present in all the wonders that Science surveys. Look for it in the sovereignty of a spiritually enlightened Reason which, repudiating fear and all superstition, will wed the intellect of Man to spiritual Intuition, and bring the powers of a true imagination into co-partnership with its own.

Then the Conscious will pierce the veil of the Subconscious, and within the veil will be found the lives of all who have thought and laboured in the past for the same spiritual ends, and their hands will be stretched out to us in welcome on the other side of the misty barrier. Their genius will enlighten us, and their experience will guide us. Their spiritual presence within our consciousness will be an ever-present stimulus and consolation for the difficult work which the Race will now be called upon to undertake in the furtherance of the great Design, the End towards which our evolutionary course is set.

The ethereal Form which is the permanent and complete expression of the Ideal ever present to the liberated vision of the Company cannot be communicated to us in its entirety, but only as a successive series of pictures apparently disconnected — visibly different, but ideally linked together. The image in its fulness is not limited by the laws of Time and Space as we know them. We may consider, however, that to the liberated faculties of perception, this series of pictures become blended in one symmetrical figure of a type inconceivable to us. So the rude wattle church of the earliest days becomes, strangely enough, an integral part of that greater Picture which includes all successive phases of development achieved in later historical epochs, and carries the promise of a yet more perfect interpretation and fulfilment in times to come.

Accordingly we take up the story of the development of the Ideal by tracing the various stages of its shaping in physical form.

The Shaping of the Wooden Church

Authentic records tell us but little of the building and improvement of that church of wood, for which so many centuries stood over and protected the sacred walls of Joseph's Chapel. St Patrick, after his Irish mission, was for many years abbot, but nothing seems recorded of any buildings by him. St David, who ended his days in Glaston, AD 546, was supposed to have built a church near the Old Church, but not to have touched the Old Church itself, having been warned by a vision to desist from his plan. According to the Fathers, St Paulinus (625–44), Bishop of Rochester, in the time of the Augustinian mission, cased the Old Church with boards and covered it wholly with lead. Such is practically the extent of our knowledge until the time of the Great Fire.

And now let us see what the script has to tell us on the subject.

SCRIPT of 30th August 1921. (First Part.)

(*This is communicated by GALFRID by the hand of S.*)

S. 'After ye coming to Ynyswitrin of ye Apostils, some of ye heathen to Christe Oure Lourde came, and were baptized and chrisomed, and after, byshopped. But of these, no great number. Then was there but ane of the fyrste twelve lefte, and hee aged and weake. But hee all ye celles in grete order kepte, and ye holie chirche as beste hee it myghte: and ye Brittesc folk him y buried nigh to chirche walle. Then, for long, none came: but at last some, and again-bulyded huttes and repayred ye Church. And Brittesc [folk] and menne of Rome worschypped thereby, so loste hitt never were altogether, albeit muche of ye wysdome of ye Apostils and of Sanct Josephus and of Natan-ael menne forgot. This is alle wee canne of old tyme tell.'

Next may be given a script received through J. A. as long ago as 1910 (7 September). This seems to refer to a company of holy men who came later.

'The Ermits did dwell in the place ye call the graveyard, and wherein was ye garden they hadde, neare by the old road made of olde tyme from the sea over the hills: and coming thither, they came to a place by the roadside where there was a little brook, and there they stayed and builded little houses hard by the road which they called STRETE. And in the woods hard by they made a lytell churche, and soe it was for a long tyme. After this, they dyed and it was forgotten, but in after tyme came others and builded not there agayne, but digged and builded ye old church, and so the place where they others lived and dyed was holy ground and they were fain to find sepulture there, although of a truth it was marshy ground, and they who were buried there were oftentimes buried in water and not in earth. Herlewin and Brighere[3] did make drains and soe the place was consecrated. BRIGHERE was one of the order of old tyme: after came Herlewin who builded the grete church and did drain all ye ground that Brighere had left.

'Brighere[2] builded some: and they who came out of the seas did burn it with fyre. Then builded Herlewin the grete church, and he was two hundred feet. No church was lyke hym in all Angleland: not Winchester was so grete. But we have said, ye lytel churches in ye graveyard were seven, and ye will find their walls deep down by the old church which Paul builded. He was the first stone [church], and he was of stone squared like the old tyme and very fair as did the Romans. There was in old tyme a faire Temple to their gods, the strange gods. The old road they made it and builded an oppida and there were legions there. They builded a temple to their god Jove and then to Mars. The Romans builded houses where four roads meet, and round them a wall, and the place where the church did lie was without the gate of the city, and they who passed by saw them in the bog-land and the woods, and some would slay them. Others laughed. But the holy men were Cives Romani coming out of a province they hadde in the eastern parts, and so they spared them.'

Q.: 'Can you tell us anything of the little wooden church?'
'They say the people who dwelt there builded it long since. Paul builded it over with stones, so I have heard.

Q.: 'To what Paul do you refer?'
'EBORACUS. He builded in hewn stones after the manner of the Romans. There was a temple to their gods at Eboracum. They say Paul builded in this manner. There was fine work in hewn stone, very wonderful. Of Roman blood was he. "Centurio pater meus fuit," dixit, "centurio Romanus".'

We must not be too readily influenced by the suggestion that Paulinus, Archbishop of York, built over the Ecclesia Vetusta *in stone*. In our analysis and estimate of these scripts, it must always be remembered that individual memories are imperfect. Morover, in this case, our

[3] Bregoret in Malmsbury.

communicator is careful to tell us that his information is hearsay only. On the other hand, we have Malmsbury, who, although himself obliged to lean upon tradition and hearsay in many points, is to be regarded as a historian careful to be accurate according to the habit of his time.

But the time of Paulinus is comparatively late. There is a long gap between the building of Joseph's Chapel and his day — nearly six hundred years, in fact. What had happened in the interval? St David clearly had meant to re-edify the little old church, since he desired to re-dedicate it. He comes a hundred years after Patrick. The wattle church could not have stood all this time without repeated renovation, that is clear. So we shall examine S.'s script with interest, and also must see whether the script of John Alleyne has anything further to impart of a nature to enlighten us further as to pre-Christian times.

According to the story as received through J. A. from the 'Watchers', we are to regard the coming of Joseph and his companions as but one episode in a long sequence carrying us back to most ancient times. It is claimed that Ynyswitrin or, as we know it, Glaston, had been from distant ages a powerful focus of spiritual teaching and nurture. Light had come to Britain from the East, by mercantile channels, for centuries previously, and the traders who brought it, themselves of Semitic blood and sharing the pure monotheism of the Hebrew, carried to these islands a religious ideal which took root among the British and made them peculiarly ready for the reception, in fullness of time, of the Christian aspect of their cult. It is clearly stated in these scripts, and those of Philip Lloyd appear unmistakably to affirm the same, that the British Isles have been, under the great evolutionary plan, the seed-bed of a select branch of the true Israelitish race (of which the modern Jew is a section largely diluted with alien blood intermixed during the Captivity and otherwise). Consequently we bear in our racial faith a large and necessary ingredient of sympathy with the pure monotheism of the Hebrew race, and this was expressed in the flower of Druidical culture. The Phoenician voyagers coming to these shores thus found themselves among a people whose ideals and traditions were so nearly related to their own that they were able, without difficulty, to propagate their more developed teaching. With this teaching there was blended a great deal of the finest of Greek philosophy, and this philosophy was carried to its utmost limits in the Druidical schools. But again, it was coloured by the traditions of the temple worship of the Hebrew, and so we find the script speaking of the same tradition in connection with a temple at Glastonbury. This tradition remains, and may be traced through the mediaeval times.

In the time of King Solomon the Hebrews and their cousins the Phoenicians had a joint navy. The Phoenicians colonized first Cyprus, then Crete, then Sicily and Spain, and finally the 'Cassiterides' (our own southern coasts), whither mercantile adventure had beckoned them.

'It is surely no accidental circumstance, ' says the author of *The Coming of the Saints*, 'that the traditional Hebrew missions follow exactly the same course as that of Phoenician colonization, and that the traditional sites of these missions are found accordingly, first, at the Syro-Phoenician towns along the coast border as far as Antioch; and secondly, at all the main Phoenician or Phoenician-and-Hebrew settlements in Cyprus, in Sicily, in Crete, at Cyrene, in Sardinia and Spain, and finally at the so-called "Cassiterides," or Cornwall.'

SCRIPT of J. A. April 24th 1918. (Extract.)

'They whose habitation was in Crete, moved by the memories and traditions of others of their own race and civilisation who had long before been impelled westward . . . followed once more the interminable route, ever westward beyond the Gates of Hercules to the islands where the fire-drawn metals be . . . Phocis, of the race of Crete, trading with Poseidon and seeking Tyrian purple, was thus brought into contact with them that worshipped the One True God in contradistinction to the Many. And being much impressed by this fact, and the beauty and the idealism of the worship of that poetic nation, he prepared the way for the building of a Temple in his settlement at Tintagella. So at Tintagella was the Temple, a place of the shrine of the Most High God. And the same — a reproduction accurate in every measurement — was established at Glaston on this foundation. Those who came long afterwards in the times of Romans built a Chapel,[4] which is the first of which ye have a record. So that cult which followed the teachings of Paul came and settled and preached, bringing with them the full knowledge of the New Philosophy wedded to the old monotheistic teachings of the Hebrews.'

The first temple, and its history, are swallowed up in the oblivion of the past. There is no hint even of the ruins of a temple here when Malmsbury tells his tale of the coming of Joseph. So with Joseph's rude wattle church our record begins. Malmsbury himself suggests that the Chapel of Joseph was circular, as S.'s script so constantly affirms. But at some subsequent date a rectangular building was placed over the circular one, and was accorded a peculiar veneration in its measures and proportions. So much so, that when subsequent additions were made to the east, a pillar or pyramid was erected on the north meridian line of the eastward termination of the sacred rectangle, that those who came after might not fail to know the exact extent in this direction of the Holy of Holies.

---

[4] This is, of course, Joseph's Chapel.

Figure 16: 'View of Glastonbury Abbey Ruins in 1723' from Stukeley's *Itinerary*

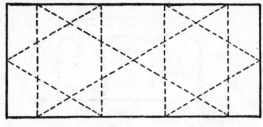

FIG. 17

The dimensions of the new Chapel of St Mary, built after the fire, and now standing, are claimed to accord precisely with those of the sacred site. The interior measures are the critical ones. The width is about 25 feet, and the length just under 58 feet, the proportion being exactly that which will allow of two interlaced pairs of triangles to be inscribed within its length, as shown. The external measures are also perfect in their geometry, as has been demonstrated in *The Gate of Remembrance*.

This system of interior measure would accord with what is known of the mystery of the temple builders preserved by the guilds during the Middle Ages, and the Double Equilateral Triangle is the mystical key of the design, and the symbol of things spiritual associated with the pattern.

On 27 September 1921, S. obtained a script signed by the monk Patriac. This was given in response to certain questions she addressed the brethren as to the measurements of the earliest churches and especially that of Paulinus. I give the transcript as follows:

'PATRIAC speaketh. Lo! now, hard it is to remember me of ronde chirche ne large and great. XVIII. easte to weste: XVIII. nord to sud, wee thynke Ecclesia Lignea (the wooden Church) twice as long — inside walls XXXVI. long, XVIII. wide: but of this, ne sure.

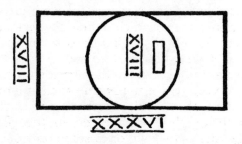

FIG. 18

'See now, brother, thou knowest naught of ye measures: difficilimus est!'

'Walles of ronde chirche gainst walles of Sanct Paulinus (were) pulled part down. They on bank of earth and stone stood: that alone, and a small part of twiggen [were] left. Wall 3 feet thick of earth and stone, as

FIG. 19

ye hit measure. Men buylded round huttes for celles as if measured by eye — so goode a ronde! This chirche of Twelve Apostles of Sanct Paulinus [was builded] by rod and plump-line.

'Walles of trees at base: wood slats over, 2 feet thick at least. That [makes] XXXVIII outer by XX outer, but ye know not our measures. Romualdus [has] oder measures like to yours — less. Ours [are] greater by two.

'Ronde more to easte, as see in Sanct Paulinus: more place for folk at the west [ad occidentem].

'ROMUALDUS speaketh. Wherefore can ye not measures take?

'Walles, brother, nord and sud, with doors of Sanct Marie on ye lines of Sanct Paulinus [measure] xxxvi.: but to the east [ad orientem], nigh on xx. more, so that Ronde Celle in midst should be — as we did it guesse.

'Thys wherefore Patriac cannot make thee to comprehend. So [ye whole length is] circa lvi. [56 feet] inner measure, nearer [to that] of Sainte Marie, but [the] breadth near yatt of Sanct Paulinis, xxiii. in oure day, or more.

'XII. ronde cells: ane apostil ever kept watch in ecclesia — xii. moons — eache watched one moon. Lamp lighted by Aulter: more to sud — for sunne. This alle I canne-by measure: Brittsec folk could.'

Patriac speaks as a monk of the eighth century, and would thus be in a position to tell us of the work of Paulinus, about a century old in his day. S. had a strong impression that there was some sort of rectangular encasement to the circle before Paulinus's time, but this was not clear from the script, which merely shows that its length was altered from 36 to 56 feet in Paulinus's day, by the addition of a sanctuary space of 20 feet at the eastern end. A later script, however, affirms the earlier rectangle to be of St Patrick's time.

The later addition brought it to the true ancient limit of the sacred ground, and in line with the pillar erected by St David to mark this line, which had evidently been merged in the general range of buildings added either in his own or in some previous day.

A likely reading of the story would be as follows: First the temple, nigh 60 feet long. This disappears, but the holy site and its measures are remembered. Next, after a long lapse of time, the coming of St Joseph and the building of the circular Chapel. Third, the enclosing of the circle in a wooden church, 36 feet in length, the altar remaining within the circle. Fourth, the building of a sanctuary at the east end —

an extension of indefinite length, perhaps at first in wood, and then in stone by St David. Fifth, the recasing of the 36-foot wooden nave by Paulinus; and lastly the extension of the wooden basilica to embrace the whole of the sacred site, under the same great Bishop.

Two Glastonbury Sonnets[1]

THOMAS SAMUEL JONES

YNISWITRIN: GLASTONBURY ABBEY
Dim watered vale whose clear streams seek the sea,
  At gray of dawn strange gods walked in the wood
  Before Saint Joseph's wattled chapel stood
Woven with green wands from some Druid tree;
The fragrance of a lost simplicity
  Clings to the tomb of the white brotherhood
  That wandered through wild lands, yet found it good
To linger here apart with Calvary.

The feet of frost have touched you, now you wear
  Autumn's rich ruined splendor and soft haze —
  The memory of immemorial fires;
But as you dream alone, the sea-winds bear
  A whispered promise from wide starry ways
  Of new songs that shall fill those fallen choirs.

THE HOLY THORN: GLASTONBURY
Long centuries past by lonely barrows grew
  The faery hawthorn boughs of haunted green,
  Beneath whose shade the Danaan gods unseen
Awoke slain heroes dark with battle-dew;
Their gilded shields of apple-wood and yew
  In time's deep tumulus have lost their sheen,
  Yet where these blossom-laden branches lean
The faith of vanished ages blooms anew.

One ancient miracle enduring still,
  Though earth's old magic seems a myth outworn,
Has hallowed Avalon's enchanted hill;
  For when men hymn the Son of God reborn,
Although December woods are bare and chill,
  At wintry Christ-tide flowers the Holy Thorn.

[1] Originally published in *Shadow of the Perfect Rose* (New York, Farrar & Rinehart, 1937).

From Avillion or the Happy Isles[1]

DINAH MULOCK

CHAPTER VI

Out into the dim obscure, guided and sustained only by that slender moonlight line, I passed without fear. As I went, olden thoughts entered my mind; and this strange journey seemed a shadowing of something on earth — some wild ocean of fate, to be crossed by one pale ray.

Gradually the moon set, and the path was gone!

I felt it vanish from beneath my feet — with the darkness came imminent death! I cried out aloud, and the cry brought to me the knowledge that I had passed into another sphere of being — for, lo! in my despair I called upon God — the Christian's God!

At once, in a moment, the abyss of darkness was ablaze with light, showing me that I had almost reached the land. Looking up, I saw on the near shore a palace whose splendour lightened the whole isle, and glimmered even on the waves. But amidst these waves I was struggling still. I saw afar off life, safety, bliss, and yet Death was ready to engulf me.

There rose by my lips words faintly remembered as being known of old, solemn and holy —

'*What shall I do to be saved!*'

But still around me the greedy waves hissed and roared. Then the cry at my heart changed to one humble, helpless, yet not hopeless —

'Lord, what wilt *Thou* do, that I may be saved?'

Instantly I saw a light boat crossing the seething waters. In it stood a youth, pale, beautiful; serene and holy as he who abode at Patmos — the beloved apostle John. Again I cried, and the answer was —

'Brother, peace! Help is near.'

Then, his blessed hands lifted me out of that yawning grave, and I sank before him — saved!

He made on my forehead the sign of the cross, saying —

'Welcome, brother! This is the island of Avillion, where dwell many good Christian knights, with those knights of Faërie who serve God, and believe in His word. I, too, abide among them, because my life on earth was spent in faith and purity, and in the quest of the Sangreal.'

[1] Originally published by Smith, Elder & Co. (1853).

'Who then art thou, my preserver?'

The youth put aside his shining helmet, looking upward a holy yet humble joy.

'I am Galahad, the only one of King Arthur's knights to whom God gave strength and patience to find the holy Greal.'

As he spoke, the boat touched the strand. He signed me with the cross once more, leaped on the shore, and disappeared.

'Oh, leave me not!' I cried. 'Good knight and true, I need thy guidance even here! How shall I tread alone the unknown isle; how enter the shining palace?'

And I looked tremblingly at the castle where dwelt King Arthur and Morgue la Faye; I knew it was so; for now all my prescience came back upon me, even as in the Island of Ulysses. But while I gazed, not daring to approach the presence of so great a hero, that which I had deemed a king's palace became a temple of the King of Kings. From the cathedral windows gleamed the altar lights, which I knew were burning round the Sangreal; and through the wide-opened doors came the holy matin-hymn, lifted ere yet the sky was purple with dawn. 'Dilexi quoniam' began the psalm; and as it proceeded, verse after verse pealed on my heart and memory.

'*The sorrows of death compassed me, the pains of hell gat hold upon me. . . . . Then called I upon the name of the Lord . . . .*

'*Thou hast delivered my soul from death, mine eyes from tears, and my feet from falling.*

'*I will walk before the Lord in the light of the living.*'

I entered the open temple-gate, and paid my vows at the threshold of the King of Heaven.

From thence I passed amid the train of worshippers — men and women, Christian knights, and ladies pure and fair — to the presence of Arthur and Morgue la Faye. They sat together on a throne, alike, and yet unlike; for she was the most beauteous dame in the whole land of Faërie, while on the face of her mortal brother lingered still the traces of his long warfare on earth. Yet he was a noble king to behold; and as he sat leaning upon Excalibur, his fair hair falling on either side his broad forehead, and his limbs showing grand and giant-like through his garments' folds, I felt rising within me the same ardour which had impelled so many brave knights to fight, bleed, or die, for Arthur of Britain.

Around the presence-chamber were grouped the most noted of the dwellers in Avillion. I beheld and knew them all. Side by side stood the two bold adventurers from the land of the Cymri, who sailed westward in search of the *Gwerdonnan Lian* — the Green Isles of the Ocean — and returned no more; Prince Madoc, and Merlin, the mightiest sage of those early days. Afar from these, half hid in a delicious twilight shadow, Sir Launfal, the pure and faithful knight, lay resting at the feet of the beloved Tryamour. Near the throne leaned Ogier le Danois, the valiant and pious, who at his birth was chosen by Morgue la Faye to be her *loyal amoureux*. He ever kept at her side, looking up into her calm, queen-like eyes, and ready to obey her lightest behest, as true knight should for the sake of his dear ladye. But apart from all, kneeling in a little oratory, I saw Sir Galahad. His face was turned eastward, and the early sunbeams fell around his head like a glory. It seemed like the smile of God's love resting first and nearest upon him who on earth had loved God only.

Concealed behind the massive pillars which sustained the hall, I beheld all these, and then felt, piercing even to my hiding-place, the eagle glance of Arthur the king.

'Come forth!' he said. 'Whence art thou?'

I answered trembling; for his voice was loud and deep, as the noise of many waters; and yet it sounded familiar, for the accents, though stronger and more rugged, were those of my native speech. The long-forgotten world, with all its memories, all its ties, rushed back upon my thought.

'Great king, I come from thine own far-off island in the northern seas. There, Arthur of Britain is remembered still.'

His countenance changed, and his mailed fingers tightened over Excalibur.

'Is it so? Bringest thou tidings from my kingdom? Do the men of Carlyon ask for Arthur to return once more?'

And his frame, hitherto calm as a giant image of a marble knight, was stirred with human emotion. This land, then, was not like that of Ulysses, an elysium of undesiring repose.

'I cannot answer thee, O King!' I cried, while a confused mass of earthly memories struggled dimly in my brain.

But Morgue la Faye arose, and struck her wand on the area below the throne. Immediately the ground divided, and formed a deep crystal well.

'Look down, and tell what thou seest,' said the sweet tones of the Queen of Faërie.

'I see a land where men run about like ants, each laden with a golden burthen, or struggling to gain the same; I see palaces built for and inhabited by fools, and squalid huts where great and wise men grovel in misery.'

'Oh, my Britain! oh, my country!' groaned the king. 'The time is not yet come; they look not for Arthur!'

But his immortal sister said tenderly —

'Wait! The ages that pass by but nearer bring the joyful day, when Arthur shall come on earth again. Child of man, look into the spring once more!'

'Aye, look!' cried the king. 'Tell me of my palace, the many-towered Camelot; of Tintagel, fair home of my mother Igrayne; of the plain near the sea, where my brave army fought with Mordred; of the valley, where I lay wounded and tended by Sir Bedivere!'

'I see a castle on a cliff.'

'Ah!' eagerly interposed the king of knights, 'it is my ancient castle of Dover, where Sir Gawaine's ashes lie. Do they still say the masses for his soul, and does the passing bell ring nightly over the desolate seashore?'

'It is a shore, not desolate but thronged with human habitations. The sea is black with ships, the hum of commerce rises up to the castle-wall. Men and women, their souls and bodies alike enfeebled by luxury and thirst of gold, tread mincingly over the bones of the stalwart-limbed and noble hearted-knight.'

'Alas! alas!' Arthur again began, but the Faërie lady's hand was on his lips.

My vision continued. 'I behold a plain, intersected far and near with iron net-work; over it speed, thundering and howling, breathing smoke and flame, giant-steeds stranger than those which Merlin harnessed to his chariot. He claimed demons within the centre of the earth; this generation has created subject-demons from the dull dead metals that lie enwombed there.'

'And these mighty dwellers in Britain have forgotten their fathers. Of Arthur and his bold knights no trace or memory remains on earth,' said the King, while a shadow gloomed on his brow, like a cloud sweeping over a gray mountain-top.

'Not so,' I answered. 'The world's truths of mystical allegory are enduring as itself. The Round Table has crumbled into dust, and the raven hoots where stood the towers of Tintagel; but still many an old romaunt, and many a new poet's songs, keep up the name and the glory of Arthur.'

The king folded his hands upon Excalibur, and leaned his forehead against the hilt. 'Then I have lived,' he said, and peace again stole over his majestic countenance.

Turning from the scene around me, I again sought the depths of the magic well. My vision obeyed now, not the command of Arthur, but the impulse of my own being. I saw no land, but a black heaving sea, upon which rode a single ship. Within its darkest cabin I beheld a woman sitting alone. She rocked herself to and fro in her desolation; she lifted helplessly her pale, sorrowful face.

Then I leaped up with a great cry, and from my now conscious heart burst forth the name of *Lilias*.

But immediately Morgue la Faye bound round my temples a slender circlet of gold. As it touched my brow all memory vanished, and I fell down in a swoon.

CHAPTER VII

When I awoke, or seemed to awake, the presence-chamber, and all the beautiful and noble forms with which it was thronged, had disappeared. I lay in a dim cavern that was hollowed out of a basaltic rock. Huge pillars sustained the roof; glistening stalactites peopled the place with fantastic images of natural objects; animals, and even the human form. These icy phantasms of life grinned from dim hiding-places, making the solitude horrible. It was as though a troop of spectres had suddenly been congealed into material form; each grotesque or ghastly shape still transparent as air, but fixed in an awful immobility.

As I beheld, it seemed that the most fearful vision that ever startled human eye, would be less terrible than these embodied phantoms. I strove to break the spell. I called aloud, but the echoes of my own voice rang through the cavern like the shrieks of innumerable spirits. Then I felt the thin golden thread on my brow, and remembered all that had chanced since I clung to the saving hand of Sir Galahad, within sight of the island-shore. And while I pondered, it seemed as though my nature had become like that of the other dwellers in Avillion, and I had entered on a new sphere of being. In this sphere, my memory, alive to the past of others, was utterly dead to my own. From the golden thread a balmy influence passed into my brain, stilling all those pangs which in the human world so often teach us that to suffer needs but *to remember*.

My life seemed only to have begun from the moment when my feet touched the shore of Avillion. But from that time it was a full, real life, acute to enjoy, and as acute to endure. Kneeling on the floor of the cavern, the terror that convulsed me plainly showed that I was human still. And like the cry which weak humanity sends up to heaven, was that which, bursting from my shrinking soul, became a prayer to God.

'O Thou, who tookest me out of the deep waters, save me from this hell!'

I lifted up mine eyes, and saw standing beside one of the gigantic pillars, a form of flesh and blood. I knew it well — the dark, sombre face, in whose upper lineaments was stamped the impress of intellect and beauty, equally divine, while the lower features denoted stormy human passions — ambition, sensuality, and obstinate will — a mixture of the angel and the beast. It was Merlin the demon-born.

Still, to behold living and breathing man was bliss unutterable in this horrible place. I leaped forward and clasped the knees of the enchanter. He looked down upon me with contemptuous triumph.

'Weak child of the after ages, how thou quailest with fear at these poor shadows! With all the boasted glories of thy modern time, the magician of the elder world is greater than thou.'

At this scornful speech, I arose, trembling still, but striving to answer him boldly. 'Merlin, why comest thou to mock me, after affrighting me with thy horrible phantasms? What sent thee thither?'

'The merciful tenderness of Morgue la Faye, and mine own will. I desired to see if one of the vaunted later world was bolder than the greatest magician of ancient time. I am content: now let there be peace between us.' He reached his hand; but I paused irresolute. 'Thou fearest to clasp the hand of Merlin, the demon-born!'

He had spoken aloud the words in my heart. I dare not deny them.

'Fool! I *am* the son of a demon — of a spirit great, strong — and good, because he *was* strong. What is virtue, but that power which is the mightiest? Therefore my demon sire was as worthy of worship as any of your angels.'

I shrank aghast, and instinctively made the sign which was used as a symbol in those olden times to whose simplicity I had apparently returned — the sign of the holy cross. The magician made it likewise.

'Fear not,' he said: 'I, too, worship God. I, with men and spirits, must needs revere the one Omnipotent Spirit, the origin of all.'

As he spoke I regarded him with less of dread; for upon his dark face had dawned something which made it like unto an angel's. Such a light might have irradiated the brow of the great Hierarch of heaven, before he rebelled and fell.

'Merlin, I fear thee not, nor hate thee: God made us all — men, angels, and demons (or, as thou callest them, spirits). We are alike His children, or may become such, one day. Give me thy hand, and guide me from this dreary cave once more into the fair valley of Avillion, if indeed I am still near there.'

'This is Avillion. Thou art in the island of the blest,' said the magician.

I marvelled greatly. 'How can it be so, when I suffer trial, and terror, and pain? Dost thou call this happiness?'

Then Merlin answered, taking up his parable. like the prophets of olden time:

'Can the day exist without the night, or the sunshine without the shade? Does not good itself need the opposition of evil? Far higher than a dull life or perpetual selfish bliss, is that state of being which consists of temptation and triumph, struggle and victory, endurance and repose. Thus, in our life here, is intermixed just so much of evil and of suffering as will purify and lift us one stage nearer to divine perfection.'

'Then all suffer, and are tempted, and must be?'

'Thou scarce knowest which thy words imply,' replied Merlin; and now his speech was soft, almost heavenly, so that I loved to listen to him. 'Here, as on earth, temptation comes from man, suffering from God. One is a torturing flame, the other a refining fire. In Avillion, some have to struggle against the evil within themselves: some are ordained to suffer for, with, or from their brethren.'

'Which, Merlin, is thy destiny?'

'It comes upon me now!' cried the enchanter, while the heavenly influence passed from his face, and it kindled with lurid fire. He gnashed his teeth, and his glaring eyes were fixed upon a dim alcove, where stood among the stalactite images one that was likest to humanity.

Horror! while we beheld — for my gaze was rivetted too — there was a change in the icy phantom. The indistinct thing took form like a statue; the statue seemed transforming into flesh; roundness and colour came into the transparent limbs; the rigid hair stirred with life. Momently the icy shape was becoming a beautiful woman.

Merlin looked, and his face was like one struggling with the death-agony.

'Vivienne! for whom I burned in such mad passion, art thou following me still? Look!' and he clutched my hand. 'Dost thou not see her, with her bare, white-gleaming limbs; her floating, perfumed tresses, in every golden thread of which she netted my soul? Dost thou not feel her young breath, that once came upon my already wrinkled brow like the breath of spring? Vivienne — my love, my beautiful: it is she — it is she!'

He drew a long gasping sigh, and stretched out his arms with a gesture of incontrollable passion. But still his feet were steadfast: he approached no nearer to the alluring phantasm, which appeared continually changing from crystal to flesh, and then back again into crystal. Merlin's gleaming eyes drank in athirst every varying line of the lovely form.

'See!' he cried, 'her brow unbends, she will smile soon; she who was so harsh, so cold! Her ripe lips part sunnily; she leans forward, her lithe form drooping like an aspen. Vivienne — Vivienne, come!'

But that instant, the cry of delirious joy became a shriek of horror. He pressed his hands upon his eyes.

'Temptress! fiend! nay, I mingle all foul names in one, and call thee *woman*. Begone!'

He clung to the basalt pillar against which he had leaned. His face was hidden, but I saw that in the stalwart arm every muscle and nerve was quivering.

'Still there? Is not the struggle ended yet? Be thyself, Merlin! Remember the time on earth: thy mad passion that counted a life's wisdon as nothing to one heartless woman's love. Think of the long wanderings after her fair, cursed footsteps — cheated, befooled, mocked — think of her treachery at last. Ah, Vivienne, smilest thou still? So didst thou, luring me to enter the magic cave — so rung thy light laugh: I heard it as the spell-closed rock shut down upon me, writhing in a darkness that might have been eternal. Murderess, I defy thee! Thy tortured slave is thy victor now!'

He sprang away, and disappeared in the gloom. Immediately the woman's form became congealed once more into its semi-transparent substance. There was a sound like the roar of many floods, and the whole scene melted away.

I found myself on the margin of a lake, surrounded with mountains.

Silvery mists hung over the water, and trembled on the hill sides: all things looked pale, shadowy, and pure. At first, I seemed to be in a deep solitude; but presently I became aware of a boat gliding over the lake. There, reclining on a golden bed, even as that wherein he traversed the sea to the city of Sarras, I saw the form of him who alone was pure enough to behold the Sangreal — the virgin-knight, Sir Galahad.

CHAPTER VIII

As Sir Galahad neared the shore I saluted him with a reverent and joyful heart. In him seemed perpetually to abide the spirit of holiness, and that love of God which is the fountain from whence diverge wide streams of universal love. He was at once Galahad the Christian champion, before whose righteous arm fell alike the world's temptations and its opposing powers — Galahad, the pious knight who saw appear the goblet which held the Holy Greal, in the mystic covering of white samite — Galahad the youth, at once loving and pure; devoted to heaven, yet not free from human ties — witness his friends, Sir Bors and Sir Percival, and the holy self-devoted maid, Sir Percival's sister — Galahad, the tender son, who dying 'kissed Sir Bors and Sir Percival, saying, "Salute my father, Sir Lancelot, and bid him remember this unstable world," ' and then was borne upward by angels.

All these things, as I had read of them in old romaunt and history, returned vividly to my memory. I said unto him —

'O Galahad, knight beloved of God and man, is this indeed the form whose breath parted while yet in prayer before the holy table, in the sacred city of Sarras? Did the angel-hands then bear thee, not at once to heaven, but to this happy Island of Avillion?'

He smiled serenely, and answered — .

'Yea! It was God's will that I should still serve him in the flesh, and so I dwell in Avillion, among those who have journeyed thither, like Arthur, without seeing death.'

'And is thine, like theirs, an existence whose bliss consists in trial conquered?' I asked, remembering Merlin and the horrible cave.

A faint shade of sadness overspread the beautiful face:

'Not for myself I suffer, but for my brethren. I minister here as angels do on earth. They weep over human sin and sorrow; but their tears are holy, and soon dried — they know that the All-wise and All-merciful cannot but make all clear at last.'

'But, save thee, the dwellers in Avillion have each this mournful doom of trial?'

'Call it not *doom*," he answered gently, 'since it is God's will, and therefore must be good. Now, of all whom thou hast seen here, whose inner struggle wouldst thou behold? Desire, and the desire will be fulfilled — it is ever so in the Happy Isle of Avillion.'

'I would see Arthur,' I said.

The young knight lifted me by the hands, and instantly, with the speed of a winged thought, we stood unseen by the couch of the son of Uther Pendragon.

The King seemed to strive with troubled dreams. His huge limbs tossed restlessly, and his sleeping fingers ever sought blindly the renowned Excalibur, which lay beside him — at once his sceptre and his sword. He called oftentimes upon his good knights of the Round Table — Tristram, and Launcelot; also, Gawaine, his near kinsman, so well beloved, and by Sir Lancelot's fatal hand slain. Then, suddenly awakening, he lifted up his voice and cried —

'O valiant companions of old! O dear land of Britain! when will Arthur revisit ye once more? Why must this yearning never be allayed? — even in the happy vale of Avillion it brings perpetual pangs!'

And he smote upon his manly breast, that was long since healed of the 'grievous wound', but rent with an inward struggle, harder perhaps to bear.

Galahad came and stood beside him. I wist not whether Arthur beheld the vision; but his countenance softened into peace — even as that of a sleeper when an unseen angel passes by. He took Excalibur once more, but used it neither as a sceptre nor a sword. Lifting up the hilt, which was made in the form of a cross, he kissed it with devotion.

'O Thou, for whose blood in the Sangreal my good knights spent so many years in a patient quest, give me patience too, that I may wait until Arthur be worthy of his kingdom, and his kingdom of him! Quell this impure earthly ambition, both in memory and in desire — let me grow meek, and pray, until the time comes when the son of Uther shall reign again in Britain.'

He kissed once more the battle-cross formed by the elfin sword, and then lay down and slept like a little child.

As Galahad passed out, the whole chamber was lightened by the holy gladness of his smile. Truly it might be seen that he had been among the angels; that in the eyes which had beheld the shining of the Sangreal dwelt the reflection of its brightness evermore.

I followed after, traversing with him the blessed isle. For it was blessed, even though it was not a region of unmixed joy, or perfect repose. Each human soul was pressing onward, and on each brow was the divine light of Hope. They drew strength even from the trials endured — as he who pushes forward in a race feels his cheek fanned by the fresh breeze into health and beauty, while the listless lingerer on perfumed banks droops wearily, howsoever the sun may shine.

'But,' I said to Sir Galahad, 'when the trial is over rest comes? I would fain see this rest.'

He took me to a bower where reclined two lovers in the cool of day —

'Enter, brother!' said Galahad, 'my ministry is needless here.'

So I passed, alone and still invisible, to the presence of Sir Launfall and Tryamour.

As grief grows keener from the memory of joy, so happiness is deepened by the remembrance of vanished sorrow. I felt this when I beheld Launfal and his beloved. He talked with her of the troublous time on earth; but he spoke even of suffering with a smile.

'Dost remember, love, the Forest of Carlyon: how I lay in poverty, despondency, and pain — when the three Faërie maids came riding by, and brought me unto a region of peace and beauty, even to thee? O dear eyes, that looked upon me in my darkness and my misery, and loved me amidst all!'

And, as he lay at her feet, he drew down to his own the lovely head, and kissed the drooping eyes — radiant as those of a princess of Faërie; but tender as those of a loving woman.

The again spoke Launfal:

'How hard it was, after that season of bliss, to mix once more with the vileness of earth — how bitter, save for those hours when a wish brought me the dear presence of my Faërie love. Then, when for that pure smile I had to endure the false queen Guinever's — more cursed in her love than in her hate —'

'O my faithful one! yet thou didst remember me!' And as Tryamour bent over him, her long locks, dropping immortal balm, fell in golden waves on the bosom of her knight and love.

'I remembered thee? Could I forget my life, my other soul? Yet in the dungeon and at the stake did I endure, nor implored thee to come and save me: I never asked of thee aught — not even love — yet thou gavest me all.'

She smiled upon him with her heavenly eyes, and bade him remember earth's sorrows no more.

'Nay, it is sweet to remember,' answered Launfal. 'Here, in this dear bower, let me think of the lonely dungeon where I lay in perpetual darkness, knowing that the first entering gleam of daylight would be a signal to guide me unto death. Let me call back the moment when dazzled, blinded, I staggered forth at last. By degrees, all grew clear: I heard the leafy rustling of the great pile formed of yet green trees — ah! cruel lengthening of torture, planned by that revengeful woman-fiend! I saw her sitting on the polluted throne, beside her deluded spouse, my dear lord King Arthur! He loved me once — even now he blenched at the sight of me, and turned away his troubled face; perchance, he could not yet believe that I had so wronged his honour. Then came the chains, the lighted torch, the approaching flame —'

'Speak no more!' shuddering said the Faërie lady — with the woman's heart.

'Yet a little; but only of thee — of thee, Tryamour! — as the steps of thy fair palfrey sounded musically along the palace terrace, and thou stoodest forth with thy immortal beauty to proclaim the honour of thy true knight. Oh! the rapture, when I felt the cool breeze wrapping my freed limbs as with a garment, and the swift steed bore me on, ever following thee, past the gleam of the now harmless pyre, past the shoutings of the multitude, far, far over forest, mountain, and sea, into the happy vale of Avillion.'

He looked up; first heavenwards, and then into that earthly heaven, the eyes of her he loved. As I beheld him, it seemed that his face, sublimed by past suffering, was more beautiful even than hers, which bore the cloudless aspect of perpetual bliss. I saw how it was that, in some things, *a man* is greater than an angel.

As these two sat together, leaning cheek to cheek in the silence of perfect love, the birds in the linden-trees over-head broke forth into singing; and lo! amidst the marvels of the Happy Isle, I distinguished one more — that their very song was speech. Thus it ran:

'But for the rain, the green earth would wither; without the evening gloom, man could not behold the stars. So, storm bringeth freshness; night, dawn; trial, peace; and death, immortality!'

I fell on my face, praying — nay, almost weeping, as one sometimes does in a heart-poured prayer such as was mine. When it ended, I arose; but the marriage-bower, and those happy ones who abode therein, I saw no more.

CHAPTER IX

I stood once more beside the lake amidst the hills. I was still veiled in that perpetual mist; and the solitary marge was dimly illuminated by a light like that of a gray June midnight, when the pale half-moon has just set. There was no sound, not even of a stirring leaf; for the hills sloped down to the water-side, bare and treeless; lake, mountain, and sky — sky, lake, and mountain — reflected each other in a ghost-like silence and repose.

At length, through the mist, I heard a sound of many footsteps. They came nearer; and I distinguished the form of Merlin, leading a mounted band of the dwellers in Avillion. Suddenly he paused, and the loud trumpet-tone of his voice rang over the still shore:

'Who will go with me across the Lake of Shadows?'

There stepped forward the giant figure of King Arthur — Morgue la Faye following. Behind them Sir Galahad stood, meek, yet fearless; and these three alone answered Merlin's summons. But the King paused, and said —

'How shall we cross the awful lake? Galahad, thou only among us who has known death, aid us now.'

The young knight advanced to the margin, and stretched his arms out over the water that lay before him, solemn, soundless, unrippled by a single wave. Then I saw glide towards him the boat in which he had formerly reclined, with its purple sails shadowing the golden bed. It came on, impelled invisibly; for there was no man therein.

'Enter!' said Galahad, in his angel-voice; and immediately the vessel rocked beneath the great bulk of the two mightiest of Britain's ancient sons, Arthur and Merlin. 'Enter thou, too, my brother,' said they to me.

So I entered tremblingly, yet eagerly, after Morgue la Faye. Then Merlin uttered a spell, and the boat darted forward from the strand without either wind or tide.

Far out into the lake we sailed. The silvery vapours shut out from my vision alike shore and sky. I cast my eyes downwards; and lo! it seemed that, like a bird of the air sweeping over a city of earth, the boat glided over a new world lying beneath the waters. In its mysterious depths, I saw palaces, towers, tombs, outlined dimly through a gigantic shroud of mist, like that which hung above the surface. At times, stirring amidst this shoud, I distinguished denser vapours, which scarce bore airy form, but resembled the *cirri* that float in a summer evening sky.

Merlin arose. As the masses of his black robe fell heavily around him, he might have been likened to a thunder-cloud lifting itself slowly from the horizon. He wore no magic symbols; he held no books of power. In the strength of his soul alone lay the necromancer's might.

'Ye who desired to visit the Lake of Shadows — say, who among you seeks to call up the ghastly habitants of the City of the Dead?'

King Arthur spoke first:

'I yearn for tidings of my kingdom on the earth. Therefore I would fain summon those who lie buried in Britain, and whose spirits may still hover around the spot where their bones repose. Which among them, deemest thou, is most able to answer my summons?'

'Love only has power over death,' replied the enchanter. 'Call one of those who were dearest to thee on earth.'

'They were few indeed!' And a grim, almost scornful smile swept over Arthur's face. 'Ambition was all to me. I loved my royal kingdom more than any of its subject dwellers — save, perhaps, Guinever and Gawaine.'

'Choose between them!' said Merlin's stern voice.

The monarch paused, irresolute.

'Gawaine, thou wast a valiant knight; indeed I loved thee, my sister's son! But Guinever sat with me on that dear-prized throne. I summon her, not as the wife of Arthur, but the Queen of Britain.'

Morgue la Faye's hand dropped from her brother's, and Merlin's dark brow was knitted in wrath. Nevertheless he leaned over the vessel's side, dipped his fingers in the lake, and uttered the spell:

'Soul of Guinever Queen of Britain, arise!'

Slowly lifting itself out of the deep appeared one of the cloud-like vapours. Gradually it became a human form, wearing a nun's garb. Then I remembered the story of the death of her whose spirit parted ere Sir Launcelot came to Almesbury, over whom *'he wept not greatly, but sighed.'* Perchance that one long tearless sigh followed the frail Guinever's fleeting soul even to its resting-place; for in the wail that arose from the waters, I heard evermore the words —

'Launcelot! Launcelot!'

'Peace, complaining spirit! False queen, false wife, false woman, answer thy Lord!' cried the enchanter.

Arthur spoke — stern, cold, passionless. He thought neither of pity, anger, nor revenge — only of his Britain. But to all his questions came from the suffering soul no word, save the cry of 'Mercy, mercy! I repent! Let me rest!' And ever and anon, in mournful plainings, was repeated the wail, 'Launcelot! Launcelot!'

The king sat down wrathful and silent, and the phantom faded into a wreath of mist that seemed continually to hover round the vessel.

Then Sir Galahad arose, and stood before Arthur and Merlin, meek reproach, mingled with sorrow, clouding his eyes.

'Oh, men!' he said: 'sinful yourselves, yet so harsh to judge the sinning — is there no pity in God's dear heaven for such as these? The convent-cell at Almesbury yet bears record of the tears, the sackcloth, the bloody scourge — sad portion of her who was once a queen! The aisles of Glastonbury yet ring with those funeral orisions wrung from the penitent despair of the knighted monk!'

And turning from where Arthur and Merlin sat together — both shrinking into silence before his words — Galahad dipped his hands in the lake, writing in the stirless waters the sign of the holy cross.

'Oh, dear father, my lord Sir Launcelot, whose sins may God pardon! no voice but mine shall summon thee here. Let me look on thy face once more!'

There was a pause; and then rising from the misty depth, I saw the mailed image of a knight. It was Guinever's lover — faithful in sin, but yet most faithful — the bravest of the champions of the Round Table — Sir Launcelot du Lac. Beneath the shadowy helmet were the features — still, and ashen gray — as they might have appeared to his brother monks who gazed down weepingly into the deep grave at Joyous Garde.

He spoke not, and none spoke with him. Only his son Galahad, with clasped hands, knelt and prayed.

Even while the spirit lingered, there came and hovered over his helm a cloud-like shadow; and through the silence was heard that continual wail — 'Launcelot, Launcelot!' But it won no answer, either in word or look, from the pale spectre of Guinever's knight.

The phantoms both grew dimmer; and then I was aware of another sight coming near the vessel. It seemed an open boat; and therein, resting on a bed, was a women dressed in fair array; and *'she lay as though she had smiled.'* By this, and by the writing in her hand, I knew the vision was she who had died for love of Sir Launcelot — Elaine, the fair maid of Astolat. I looked on the beautiful dead image, and thought of the time when the waters of Thames had floated up to the feet of Sir Launcelot this poor broken lily, that asked no guerdon for love faithful even unto death, but burial from his hand. And when I remembered this, my heart melted with pity, and I wept.

'Dost thou weep for me?' said a voice, sweet in its sadness, like a vesper-bell heard over the sea at night. I felt it came from the pale lips that looked *as if they smiled.* 'Weepest thou for me, because I died? Nay: for love's bliss was greater than death's pain.'

'How so — when the love proved vain?' I asked.

She did not answer my words; but went on murmuring softly, as one does in musing aloud:

'Dear my lord Sir Launcelot! was it sin or shame that I should love thee, who came and stood before me like an angel in a dream? I never thought tenderly of living man, save thee. Thou wert the sun that unfolded my life's flower: when the sun set, it faded and died.'

The voice was thrilled with a meek sorrow that roused my pity into wrath.

'Surely it was evil in the sun to scorch the poor flower,' I cried, remembering how the concealed knight took and wore in the fray the token of Elaine la Blanche; and how, when she swooned at his wound, he, saying no word of any former love, prayed her brother, Sir Lavaine, to bring her to him, and took her in his arms and kissed her. Then I thought of all the days of fondest tendance which to the knight brought renewed life, to the fair maid death. And lastly, of the cruel scorn which, knowing her pure love, instead of requital offered pitiful gold. And my swelling heart told me that Sir Launcelot had done a grievous wrong.

But again the voice seemed to answer my thoughts, though it spoke not to me, but dreamily and vague:

'Was it, then, so sorrowful to die for thee, my Launcelot? or did my death lay aught to thy charge? Nay: it was no sin of thine. I worshipped thee, as one should only worship Heaven; Heaven punished me — then pityingly took me home: I am content!'

Again my tears fell to hear that low, tender voice; and I marvelled in my heart whether on earth it had been ever thus uncomplaining. The spirit answered once more:

'What was I, that I should murmur against thee, O my lord Sir Launcelot? Only once — when I lay in my tears, and darkness, and despair — I heard the blithe sound of thy trumpets, and saw thee going forth again into the fair world; while I — forgotten, forsaken — was to thee less than the grass under thy footsteps. Oh, forgive me, my lord and love, for that one cry of reproach against thee! I *would* have been — aye, ten thousand times — that trodden grass, if for a moment it gave freshness to thy feet?'

I looked on the calm features, where no movement of the lips gave token of the voice which spake. But the deep peace of the smile that sat on the dead face was an echo of the words which the spirit uttered. And when I thought of the pure soul which had departed in the tower of Astolat — praying and confessing meekly unto God, and remembering with tender and forgiving love Sir Launcelot — I said in my heart that unto such, against whom earth's hopes are closed, does the kingdom of heaven open.

While I watched this vision, Arthur, Merlin, and Sir Galahad sat at the vessel's prow, each absorbed in thought; little to them was maiden's love or maiden's woe. But Morgue la Faye came near with her woman's soul shining tearfully in her majestic eyes, and cried —

'Tell me — thou pure and meek spirit, whom I have summoned from thy rest — does the remembered love of earth wound thee even in Paradise?'

Elaine la Blanche answered:

'I love still, but I suffer no more: God looked on me in mercy, and drew wholly unto Himself that love which in life was divided. I am happy — yet I forget thee not:I never could forget thee, my lord Sir Launcelot!'

While the voice yet spoke, there stood beside the bed another spirit — also in woman's form. Before its glory the mists dispersed, and light broke forth upon the waters. Soon another voice was heard, sweet as that which had murmured its patient sorrow; but clear and joyous as the angels' harping before the throne.

'Galahad, dear brother of my soul, say unto my brother in the flesh, Sir Percival - and to that true knight Sir Bors — that far exceeding the holy city of Sarras, to which we four journeyed together, is the Eternal city, New Jerusalem. Say, I rejoice that I died, a willing sacrifice, for the glory of God.'

Galahad lifted his brow, radiant with exceeding joy.

'Maiden — through life pure and heaven-devoted, as was the virgin-mother of Nazareth — say, where does thy soul abide?'

'In Paradise; ministering there as many of God's servants do on earth, and as thou dost in Avillion. Therefore my spirit, inter-penetrated and made strong by its love of God — which in life was entire and undivided — is commanded to succour this soul, once tortured by earthly love. Sister, come!'

Over the bier she bent, lifting by the hand the pale form, even like Him who lifted the dead, and said, 'Arise.'

Elaine arose. To the opening eyes came a brightness, less of earth than heaven; to the lips came a voice — no mournful complainings, but melodious hallelujahs. And so, linked hand-in-hand the sister-souls passed from sight, not sinking like the rest into the dim city of the dead, but soaring upwards unto the mount of God.

CHAPTER X

As one who falls, flooded and dazzled by a sunshine cloud — or as Paul
fell, blinded by the heavenly vision near Damascus — so sank I.
Human eye and ear could not endure the glorious radiance, the
angelic melody. Beneath them, my brain and sense seemed numbed —
or rather exhaled into delicious death.

From this trance I awoke, feeling on my brow the light touch of a
woman's hand. It brought strange, undefined remembrances.
Wistfully I looked up.

I lay in the midst of the great hall, once filled with many knights and
ladies.It now held only the fair presence of Queen Morgue la Faye. But
she stood beside me less as a queen than a woman. Her gorgeous robes
were thrown aside, and in her white garments she seemed a simple
earthly maid, even resembling — I strove to remember what or who
she resembled; but my thoughts fled away, like winged birds, ever
fluttering on before, yet impossible to seize. Amidst them I heard
continually the murmuring of the little fount which had sprung up at
Morgue la Faye's bidding from the cloven marble floor. It seemed
singing to me an olden song of some long-past existence; and yet,
when I drew nearer, its waters were as smooth and as opaque as the
marble which encircled them. But still, rising from their depths, came
that mystic murmur, as it were a voice from the inner earth.

I leaned eagerly over the well, and my greedy ear drank in its musical
whispers. Morgue la Faye said to me —

'Child of man, what dost thou hear?'

'I hear a sound, like the evening wind in the full-leafed linden-trees
that grew — where was it they grew? Or like that Eolian harp we put
between the ivied window, and listened — *who* listened, and *when*?
Alas! alas! the thoughts slip from me; I cannot grasp them!'

'Bend down thy head again over the water.'

'I feel — I feel a perfume; it comes from a violet-bank, the bank
where — but no, all is gone. Again, it is like a rose-garden; I am
walking there in sunshine and gladness; and now it changes to a sweet
clematis-breath — wafted through that still autumn night, with the
stars shining coldly overhead, and the waning crescent glimmering
through the trees. Ah me! ah me! it is fled from me! No more! no
more!' And uttering these mournful words, the perpetual dirge of life,
I fell down weeping beside the mysterious spring.

Morgue la Faye stood on the other brink; for the well had grown
wider and broader, and even now was swelling out into an infant
stream. She stood, her falling hands meek-folded, her head half bent,
watching me. A gleam of womanly pity softened the steel-like
brightness of her eyes.

Perceiving it, I cried imploringly —

'O Queen of Avillion, I am not of thy nature, but only mortal man!
Why dost thou try me thus?'

'Because, as thou sayest, thou art not of our nature,' she answered softly. 'Thou canst not stay in our happy isle; but I have no power, nor yet desire, to cast thee thence. Thou must depart of thine own will.'

'Depart!' I echoed sorrowfully; for now that the spell had ceased, I felt no more the vague memories and wild longings which it had awakened. I thought with fear of quitting the beautiful island for some unknown region, perhaps of horror and woe.

'Poor mortal!' Morgue la Faye continued. 'Art thou then so loath to depart? Do the sounds and sights of former times, which I have raised up before thee fail to win thee back to earth?'

'I know not of what thou speakest,' I answered, trembling. 'True, I had a vision; but it is gone now. I would fain stay in Avillion.'

'It cannot be,' said the firm but still gentle voice of King Arthur's sister, as she crossed the spring, its waters sinking not beneath her airy footsteps. Then she bade me kneel, and took from my head the slender thread of gold which continually encircled it.

Instantly my brain reeled beneath the thronging memories with which it teemed. All came back to me — my land, my home, my Lilias — each thought piercing my soul like arrows tipped with that bitterest poison, the remembrance of eternally-lost joy.

I dashed myself on the ground at the feet of Morgue la Faye:

'Cruel queen, why didst thou take from me that blessed spell of Oblivion? Why torture me with these memories of earth? O Lilias my wife! my love! my beautiful! would to Heaven that I might see thy face once more!'

Morgue la Faye lifted me from the earth, where I grovelled in mad despair, and led me to the brink of the magic well.

'Now, poor child of mortality, cast thine eyes down once more.'

I did so. Oh marvel! As the clouds of oblivion had passed from my soul, so passed the dusky shadow from beneath the water, which became crystal clear. While I gazed, there grew defined from out its depths the image of a scene — an earth-landscape — one that I knew — oh how well! Blue and dim rose the mountains — those giant spectres of my childhood, which, night after night, enclosed the descending sun in their craggy, ghostly arms; beneath them lay the valley, and the broad river, and the woody slope, where stood — a Home.

We had chosen it as our home, our wedded home, when — the melancholy voyage ended — Lilias and I should return to our own land and our own people. There it stood, near the spot where we had both dwelt from childhood — a house reverend and beautiful with years. Over its brown walls climbed the ivy, mingling with the dear clematis, cherished of old; its painted gothic windows transmitted every sunbeam in rainbow-tinted glory; and from its protecting eaves the brooding swallows merrily flew — their cheerful homes without being meet emblems of that most blessed one within.

A moment, and the scene changed to the interior. I saw the quaint labyrinthine chambers, whose gloom was made beautiful by the presence of youth and happiness. Pictures shone from the dark-panelled walls; in a recess, the ivory-keyed instrument smiled over the soul of music shut up within it; above the green, branch-adorned hearth, fresh-gathered flowers bent to their own fair images in the mirror.

And near them, pure and lovely as they, was my own life's flower, whom I had chosen to adorn and bless my home — my wife Lilias!

She sat droopingly, her cheek resting against the crimson chair — the same where mine had rested in many an hour of mental and bodily suffering. The remembrance seemed to strike her then; for suddenly she lifted her face, wherein was love so intense that it almost became agony, and cried — aye, *I heard the very tone* —

'Wilfred, beloved, come!'

I would have plunged into hell itself to answer that call! Hearing it, I sprang madly into the waters, there to seek the vision and the voice.

In a moment, Avillion and its dwellers had vanished from me for ever.

20

The Glastonbury Scripts[1]

FREDERICK BLIGH BOND

No. 5
The Vision
of
the Holy Grail

I

I speak, to whom the Vision of the Cup
In Eirenn came: Mathias is my name.
I came from Connaught in the Holy Isle
Unto that place that Holy Rood is named
To take my vows, and there was I received
Into the bosom of my Mother Church.
Holy Saint Patrick was the Father there
The name Mathias gave he unto me.

II

Now would ye hear my Vision of the Cup
And the device upon it blazoned.
It came about that on a certain night
While I within my cell asleep did lie
A Voice to me did call: upon my bed
I rose; a shaft of light did on me fall;
A wondrous light, white as the driven snow
Upon the hills: and unto me the Voice
Did call in accents clear 'Arise, my Son
And see what man has never seen before.'

III

And lo! from out the shaft of light, a Hand
Was stretched to me. I trembled, and was feared
To touch the Hand; but closer yet it came
And when at last the fingers of the Hand
Touched my cold fingers, it was as a coal
Of living fire. I rose from off my bed
And forward guided by that fiery touch
Obediently I followed on my feet
Out of the door; down the long winding stair,
Until the Chapel door at last I reached.

---

[1] Privately printed pamphlet (Glastonbury, *c.* 1923).

IV

And now into the Chapel was I led
Until at last I stood beneath the Cross.
Suddenly feared was I: aloud I cried,
But lo! the Voice made answer to my cry:
'Fear not, Mathias, all is well with thee:
But raise thine eyes, thy Saviour to behold.'

V

And lo! before mine eyes I saw a Cup
Of shining gold: large as a man it was,
And in the Cup stood He Whose sacred blood
Upon the Tree was spilt: His face most sweet,
Fair as a child's, and sad beyond compare.
He gazed into my eyes. I raised my head
And looking at His Hand, I there beheld
A Stone: a precious Gem of beauty rare;
And unto me these words my Saviour said.

VI

'List ye, Mathias, I thy Lord am come
To bid ye journey far across the seas,
Away from this fair isle, unto the land
Of Anglia, for there this precious Stone
Shall ye discover, in that Holy Place
Where, in the bosom of the Father's robe,
She lieth hid, and hath been so preserved
From ancient times: this Stone I bid ye seek,
For lo! she is My very Blood and Sweat
That from Me fell in My great Agony.

VII

'When ye are come unto that Holy Place,
Seek ye the Abbot, and to him commit
My words: that in the fulness of the days
A time is set, wherein a Golden Cup
Shall carven be and in her bowl be set
The Sacred Stone, that so she may be seen
With the intent that she shall minister
And give forth healing to the sore and sick.
Note ye the pattern of this golden cup
Wherein I stand: carve ye that lesser one
In her true likeness, and upon her face
Make ye a picture of My Agony
Upon the Tree; and on the further side
Make ye the Rood, to shew My Gospels Four,
And in her central hollow lay the Stone.

VIII

'Years will pass by, and many seasons come
Before she shall within this cup be set:
But this the Sign that I shall give to ye
When in the Cup this Jewel shall be fixed.
A Mark will I make plain upon a man
Of holy mind; one without guile or sin.
Upon his feet, upon his hands and side
Shall I mark holes, the which shall signify
Those wounds the which upon the Tree did bleed:
So shall ye know that now the time is come
For setting of the Stone within the Cup.'

IX

After that Vision bright no sleep had I,
For at the cross's foot I straight did fall.
And when the dawn into the chapel crept,
I rose, and hied me back into my cell
Once more. The holy Patrick heard my tale,
And taking pen, he wrote my vision down
On parchment fair, for eyes of men to see.
And then he gave to me the kiss of Peace
And bade me unto Glaston journey forth
And there unto the Abbot tell my tale.

X

So o'er the seas and unto Britain's isle
Came I at length, and journeyed on until
The Church of Joseph stood before mine eye.
There rested I and told my tale to all.
But, mark ye well: no Brother in that House
Had sign or symbol of those blessed holes
That in Christ's Body left their bloody mark:
Yet was it written that no Cup should be
Until on one those Wounds of Christ were shewn.
Thus was the written word the only sign
Of that most lovely promise of the Grail
To Glaston's house, until that far-off day
When to a brother should those signs be given.

Brother Petrus tells his Tale

XI

I, Petrus, was right ready with the pen.
In our scriptorium I loved to sit
And blazon in our holy missal-books.
Right cheerful was I when at eventide
I wrote the sacred words, and blazoned them
With images arising in my mind.

XII

Now unto me it came that, on a day
When in the Chapel, bending on my knees
I prayed, that, looking up, I saw a light
As of the sun at even, which did fill
The chapel, and within the light there stood
He whose sweet face brings peace to all the world.

XIII

'Petrus,' quoth He. 'I give to thee the care —
Of that most precious Stone the which doth rest
Within this House: this shall a token be
That I have chosen ye my messenger.
Forth to the world My gospel shall ye send;
And as the witness of My Will in this,
A holy Symbol shall to thee be given
So shall the hearts of savage men be tamed
By a great Miracle in Glaston wrought.

XIV

'Fear ye not, Petrus, to your Father go:
For with him in the Spirit have I striven
So that in faith he shall accept thy tale,
And to thy hands he will commit the Stone
And cause a holy Chalice to be wrought
Wherein she may be set, that, shining there,
Her Virtue may be manifest to all
That on her look. Take thou the Stone, My Blood,
And in the centre of a carven Rood
Set her, and lay her in a secret place
Behind the altar: keep her there with care
And, on the solemn feast-days let the Cup
Be raised aloft that all men may her see.'

XV

I, Petrus, bent my head unto the ground
Hiding my face in awe and wonderment;
Then to the Abbot hied I in hot haste.
To him I told my tale, who, marvelling
At this my vision, did, with mind prepared,
Study the parchment by Saint Patrick writ
And fall to prayer. Full earnestly he gazed
Upon me, then he lifted up his voice
In praise of God for that the time was come
When in a humble Brother of the house
The promised tokens should be manifest.

XVI

Naught knew I of the nature of the Sign
That by the Spirit should in me be wrought;
Yet I believed a miracle should be.
And now my Father called unto him
A learned Brother, skilful in the arts,
To whom the antique draft he did submit
That held the characters of that design
That was in vision to Mathias shewn
In the far distant days of Patrick's rule
At Holy Rood in Eirenn's holy isle.

XVII

Now I in metal had not learnt to carve.
So, while the golden Cup was fashioned,
I sat beside, and waited for that time
When to my hands the Treasure should be given.
Thus, day by day, the Cup was perfected
And, as her beauty grew, so grew my joy.
But ye shall hear the tale of her design.
And of the Holy Symbols that she bore.

XVIII

The Holy Cup was large: it could contain
A measure equal to a bowl of wine.
Burnished her face, and all of molten gold
Was made, from moneys that had long been stored.
Round was the bowl; yea, round as any pearl;
Slender the stem and long; and at her foot
A heavy plate was laid for steadying.

XIX

Now on the forefront of the bowl was carved
The Agony of our most Blessed Lord.
The Cross on which He hung: right simply this
Was carven, yet with most consummate art:
For on the Saviour's face a smile was seen:
No downcast look — His eyes up-turned to Heaven
Shewing the Joy that conquered agony.

XX

A Rood was carven on the further side —
A Rood: no other ornament beside.
Yet was this rood a work of beauty rare
And great enough to fill up all the space
From lip to stem: and, at the very heart
A place was kept for that most precious Gem
Of which ye wot: a heavy ring was wrought
To hold the sacred Treasure in her place.

XXI

Equal the four arms from the centre spread
And each one at her end a jewel held
Firm in the head, and these did signify
The Four Evangelists: so mark ye well
The colour of these stones: The first of these;
He at the head, a Persian ruby was,
Which, shewing forth the colour of the rose,
John the Divine of Mystery portrayed.

XXII

Next, at the foot, a purple amethyst
Marcus the Scibe did truly symbolize —
The Road of Learning and Authority.
With pink and yellow stones the arms were decked
Symbols of sun at morn and setting-time
And these for Luke and for Mathias stood.
Last, in the centre, was the Holy Stone
That was the Blood and Sweat of Christ congealed.

XXIII

And all the space between the arms was filled
With carven gold, wrought with entwined snakes
Coil within coil, and plaited cunningly
And with such curious art that none could find
The head within their coil. Now, one thing more
Must I narrate, for underneath the foot
Were certain words writ in the Roman tongue;
But what their meaning was I cannot tell.

XXIV

Now while the Cup was being perfected,
My silent heart did cry unto the Lord
To give me strength that I might hold and keep
The Treasure of our land of Anglia:
That in His service I might never fail
But in fidelity my Trust fulfil.
Sore was I: sad in mind and joyful both:
I could not rest: I might not eat nor sleep
Possessed with that most joyful agony.

XXV

And when at last the Cup was fashioned
And in the centre of the Holy Rood
Was laid the Stone, weary was I and faint.
Upon my feet I scarce could stand upright.
My brethren James and Joseph lifted me
And bare me to the chapel in their arms.
There in my hand my Father placed the Stone.

XXVI

And, as it touched me, lo! to outward things
Was I a moment lost; of sense bereft,
Yet inly conscious; and within my heart
As in a tomb, unto the Lord I cried;
And lo! again was I a living man
And thro' my body shot a piercing pain.

XXVII

The Stone had pierced my hands, my feet, my side,
And on my brow had left a bleeding mark.
So cried the brethren all 'God's Mercy! See!
The Wounds of Christ upon a living man!'

XXVIII

With bloody hands I laid into her place
The Stone: the golden Cup was washed with blood
When high I held her to the eyes of all.
The brethren, with my Father, gathered there:
With long and solemn rite we laid the Cup
Within the altar shrine, a holy place
And secret. Meet it was the Cup should rest
In such a house. I, Petrus, had in charge
The holy Vessel.

XXIX

                    Never from my hands,
My feet, my side, did vanish those sweet wounds,
Nor did they heal: full feeble I became,
And weary oft; and never more did use
The pen for blazoning. One task alone
Was by the High Lord Abbot set for me;
And this it was: To shield the Cup, and pray.

XXX

Now, in those days, before the savage hordes
Did border on us, were my days in peace
And service spent: for I was young, and all
My days of vigour and of youth were given
Unto the service of the Lord Most High.
But after this there came a dreadful time.

XXXI

Ye know how savage men upon us fell
And how they spoiled our house. Afeared was I
Not for my body, but the Holy Cup
And those sweet wounds of mine; and so I hid
In secret crypt below the Altar High
Holding the Holy Vessel in my arms:
And never did I in those days of fear
Let man put hand thereon: so was it saved
From all defilement. Many a weary day
Had I lain hidden in that secret crypt
While dreadful men did run about our House.
Yet all our treasures had been safe bestowed.

XXXII

Upon a certain day, as wearily
I sat and closely held the precious Cup,
A Voice cried 'Petrus, to the Chapel go;
There kneel, and hear thy Lord declare His Will
For He shall tell thee where the precious Blood
Shall be bestowed.' I clambered from the pit,
And hied me to the Chapel, where I knelt,
Kissing the foot of the most Holy Cross,
And prayed that I the knowledge might receive.

XXXIII

Before mine eyes a picture there arose
As of a narrow chamber, secret, dark,
Within the ground. Then spake the Voice to me
From out the Cross: 'The chamber that ye see
Must builded be full deep within the earth
To house My cup. Deep let her rest, and there
For many a year a-sleeping shall she lie.
Full many winter rains and snows shall fall
Upon her bed, and little flowers shall bloom
When summer comes, to deck her resting-place.
And hark ye, there shall come at last a day
When by the hand of one of perfect faith
And pure and simple mind, the Stone once more
Shall be revealed unto the eyes of men.'

No. 6
The Rose Miraculous[1]
PREFACE TO THE METRICAL VERSION

The story of the coming of Joseph of Arimathea to Britain bringing with him the Blood of Christ, and of his founding of the first Christian Church at Glaston is a most ancient and venerated tradition, securely established. In the monastery, the story told was that Joseph brought with him the Blood and Sweat of our Lord in two little silver cruets, and that these were buried with him in the consecrated ground. The mystery of the Sangreal and its spiritual virtues underlie all the legends of the Holy Grail in its Christian form.

The story here presented is found for the first time as a consecutive and coherent narrative in the script received through the hand of H. T. S., a lady well known as a very perfect channel for these involuntary writings. The script was received in my presence and was obtained at a uniform rate of some 2,200 words per hour. The substance of the narrative was unknown to her and equally unfamiliar to myself, since neither of us had been students of this branch of Glastonbury lore or of the Romance writings of the early mediaevel period.

No claim is made for the authenticity of the story here given. It is submitted as literature, and the judgement of the literary critic is asked for on its intrinsic character alone. It has been greatly condensed, and emphasis given to the essential features of the story, but in faithful adherence to the original. The final verdict to be passed upon such a tale will depend upon the extent to which scholarly analysis may prove its accordance with what is most fundamental in the great cycle of 'Grail' literature, and what is most probably historically in the traditions of the mission of Joseph. I have put it into metrical form, as this was strongly suggested by the rhythmic flow of the original prose, which in some passages actually falls into pentameters.

FREDERICK BLIGH BOND
London, October 1924

---

[1] Originally published as No. 6 of *The Glastonbury Scripts* (Privately published, Glastonbury, 1924).

The Story of the Sangreal

PART I

*Relating how Josephus preserved the Blood of Christ
and carried it with him in his bosom
to Aix in Provence.*

I

When that Our Lord upon that Tree did hang,
And from His side, the sacred Stream did pour;
JOSEPHUS, he that gave His Body rest
In his own tomb, did from that Body take
Within a cup of wood, that stream of Blood:
And, with it mingled, was the Sweat that ran
Down from the Christ in His great Agony.

II

With this most precious Stream the Cup was filled.
Josephus sealed it safely, and with care
Within a Shrine of silver and of gold
Places he that Cup of wood that did contain
The Holiest of all Relics of the Lord.
This by a cunning worker carven was
With pictures of the Miracles of Christ;
The Loaves and Fishes, that the people fed;
The Turning of the Water into Wine;
The Raising from the Tomb of Lazarus;
Symbols and Spirit's threefold dominance
O'er Substance; giving Increase, Change, and Life.

III

JOSEPHUS the shrine within his chamber set;
And, of an evening, would he enter in
Unseen by any, and upon his knees
Would offer prayer and thanks before the Shrine,
Opening her gates to view the treasured Cup.
But, on a day when he had come to pray,
And with full reverence, had unlocked her gates
And looked within, a Wonder met his eyes

IV

For, from her treasure-house inviolate
The Cup had vanished, and a Stone lay there;
A limpid stone, like to a beryl pale;
And thro' her heart there ran a ruddy streak.
Now Joseph, wondering how thieves had come
Into his chamber, ready made to cry
About the house, when unto him a Voice
There came, which said:

V

'JOSEPHUS, HAVE NO FEAR
NOR BE YE TROUBLED: 'TIS THY LORD THAT SPEAKS
THIS STONE THOU SEEST IS MY BLOOD AND SWEAT
TURNED INTO STONE, THAT SO IT SHALL ABIDE
UNTO ALL TIMES, A TOKEN UNTO MAN
OF MY GREAT AGONY: AND SHALL IT BE
A SIGN THAT WILL GIVE FAITH UNTO THE WORLD
AT TIMES WHEN FAITH HAS ALMOST PERISHED.'

VI

Thus was the soul of Joseph comforted,
For, though the simple cup of cedarwood
Had vanished, yet his Treasure still remained
Imperishable to the ends of Time:
And a great joy and thankfulness were his.
Yet, greater was his joy and wonderment
When, as he knelt and prayed before the Stone,
There shone within her heart a rosy fire
That quickened ever to a mighty glow.

VII

And, all around, there breathed a Perfume rare
Fragrant of spices, and of precious balm
And sweetest savour of the Rose in June.
Then spake again to him the Voice of Christ
Saying 'JOSEPHUS, SERVANT OF THE LORD,
TAKE THOU THIS STONE THAT IS MY VERY BLOOD
AND SWEAT THAT FELL IN MY GREAT AGONY:
HOLD THOU THIS STONE, AND BE FOR EVER STRONG
IN FAITH, FOR THUS WILL MUCH BE WORKED BY THEE.

VIII

'WITH THIS GO FORTH AND CONQUER FOR THE FAITH,
FOR LO! THIS JEWEL AS A SWORD SHALL BE
WITHIN THY HAND — THE WHICH CAN NEVER STRIKE
AS WEAPON OF OFFENCE TO HURT OR WOUND,
BUT HEAL THE SICK AND THEM THAT SUFFER WRONG,
AND RECONCILE ITS DOERS UNTO GOOD.'

IX

'AND FOR THIS COSTLY HOUSE THAT THOU HAST BUILT
FOR THIS MY BLOOD, THIS SHALT THOU SELL AND TAKE
THE GOLD THAT THOU RECEIVEST AND GO FORTH
UNTO A PLACE I HAVE APPOINTED THEE
FAR OFF, WHERETO THY FOOTSTEPS SHALL BE LED
THERE SHALT THOU REAR ANEW, TO HOUSE THIS STONE,
A SHRINE WHICH NEVER SHALL OF GOLD BE BUILT,
NOR YET OF SILVER METAL, BUT OF FAITH.
SO SHALL IT NOT BE SUBJECT TO DECAY,
BUT, BEING BUILT OF FAITH, SHALL AYE ENDURE.'

X

Many a prayer JOSEPHUS offered up,
Asking that guidance might be given him
As to that Land where he should build this Shrine;
And always did the self-same answer come:—
'MY TEMPLE IN A COUNTRY SHALL BE REARED
WHERE BLOOD-STREAMS FROM THE INNOCENT DO FLOW
AS DOTH THE JORDAN'S STREAM THRO' JUDAH'S LAND.'
No more: so must Josephus seek a land
Where cruel brethren usage should prevail,
Claiming a heavy toll in human blood.

XI

Now Joseph, after that his shrine was sold,
Did wrap that sacred Stone within a cloth
And bear it in the bosom of his robe.
And ever since that Miracle, his zeal
Was much enkindled in his Master's cause;
So that he preached the Gospel openly
And with much fervour, in the market-place.

XII

Now, at this time, the priesthood were alarmed
To find this teaching had not died with Christ;
For its adherents grew and multiplied.
Thus gave they letters from the Synagogue
To agents bid to persecute the Church;
And Joseph, deemed by them a dangerous man,
Was stripped of his possessions and was cast
Into a prison cell; there to remain
For well-nigh half a year, until his friends
Counselled with men in high authority
To set him free: to which they gave consent
On one condition: that he leave the land
And never more return:

XIII

And, since his mind
On a far journey was already bent,
He was made free to travel where he would,
And gather such possessions as were his
Finding a guardian for his infant son
With brethren who to Gaul were journeying.
For now the Church had fall'n on evil days
And those that held the Faith were scattered far
To distant lands to find a resting-place
Where they might preach the Gospel of the Christ
To those by cruel heathen faiths oppressed.

XIV

So Joseph made him ready to depart;
Bartered his goods and settled his affairs;
Full joyful he, that now the time was come
When he might bring the Word to heathen lands.
Some jewels he secured within his robe.
But that MOST PRECIOUS JEWEL of them all
Was tied within a cloth, and held secure
From misadventure or from robbery.
Well that Josephus to another's hand
His more material treasure did confide:
For nigh unto the shore of Cyprus' isle
His boat was wrecked, and he, half drowning, saved
By the prompt hand of some poor fisherman.

XV

Now by another vessel journeyed he
To the Cyrenian coast, and thence to Crete;
And onwards, past the isle of Sicily
Unto a towered harbour on the coast
Nigh to Massilia's city; where he found
Lazarus, he whom Jesus from the tomb
Had raised; with Mary, she whom Jesus loved
And who His feet anointed with the balm.

XVI

Here too was Sarah, sister of the one
Whom ye call Peter. To the Faith she came
After that Christ had died upon the Cross
And here, Josephus found again his boy;
With him a faithful Nubian serving-man
Who to his household long had been attached,
Nor would from young Josephus parted be;
So dearly did he love his infant charge.

XVII

And now Josephus made the town of Aix
The head and centre of his mission work,
And here became the Father of the band
That, to a people partly civilized
By Roman culture — in an earlier day
When Rome was stronger — brought the light of Christ.

XVIII

This was a generous and kindly folk
Who, since the Roman order was withdrawn,
Were slipping back into barbarian ways
And relics of a bloody primal faith
That yet had grown less stern with lapse of time.
And thus their mind was lent to Christian love
With greater ease, for that the seeds of Love
And Brotherhood in them had taken root.
Hence did the mission flourish in Provence
And spread from thence throughout the land of Gaul.

XIX

Now Joseph travelled much from place to place,
And, as he journeyed thro' the countryside,
Heard he the rumour of a holy man
Who healed the people and did miracles:
Neither a Roman nor a Druid he;
Or so they said; and Joseph fain would know.

XX

And thus, one day, upon a river bank
Saw he this man, amid a multitude,
Administering the baptismal Rite
As John had done within the wilderness;
And this was Philip of the Holy Twelve;
One that had been a carpenter by trade,
And a most true disciple of the Lord.
Now at this meeting both were filled with joy.
And with him Joseph many days did dwell.

XXI

But of a second PHILIP we would speak;
He whom the Churchmen call 'Evangelist'
This, a young man of Grecian parentage
Son of a lawyer in Jerusalem
Who unto Jesus' teachings had been drawn —
Though not a close disciple of the Christ —
But who, thro' love of all things beautiful
Became a bondsman of that Higher Love,
Ev'n of the Spirit that doth lie within
All that hath Beauty: so he followed Christ.

XXII

Now, when the Church was scattered, Philip went
Into Samaria, where he did baptize
And minister with apostolic power.
Later, to Egypt went he; then to Greece;
And afterwards to northern Africa;
Then unto Spain awhile. But he was led
To cross the mountain barrier into Gaul
For Philip was obedient to a Voice
That led him onward to a certain field
Unknown to him, but ever to the North.

XXIII

And thus to Joseph's mission did he come
With an Egyptian convert, later known
By his baptismal name, NATHANAEL.
Now one Tobias, meeting him, did tell
Of Christian fugitives from Judah's land
That in the town of Aix assembled were
And housed in a poor quarter of the town
'And for all these,' said he, 'a home is found
By one rich man, the Father of the band.'

XXIV

And thus did Philip with Josephus meet
For he it was who for the brethren cared
So Philip took his place among the band
And with Josephus did he tarry long
Working among the toilers of the vines
Upon the hills around; and here the Word
Found ready echo in the hearts of those
Who but an outworn heathen faith possessed.

XXV

And so the time passed by, till, on a day,
After the company had met for prayer
Philip to Joseph for good counsel went.
Right willingly the people did receive
The Gospel message; yet, to Philip's mind,
Somewhat too readily the harvest sprang,
As from a seed, that on a shallow soil
Is sown and — quickly grown — as quickly dies
So minded he his Master's parable:
And how the Word might take a deeper root
And fix itself more firmly in the soil
Unceasingly he pondered day by day.

XXVI

So to Josephus he the question brought
As to what sign or symbol might be found;
What token, patent to the eye or mind,
To hold the people in their new belief
By impress on the sense or memory.
For Philip knew that Joseph with him brought
From Judah, certain pieces of that Tree
On which the Lord did hang: and so he thought
That, if those precious fragments in their midst
Were set, this simple people, seeing them —
Not worshipping — might well by these be moved
To deeper love and worship for the Christ.

XXVII

So Joseph shewed him pieces of that Tree
The which to handle, Philip could not bear,
But, on his knees, in awe and wonder sank
Before that symbol of the Agony.
But, as he knelt, Josephus set his hand
On Philip's head, and whispered in his ear:
'PHILIP, another Treasure have I here!
A Treasure greater far; concealed well
Within my robe: and lo! I shew it thee.'

XXVIII

As Joseph spake, so Philip turned his head
And gazed into his Father's eyes, which glowed
As with a fire, while, from his bosom out
Drew he a linen napkin, knotted close.
Josephus gently pulled the knots apart,
And there, upon the cloth, did lie a Stone
Like a pale beryl, of a pearly white;
Yet not a beryl: for, within her heart
Imbedded deep, a line of red was seen.

XXIX

And Philip unto Joseph raised his eyes
Asking him, wondering, what this Stone might be?
'My Son,' said Joseph, 'List ye while I tell
The great and mystic wonder of this Stone.
'Tis the pure Blood of Christ our Lord Who hung
Upon the Cross in His great Agony!
For I did take, within a wooden Cup
The sacred stream which from His side did flow:
Thus, in that vessel, most securely sealed,
Held I the Holiest Relic in the world.'

XXX

And here, the Grecian mind of Philip spake
Probing the tale with intellectual doubt.
'This be a Stone, and not the Blood of Christ!'
Then to him Joseph: 'List ye well, my Son:
Ye have a heart that is not ready yet
As garden ground, to bear the Rose of Faith;
Yet here I shew a marvel unto ye!'

XXXI

'I, in a shrine, that Cup of wood did place
Concealed from all: and, when the evening came,
Entered I in my chamber and gave prayer
And thanks before the shrine, op'ning her gates.
But lo! upon a day when I had come
To pray, and when her doors were opened
The Cup had vanished, and this Stone lay there.'

XXXII

'And I, Josephus, marvelling how thieves
Had come unto my chamber, ready made
To cry about the house my woeful loss.
But unto me there came a Voice, which spake:
'THIS IS THE VERY BLOOD OF CHRIST THY LORD
TURNED INTO STONE: THAT SO, IT MAY ABIDE
AS SYMBOL UNTO MAN UNTO ALL TIME
OF MY GREAT AGONY FOR MAN ENDURED
UPON THE CROSS. THIS SHALL A TOKEN BE
THAT SHALL GIVE FAITH AGAIN UNTO THE WORLD
AT TIMES WHEN FAITH HATH ALMOST PERISHED'

XXXIII

So spake Josephus: Philip bowed his face
Before the Wonder, and his heart was moved
For the first time with that true inward Faith
Which, for her counsel, doth not reason seek.
And thus, in him, the Miracle was wrought
Which, to the doubting heart of Lazarus
Had brought conviction at an earlier day.

XXXIV

Only to Philip and to Lazarus
Had this great Treasure been by Joseph shewn;
And this, they held a blessing most supreme:
For, from the Stone, an Incense did exhale,
Like to the scented breath of garden blooms
Sighing good-night unto the Lord of Day:
Odour of precious balm and costly spice,
Filling the chamber with its redolence.

XXXV

And, as the roseate Glow, and Fragrance rare
Grew on the outward sense, so, in the heart
Of Philip, bloomed the Very Rose of Faith;
And he, a child of the Philosophies,
Given to words, and weighing this and that,
Now knew the marvel of a perfect Faith
That answered every question of the Mind
With the more perfect Knowledge of the Heart.

PART II
The Call to Britain

Now for awhile shall Philip tell the tale
For unto him the message first was brought
That called Josephus unto Anglia.

XXXVI

WELL MAY YE ASK, why, when we rested here
So richly blest within this golden land
Where many people listened to the Word
And the faith strengthened, should we lay aside
All this rich harvest, and begin again
To sow the seed on rough unfertile soil
In a cold island, girt about with seas,
Where naught but hardship could our portion be?

XXXVII

List ye to me, and I will tell the tale;
And, for the first time, shall the truth be known
How that the Words of our most blessed Christ
Within your land were planted, and took root.

XXXVIII

Joseph my Father, Lazarus, and I
With all our company, right earnest were
In furtherance of our mission in Provence;
Having no other thought. And I had dreams
Of a great church that should be founded there:
Should spread her wings across the whole wide world.
So, Brother, can ye know how firm we stood
In this, the settled centre of our work.
Yet shall I tell ye how our purpose shook,
And how we wavered, and resolved to dare
That which seemed dangerous; and, to some, unwise.

XXXIX

It came about that, on a certain day.
When in the vineyards I had tarried late
Upon my ministry, that one there came
Who said: 'My Father did desire my speech
With one that to our mission had arrived
But could not speak our language,' Joseph thought
This stranger bore a message unto us
Of some great import: yet was no one there
Could find the words to make his meaning plain.

XI

I, after that this messenger had gone,
Lingered awhile: and then I turned to go
Adown the hill, and toward the city gate:
And lo! an omen: for, within my heart
A silent Voice cried to those hills: 'FAREWELL.'
And all my purpose — all my golden dream —
Was withered in my heart: and, in its stead,
There came one new and stern that, like a thorn,
Pierced through my mind, and wounded me so sore
That all my joy was smitten to the dust.

XLI

'THORN?' say I: 'Nay! A Sword of severance
That from my loved companions sundered me
And, by some tie mysterious and new,
Drew me afar, to regions yet unknown.'

XLII

Now, coming home, found I my Father there
And, in the room, a man of aspect strange.
Rugged was he, and wild: his garments made
From skins of beasts, and girt with little care;
Whilst, on his head, the hairs did stand upright
As stalks of corn. Vainly he strove to speak
With gestures; and, when words at length did come,
Forth from his tongue there poured a stream of sound
Uncouth, and void of meaning to the ear.

XLIII

Unto me, Philip, thus Josephus spake:
'Surely this is a messenger of God!
Coming, like John, that, in the wilderness
Did of the Spirit and the Water give
Baptismal rite. Must we not care for him
So that, by gentleness, we may in time
Learn from his lips those things he needs must say?'

XLIV

We gave the stranger rest and nourishment,
And, in the evening, when we knelt to prayer,
Came he with me and, falling on his knees
Lowly he bent his forehead on the ground.
And, as the days passed by, Nathanael
Had him in charge, and gave to him the name
JOHANNES, which he answered, as a dog
Answ'reth his master's call: and so, in time,
Nathanael gave him words wherewith to speak;
And thus, at length, we knew his tragic tale.

XLV

We learned that he had come across the seas,
Fleeing in horror from the savage rites
That stained the ancient faith of Britain's Isle.
For lo! her faith was not the faith of Gaul;
But one that claimed a sacrifice of blood
From ev'ry family; so that, of its best,
The native strength and beauty of the race
Was drained away upon the Altar-Stone.

XLVI

Youths in their prime, and children yet unborn
Became an off'ring to the Lady Moon,
The cruel consort of the Sun, their God.
And ever, when the Orb of Night rode high
At fulness, in a heaven free from cloud,
A tortured victim, shrieking, would she claim;
Demanding music with her thirsty meal.

XLVII

And thus the pains the people had endured
Had made their country barren of all joy,
And terror held them; so they feared their gods
And scarce endured to live, yet feared to die
Since, in the teaching of their Druid priests,
Yet greater miseries awaited them
When on the other side of death they came.

XLVIII

Mark ye: This was the Kingdom of the Priest.
No King, in any kingdom of the world
Held sway as did the priests of Britain's Isle.
These had the power to rule the lives of men;
Moulding the destinies of that dark isle.
RULE was the Curse that with the Druids dwelt!
The faith they held was in One Cruel God
Who had the power to ruin, and to slay;
To torture any who might shake the faith;
Not in Himself, but in his Druid Priests!

XLIX

Ye know how, in their Altars, and their Shrines,
Lyeth the strength of pond'rous slabs of stone
That none may hear or carry. Even these
Do not convey a symbol of the strength
That lay in Britain's priesthood of that time!

L

I, Philip pondering upon these things,
Bore in my mind an ever-growing thought
That here, in truth, a race of martyrs was
Who, for their Faith, would freely sacrifice
The choicest treasure of their earthly life,
Giving themselves to God: the only God
Who to their darkened vision stood revealed:
To whom they sacrificed, without reward,
Their sustenance, their children, and their homes,
Obedient to the call of piety!

LI

'IF THEN,' thought I, 'UNTO A CRUEL GOD
THIS NOBLE PEOPLE WILLING MARTYRS BE:
HOW SHOULD THEY NOT ADORE A GOD OF LOVE
AND KNOW THE VIRTUE OF THAT SACRIFICE
MADE BY HIS SON MOST DEAR, UPON THE CROSS?'

LII

And thus I felt, within my heart, a call
To go to Johan's most distressful isle
And there, upon a Rock, to build a Church
Which should endure unto the ends of Time.
Thus did a picture in my mind take shape
Of a great Church within that Island built
Upon the Rock of Faith and Sacrifice.

LIII

In secret held I this: and when I saw
That savage man grow daily full of grace
I knew I had not erred in my mind.
As a tamed beast was he: a Lion brought
Into the sheepfold: gentle he became
And all the brethren loved him; for his love
Was upon all bestowed: and in the Faith
Grew he more perfect under Joseph's care.

LIV

Upon a day, when we in converse sat,
Unto my Father felt I moved to speak:
So poured I forth the story of my dreams
And of the Revelation made to me
Concerning Britain and her destined Church.
I told him that I had in mind the thought:
'That if upon a Nation I could come
Which close was to the state of Primal Man;
There could we build a Temple to the Christ
That on a Rock enduring should be fixed.'

LV

For look ye, Brother, how it was in Gaul.
There, graven deep, the Faith of ancient times,
As in my land of Greece, had gentler grown
With passing years: and, though it cruel were
In contrast with the Teachings of the Christ,
Yet 'brutal' could it not in truth be called,
Nor yet a bestial philosophy.

LVI

Now, in such hands, the teachings of the Christ
Could nor strike deepest roots; because the land
Already, in a measure, had been tilled,
And so prepared for easy harvesting —
As of a summer crop, the which doth strike
Only in surface layers of the soul,
And must again be planted, year by year.

LVII

'But if,' thought I, 'upon a barren rock
Be sown the seed of some great sturdy Tree:
And if that Rock for planting be prepared
Because the land is spoiled, and torn apart,
And shattered to its deeps by ruthless hands;
So shall the seed take root, and there remain
Firm in the soil, unheeding winter's blasts,
And drawing strength and moisture, year by year,
Until a Tree shall grow, whose kingly height
Shall shadow all the land: and, 'neath his shade
All Life shall find protection; whilst his fruit
For all that lives shall nourishment provide.'

LVIII

So spake I to Josephus, and his heart
Was quick enkindled with a zealous fire.
'PHILIP,' quoth he, 'I know thou speakest Truth:
For, hark ye, what our dear Lord's Voice did say
When that the Treasure first to me was given,
And I had prayed that guidance might be sent
To mark that Land where I should build my Shrine,
For always did the self-same answer come:
MY TEMPLE IN A COUNTRY SHALL BE REARED
WHERE BLOOD—STREAMS FROM THE INNOCENT DO FLOW
AS DOTH THE JORDAN STREAM THRO' JUDAH'S LAND.'

Figure 20: 'The Abbot's Kitchen at Glastonbury Abbey'

LIX

Thus found I Joseph one with me in mind;
And oft we pondered on this enterprise
Debating this and that: When should we start?
And whom upon that journey should we take?
Discussing all the dangers of the road
And means of travel: How to find a ship
To carry us across the Northern Sea;
And who should lead the band. To this I said
That my good Father must the Pilot be,
And I should follow second in command.

LX

Now to myself and to Nathanael
(With Joseph making three), we added first
Eight further brethren to companion us;
Perfect in body; sound of ear and eye;
And none too young, nor much advanced in years.
My Father was the eldest of the band,
For he, full six-and-forty years had seen
When Christ did suffer death upon the Cross;
And now, another fourteen years had sped.
Thus to his sixtieth year had Joseph come;
While I but two-and-thirty years had known.

LXI

Each of our eight companions did we mark
For some especial quality of Use,
Of Training, or of Nature's aptitude:

LXII

One that could tell the stars, and find the road:
One that could build us shelters: one that could
By signs and gestures comprehension give
Of our chief needs to foreigners in tongue:
One that could fashion implements: and one
Well skilled in the preparing of our meat:
One whose broad shoulders any weight could bear:
One that by reason and good fellowship
Might smooth the rubs that ever will arise
Among a band of men on toilsome road.

LXIII

So was it planned, and finally resolved
That in the mellow harvest of the year,
Upon that day which ye do Friday call —
The day that Christ upon the Tree did hang —
We should leave Aix, and travel to the North
By Rhonus' stream, till, striking to the west,
The placid Liger thence should be our guide
Until the western Ocean meet our view.

LXIV

Thus, to the women and the brethren all,
Comrades beloved, and fellow-labourers
In Christ's own harvest-field, we bid 'FAREWELL!'
For ever! And our human hearts were stirred
By an emotion sad, ineffable;
Solemn and full of awe: for well we knew
That never should we see their face again.

LXV

And yet, with all its sadness, strangely sweet
Was this our parting: for the Comforter
Had crept into our hearts and gladdened them
With subtle whispers of the Infinite
As Spirit speaks to spirit — seems to say:
'There is no parting unto them that have
Their habitation in Eternity:
The Spirit is not subject unto Time,
And naught can from this Knowledge sever those
Whose Names are written in the Book of Life.'

LXVI

And now, unto the company of eight,
Two more were added, making Ten in all:
These, with myself and with Nathanael
Making the symbol of the Holy Twelve
That clustered round the Christ: so gathered we
Around our Father, who that Sacred Blood
Bore in his bosom as the Sign of Christ.

LXVII

And, of the twain that came into our band
One was the lad JOSEPHUS, Joseph's son
Whose earnest pleadings could not be denied.
The other was his Nubian serving-man
That had not come into the faith of Christ,
Yet from his master would not parted be.

LXVIII

So journeyed we by old Avenio
VINI, the people called her in our day —
Thence thro' Valancia, to Leoni,
Set in a district scoured by lawless bands
That sore beset our band and wounded two
Stealing the greater portion of our pack.
So, westward, till we touched the northern bank
Of the broad Liger, sometimes Lois called,
And followed this until at last we came
Unto the busy mart of OLEAN,
Set among dreaming forests, glamorous
And haunted by the spirits of the glade.

LXIX

In OLEAN we rested many days
And were refreshed in body and in mind,
For o'er the place a wondrous Peace doth brood
That lulls the spirit to a calm repose.
Fain would we linger, but the call arose
And we must journey on: our preachings fell
On willing ears, but not on willing minds,
For her most kindly people wedded were
To strange beliefs: and thus the seed we sowed
Could bear no fruit, nor even blossom here!

LXX

Next to the port of NANTI we arrived,
And first upon her outskirts, did we see
Circles of massive stones, by Druids built
In days long past, when their religion held
Its pristine vigour and simplicity.
Rootless these Circles: set on barren hills
As Temples for the worship of the Sun.

LXXI

In NANTI did we meet TIMONEUS,
A Greek, who partly held the Grecian faith,
And partly was he unto Jesus drawn.
Having in Athens heard the Word of Christ
From brethren who had tarried in that land.
This man with Joseph fell to argument,
And, with his own, the teachings would compare
Of Joseph, and would tear them into shreds,
Weaving them once again in patterns new,
Agreeing with his own philosophy.

LXXII

And to some purpose: for Timoneus said:
'It seemeth unto me that this your Faith,
Which doth accredit all that is supreme
In Man and Man's achievement unto LOVE,
Must have a meaning truer and more deep
Than that of the religion of the Greek:
For there is worshipped BEAUTY; and, in truth
Is she but the Habiliment of LOVE.'

LXXIII

So Joseph, marking him of earnest mind
And wishing to assist him in the Faith,
Did beg the brethren present to retire:
And to Timoneus spake he of that Stone,
Who, listening to my Father with a smile
That not of mockery was, but gentle doubt
And kindly questioning of that great faith
That in Josephus dwelt, did harken well
The while the tale was told.

LXXIV

Then Joseph drew
From out his robe the precious Gem, and laid
The same upon a table near at hand:
Sank on his knees, and bade us follow him
And straight, a wondrous odour filled the room
As of a shop of one that spices sold;
And, with these mingled all the perfume sweet
That breathes from roses on a day in June.

LXXV

Still did Timoneus question in his mind,
Asking Josephus 'If the Stone had been
Placed in some chamber where such spices lay?'
But, as he spake the words,the Holy Gem
Seemed suddenly to burst into a fire!
Timoneus was the first to see the Light
And thus a token unto him was given
The which did set his faith on firmer ground.

LXXVI

Mark ye! This precious Stone to none was shewn
But them within whose mind a miracle
Might kindle Faith, and kill the power of Doubt.
There was no need for those that knew the Christ
To see that Sacred Stone: the Voice from Heaven
Had warned my Father he should shew the Blood
To none but them whose faith might need a crutch.
Thus to me, Philip, and Timoneus,
Both being of doubting mind, was she put forth
That, through those Signs, Faith in our hearts might grow
And for our Mission make us truly fit.

LXXVII

'Therefore,' say I, 'Despise not Miracle
Nor think it but a weakness of the mind
That men should wonder: for, in wondering
They reach the Kingdom. I would have ye know
That Faith is but the Wonder of the Mind
A Revelation of Reality.
The mind that hath not Wonder, hath not God;
For it hath lost the Pearl of greatest price
The Substance of those Things for which we hope,
The Evidence of Things Invisible
That lie behind these Images of Time.'

PART III
*Of the death of Job: and the passage of the seas
to Britain.*

LXXVIII

By the bleak coast-line of Armorica
Where ever moans a grey and sobbing sea,
Josephus and his band pursued their path.
And now was come the autumn of the year,
Whose damp and chill brought aching of the bones,
And a strange malady that caught the breath
And made their pilgrimage a misery.
And one poor brother, Job, was lost to them:
One that had greatly holped them from the first,
Both by his faith as simple as a child,
And by his humble service, which was that
Concerned with the preparing of their food.
All night he struggled to retain his breath,
And in the early morn, exhausted, died.

LXXIX

Now Joseph laid his hand upon his head
In sign of blessing, speaking words of Christ,
And, calling all the band of brethren round,
He, for the first time, shewed them the stone
Holding it high, and said to them: 'My Sons,
Far have we journeyed: much have we endured;
And far again we needs must journey yet.
Look ye to Christ, for with us bear we here
His Holy Blood, contained within this Stone.
Grieve not for him who now from us hath passed;
For here ye have a Symbol and a Sign
That Death is but the rending of a Veil;
The casting of an earthly Robe outworn.
So is your Brother with ye even now.'

LXXX

Thus Joseph spake, obedient to a Voice
That, on the night before, communed with him
While he was watching by the dying man.
For he, when all the others had withdrawn
Had laid that Stone upon the head of JOB
And prayed to Christ for his recovery:
And lo! the Voice that spake to him had said:
'JOSEPH, PUT BACK THE STONE, FOR IT CAN MAKE
NO HOLPING FOR THE MAN THAT LYETH HERE:
FOR THIS MAN'S TIME IS COME; HIS PERFECT FAITH
AND LOVE HAVE MADE HIM READY TO RETURN
UNTO HIS LORD. THEREFORE I BID YE PLACE
THE SACRED STONE AGAIN WITHIN YOUR ROBE.

LXXXI

'AND, WHEN THE MORN IS COME, AND THIS PURE SOUL
HATH RISEN FROM HIS TOMB OF MORTAL FLESH
THEN SHEW THE STONE TO ALL THAT STAND AROUND:
FOR THEY WILL BE MUCH FEARED IN THEIR HEARTS
AT SEEING, THIS THEIR BROTHER LYING DEAD
UPON THE GROUND: SO GIVE YE STRENGTH TO THEM
BY SHEWING OF THE STONE.' And further yet
The Voice said unto JOSEPH: 'IF THEY FAIL,
AND DO NOT CARRY SURETY IN THEIR HEARTS
SHEW IT AGAIN: FOR, AT THIS SECOND TIME
A LIGHT FROM OUT ITS DEEP SHALL SHINE, AND ALL
THE FRAGRANCE OF THE ROSE SHALL POUR AROUND
UPON THIS BARREN SHORE. THIS MUST YE DO
WHEN THE HOUR COMETH FOR THE BURYING
OF THAT STARK BODY LYING ON THE GROUND.'

LXXXII

Of these instructions Philip only knew;
For he with Joseph had had argument
As was his ancient wont, being predisposed
To questionings that ever would arise
In spite of faith: so, turning to the band
Who silent stood, chilled by the morning air,
They sate to meat with sadness in their hearts,
And, seated there, their Father spake to them.

LXXXIII

'My Sons,' spake he, 'we shall commit the dust
Of this our brother, not to the hard earth
But to the shifting sands; that, in good time,
His body to the waters may be borne.
So dig ye deep a grave beside the marge,
And, having wrapped him in a seemly cloth,
Shall we, with words of comfort and of hope,
Commit him to his sleep; and I on Christ
Shall call — not help for him that is with Christ,
But help for us that work to build His Church.
This must ye know: Death no misfortune is:
Only the passing to a fuller life:
While, here on earth, we toil because our days
Are not accomplished, and we have not reached
That state in which we may approach our Lord.
We wait His pleasure, and redeem the time
In constant service, looking for the joy
Of His acceptance. So we take the death
Of this our Brother as for him a joy.'

LXXXIV

Thus saying, singled he four brethren out
All sad of face: no brightness in their eyes,
But rather, sullen in obedience
To Joseph's will: so, having dug the hole,
And wrapped their brother's body in a cloth,
They laid him in the sand. And Joseph then
Spake once again, before the hole was filled,
Those words of comfort which had come from Christ.
And finishing, from out his robe once more
Drew he the Stone. 'This,' said he, 'is the Blood
That flowed from Him, our Lord, upon the Tree;
So let us take it as a symbol bright,
That those who were His servants now are cleansed
From all the sins for which His Blood hath paid.
The Agony enclosed in this clear stone
Hath paid the price for his who prone doth lie:
And, of his freedom, lo! the Stone shall speak.

LXXXV

Ev'n as he spake, there rose from all a cry!
For there, upon his hands, the Stone did glow,
As with a ruddy fire: and, at this sign,
Their hearts with wonder and with joy were filled,
'Fall ye upon your knees!' Josephus said;
And, they obeying him, upon his word
Came from the stone the perfume of the Rose;
And all the air, on this most barren shore,
Was as a garden in the month of June,
There lay our Brother, shrouded in his tomb;
And right above his head, in Joseph's hand,
There glowed the Blood of Christ, with rosy light
And fragrance rare, that, spreading all around,
Did sanctify the place with holy power
Giving them back their faith and hope again.
So they proceeded joyful on their way,
Never again despondency to know.

LXXXVI

And so they made the passage perilous
Of that wide strait that doth divide the lands.
Four days they laboured on the tossing seas,
Taking the oars within a merchant's boat
Until at last they made the Cornish coast,
Where the great rock of Ictis jutteth out
Encircled by the waters: and from thence
Westward, then north, along a barren shore
In poverty and hunger made their way
Until, at last, provision for their needs
Was by a band of miners offered them
In barter for the labour of their hands.
So for a season, tinmen they became;
And thus, the story that is handed down
No legend is, but warranted by truth.

LXXXVII

Like to the Urim of the Jewish priests
The Stone had shewn them, with her rosy glow,
The way to travel: yet their destined home
Until they landed safe on Britain's shores,
Had never been revealed. But, on that night,
When they were sheltered in a little cove
That saw the roll of the Atlantic sea,
Philip a vision had. Before his eyes
Saw he the picture of a little plain;
Well-watered and full of gentle grass
Full sweet to look on: wholesome for a home.
Around him, in a circle, little hills,
Like to the circles that the Druids build,
Did stand: and in his dream, on one of these,
Stood he, and gazed beneath him to the vale.
There he described a host or armed men
Falling on all who passed, and casting them
Unto the ground. Then said he to himself:
'That army must be scattered; for these folk
Are slain; and for no trespass of their own,
But for the pleasure of the men who stay.'

LXXXVIII

So, in his dream, he travelled down the hill
And to the valley came, with full intent
To scatter all that host: and then a voice
Said to him: 'Philip, see, thou art but one,
And these be many hundreds: do not fear,
But go ye forth, O! servant of the Lord,
And slay these hordes who pillage and who rape
'Those that be innocent.' So sprang he down
To meet the host, and laid about him well
With but a goodly staff. But this great host
Was furnished with swords, the blades of which
Glanced in the sun: yet here his goodly staff
Soon made his mark! for every man he struck
Fell down upon his face; so, in the end,
Stood he alone amid a prostrate host.
And Philip struck his staff into the ground.

LXXXIX

But, as he did this, was a wonder wrought;
For lo! the staff bore leaves, and quickly grew
And bloomed into a tree, with kindly shade
That sheltered all around: and growing yet,
Greater and greater he became, until
He covered all the land of Anglia;
And, underneath the shadow of his leaves,
Did all her people gather and give praise.

XC

'Twas morn when Philip, starting from his dream,
Rose from his sandy couch within the cave,
To see the dawn break o'er the cold grey sea.
And, having still his vision clear in mind,
Yet knowing naught of the diviner's power,
Could he not tell the meaning of his dream;
Nor did he wish to break his Father's sleep.
And so he waited for an hour or more,
While the sun's rays dissolved the mists of morn
And Ocean's ripples ever clearer grew.

XCI

Now, close behind, heard he his Father's voice,
And turning, saw him seated on his couch,
And all his face was lightened with a smile
That wondrous seemed. 'Philip,' quoth he, 'come nigh
Unto my couch.' So Philip turned to him,
Being somewhat anxious for his Father's health
Since ague, and an aching of the bones,
Had seized upon him when the autumn came,
And, on their passage, these had been increased.
But Joseph now took Philip's hand in his,
And pressed it to his robe, and Philip felt
An unaccustomed warmth, as of a fire,
The which dismayed him, and he cried aloud:
'Father, ye have the fever back again!'

XCII

But Joseph smiled again, and Philip sensed
That holy fragrance rise that, thrice before,
Had filled the air with balm: and Joseph drew
The sacred stone again from out his robe.
And there she glowed, full crimson as the rose.
And Philip, kneeling, cried aloud to Christ:
'Is this a sign, dear Lord, that Thou hast sent
To tell me that my Vision is the Truth?
And that the conquest of Thine enemies
By our stout staves — the weapons of Thy Word —
Shall come to pass indeed? And is that Vale
So strait, so narrow, girt with little hills,
The spot, in truth, where we shall build Thine House?'

XCIII

He ceased, and ever redder glowed the Stone
And then she seemed to shoot a roseate ray
Of light into the clouds, intensely bright;
But for a moment: then, with suddenness,
The light was quenched, and all the glow had fled;
As when a lamp, that burneth in a tomb
In which a loved one lies, exhausts his oil
And, in expiring, sudden leaps the flame
From light to darkness: so this mystic Ray
Leapt forth, and left a simple stone once more.

PART IV
Of the Coming of the Company to Avalon

XCIV
Fain would I tell ye of their pilgrimage
And of the many strange and curious things
That Joseph's band encountered on their way:
Meetings with Merlin, or with Druid priest;
Of sojournings in thinly scattered towns:
Or of a certain strange experience
By Druid altar, on a Cornish moor;
But this be not the place: and we must pass
To when the summer, fading to its fall,
Found them upon the Moors Adventurous
Where the dry bulrush, quivering in the brake
Stands sentinel o'er treacherous lanes of green
That suck the footsteps into depths of slime:
Moors of the Somersoettae, fencing in
With mere and fen, the mystic guarded Vale
Towards which their footsteps ever nearer led,
Guided by signals from that holy Stone.
So we return, to find that company
Threading their way across the trackless moors
Low-lying in the heart of Somerset.

XCV
It was the close of a September day
The sunset fading into purple dusk
That the last stream was crossed; the marshy land
Traversed, and left behind: and all the band
Weary and hungered, clomb the little hill
That lay between them and their resting place.
Yet one there was that never felt fatigue;
This one was Joseph. He it was who clomb
First to the summit, coming from the south,
And cried in joy to all that followed him:
'Brothers! The End of all our wanderings!'

XCVI
Think ye of this, my reader, when ye go
Next unto Glaston: think of all the train
Climbing that little hill, and seeing there
That fair green vale, and those well-watered meads
Dusky in evening haze; and knowing this
The place indeed appointed them by Christ;
Their home; the end of all their pilgrimage!

XCVII

Here, on the hilltop, falling on their knees,
They rendered thanks to God. But Joseph stood
Alone among them, gazing on the vale,
Filled with a peace that had no utterance.
And now, he sets his staff into the ground
And, leaning heavily upon it, draws
From out his robe once more that Jewel Rare.
And all his band, knowing full well that now
The final Sign should thus to them be given
That to their place appointed they have come,
Do scarcely dare to look upon the Stone
Lest she should fail to give her rosy Light.
Then Joseph offers up a prayer to Christ
That now, if this their home be, would He give
The final Sign that this indeed were so.

XCVIII

Now ye have heard this wonder many times:
But ever, when the Stone was shewn before,
The Light that entered her shone forth and fled.
But, on this night, she glowed like any rose
And all the light that entered her remained,
Nor left her till the shadows of the night
Had melted in the rising of the sun.

XCIX

When that the Light in Joseph's hand was seen,
He held it high above the kneeling band
Until he drooped his arms for weariness.
Then all the band together placed their staves
As in a ring, their heads together bent,
And thus they made a table for the Stone,
Seated around her, as a Circle formed
Encompassing her light till break of day.

C

And ever and anon, throughout the night,
One of the band would offer up a prayer
For all the air was sanctified around;
Not as with spices only, or perfume
Such as ye find in flowers; but something yet
More precious still; that Incense, which of old
Filled with her fragrance Judah's sacred Fane.
But this more potent was, and yet more sweet
And powerful to overcome the sense;
Soothing all aches; relaxing weary limbs;
So that the brethren, drowsy, laid them down,
Rapt by the perfume in an holy trance.

CI

Such was that wondrous Vigil on the Hill:
A night long after known to Glaston's House,
And called therein 'THE WATCHING OF THE ROSE.'
This Watch they kept, and those that followed them
And they of later years, until such time
As other festivals, and Days of Saints,
With changes in the Rule, did supervene;
And Arthur, with his Queen, being buried there,
The Festival was lost, and men forgot.

CII

Yet may it be that it shall once again
Be honoured, in the fulness of the days:
For they, the Watchers, never shall forget.
They, in the Spirit, brooding o'er the place,
Await the time her glories shall return.
So shall their memories at last find voice
And, speaking to the heart of Holy Church,
Shall gain response. So ye who are attuned
To true conviction that our Master's Will
Through all the ages fails not, but must find
Perfect fulfilment in the scheme of Time,
Pray that the Circle may be joined again,
Making Two Thousand Years as yesterday:
Restoring us the freshness of the Faith.
So may her spiritual Waters flow,
Ev'n as refreshing rain on parched soil.

ENVOI

Lovers of Glaston: Britain's sons and daughters
Think of that evening, when we first beheld her:
Hold ye it sacred: even as we held it:
Keep ye our Vigil: Watch ye by the Rose!

Or on the hilltop; or within your chamber;
That night ye call the Twelfth Night of September;
Like ye with Us, in Memory Eternal,
That night we hold in Recollection True.

When comes that Day on which we kept our Vigil;
Rise ye betimes, in early light of morning;
Hold ye your fast unbroken till the noontide:
Then, like as we did, take your simple meal.

Eat then and drink no more until the evening:
This be in memory of our last day's journey;
Then, with the evening, when the shadows gather
Close after sunset, to your chamber go.

Pray ye to Christ, for welfare of His Chosen:
Pray that the Father's Will may be accomplished:
Pray that the Glory may return to Glaston:
Heart of our Worship: our Jerusalem.

Take ye nor food, nor drink, into your chamber;
But one red Rose, in memory of our Watching:
Just a red rose, full perfect in her flow'ring,
Mindful of us who to Britain brought the ROSE.

Sit ye and look, in stedfast contemplation;
Bow ye and breathe the Incense of her fragrance:
Trace in her thorns, the Nails wherewith they pierced Him
Trace ye His Wounds in the blood-red petals Five.

Pray that the Rose again may be discovered;
Brought from the secret place where She abideth:
Healer of Nations: Faith's Regeneration:
Herald of Kingship, and of Victory.

No. 7
HUGH OF AVALLON[1]
(An Authenticated Script by Philip Lloyd and K. L.)
INTRODUCTORY NOTE

The beautiful script now printed fills in the details of the life and work
of St Hugh, Bishop of Lincoln, of which a sketch only was given in the
study of these historical scripts published in *Psychic Science*, No. VI
(July, 1923), under the title 'Metagnosis'.

For detailed information as to the origin of the script and for a
detailed explanation of the story it conveys, readers may be referred
to that number and also to *The Company of Avalon*, wherein a good
deal is said about Hugh's connection with Glastonbury.

For the benefit of new readers I would briefly state that the writing
was produced jointly by Philip Lloyd and K. L., the right hand of
Philip Lloyd resting on the right hand of K. L. K. L. alone can produce
nothing of this nature and never has up to the present time. In this fact
the dual nature of the mediumship is clearly brought out, and in view
of the quality of the matter produced — its literary and historical
values — the experience would seem almost unique because in this
case neither of the two agents has any knowledge whatever of the
content of the script or of the general historical background of the
tale; also there has never been any professionalism connected with
these writings. The scripts now recorded were produced as follows:

[1] Privately printed pamphlet (Glastonbury, 1925).

the first three parts and the first two paragraphs of the fourth part were written on four successive Mondays, beginning March 5th 1923, between 3 and 4 p.m.. Part I covers fifty-five pages of script and was written continuously with great speed in less than forty-five minutes. The script is written in pencil on quarto sheets, and is similar to the specimen illustrated in the previous record. Part II, given Monday, March 12th 1923, covers sixty-one pages of script, and was written continuously in less than forty-five minutes. Part III, given on Monday, March 19th 1923, covers seventy-three pages of script, and was written continuously in about fifty minutes. The mechanical work of changing the sheets is considerable, and a good deal of energy is expended in the production of the large characters of the writing. This part was so very long that its effect upon both agents was physically exhausting. Mr Lloyd therefore asked that the final part might be divided. The first two paragraphs of Part IV, given Holy Monday, March 26th 1923, covers fifty-one pages of script and were written continuously in forty minutes. The third paragraph of this part, given two days later, covers twenty-eight pages of script, and was written in not more than twenty minutes. The last two paragraphs of this part, given on Easter Even, March 31st 1923, cover twenty-five pages of script and were written in not more than twenty minutes.

FREDERICK. BLIGH BOND
Glastonbury Easter, 1925.

Hugh of Avallon

I

Often in the wild days when the stark Lord of the Normans swept through Northumbria in a cloud of flame, and his crested warriors drave the burly thanes from blazing hall and wasted shire, the island folk longed in vain for the simpler time of the Seven Kingdoms. For now high above the little ham, where rude wains rumbled homeward as the minster bell pealed across the sunset meadow, gloomed the mysterious hold of a Jotun. Square towers, crowned with jagged turrets, rose swart against the sky; bowmen stood at ward upon the sullen battlements; strange banners swayed from the huge gray walls; and the ancient forests that lay beyond, whose Druid oaks once closed around the Roman Eagles, were become the hunting ground of a King who held the life of the dun deer more precious than the life of a vanquished foe. The quiet glades forever rang with the trumpet horns of the hunters and the deep-mouthed baying of the coupled staghounds, while swineherd and woodcutter fled to the pathless wastes. Moreover, since the autumn star shone through a crimson twilight on the broken shield-wall of the Saxons, all men groaned beneath the cruel taxes wrung from every hide of land to swell the Great Horde at Winchester.

Yet despite these ills, the lonely Chieftain of the rueful deeds grimly shepherded the conquered people. No heathen sail suddenly flamed up the tranquil reaches of an inland river, nor did any towered galley, crowded with wailing captives, bring terror to the watchers by the sea. Massive keeps guarded the Western marches and rocky headlands of the Cymri, holding the tameless Bulls of the Mountain at bay upon their desolate moors. And there was peace on the highways of the island kingdom. Because of this, it fell that when the war-worn Conqueror rode no longer to the Witan with his armoured barons, the Sons of the Raven clave to the fierce Red King and once more lifted the battle-axes of Senlac against the strong bows of the Northern earls. Right eagerly did the sturdy yeomen storm the rugged bastions that menaced their wattled farmsteads in the name of Anglelonde's King. But with the ruthless Norman, foe alike to God and man, the pledges sworn in the time of need held but a little while. Evil ways from the Southlands swayed the great Hall of Rufus. Instead of the stern heroes, destroyers of many a plumed host, before whose world-shaking onset nations trembled, long-haired courtiers, clad in the soft webs of Syria, walked by night in pointed shoon, mocking at holy things. Well was it that God's singing arrow loosed the soul of the savage Hunter, to make way for the Aetheling foretold by Merlin. Then the wise dooms of the ancient Bretwaldas were restored. The wild clearings, the woody tuns of the Saxon cynings waxed free and powerful through the craftsmen from over seas. Even though the Prince of Cerdi's line perished on the White Ship of death, even in the dark years of man-slaying that followed the reign of the Lion of Justice, years so full of horror that men cried out, 'Christ and His Saints sleep!' the race of Hengist and the race of Hrolf, Odin descended, grew closer, to battle together for the common weal.

Meanwhile, they of Glaston, remembering the noble hests of Ailnoth, found evil rede under the foreign Turstine, who leagued with the Arch Fiend set French bowmen upon his rebellious monks, until the great Rood bristled with feathered arrows. Now this baleful Abbat did strive to build after the fashion of the Prior of Bec, so that the hairy churls might marvel at long dim aisle and high vaulted roof. But nothing prospered, for there was no heart in the building. Monks used to the simple rule of the olden saints, looked askance on the stately bishops mailed like the Archangel Michael; and the mighty Fortress that shadowed hill or fen, seemed builded more for the glory of a Chapter than better to house the Majesty of the Lord of Heaven. It remained for the good Herlewin to show them how Love could speak through the miracle of silent stone.

II

The company of pilgrims, winding over the steep hills, no longer beheld a rugged Minster of Saxon wood and Roman stone, builded in a time when Caedmon's harp rang high in Hild's wide Feasting Hall. Heavy columns, broad and short; round massive arches that upheld the rude House of God with simple barbaric dignity, had vanished forever. So, like a shadow, perished the glories of Ine. In their stead the nobler work of the Norman Abbats lifted slender pinnacles to the far-off sky above the quiet vale. Here, as through his native forest-alley, the awed herdsman could walk among clustered boles of soaring spreading stone. Between the dim arches that met bough-wise above him, glimmered the veiled shrine of a saint venerable in Aelfred's reign, or the armour-laden tomb of a hero who faced the horsed here upon a bloody heath. And at the end of the long shadowy way, in the heart of the burning gold, hung the Rood that turns man's woe to weal. Though bale followed in the wake of the weak Stephen, Glaston was peaceful enow. That which Herlewin left unfinished, the Abbat of a royal race took in hand. For Henri, one eye on Heaven, one on earth, added to cloister and chapter-house, a moated palace where a Prince of the line of Blois might rest within walls covered with an arras of richly woven woof. Such was the Abbey after the harrowing of the Hunter, well worth a man's perilous riding across the dreary marshes to look upon the vast demense, whose woods and wolds, manors and farmsteads, meres and meadows, fish pools and pastures, vineyards and orchards had been slowly gathered since the Twelve Hides of Arviragus, in the Name of One Who found no place to lay His Head.

Outside the monastery gates, while minstrels sang their hero-deeds, the strong ruthless Chiefs — he of the Mighty Bow with his strange sons, and the fierce Angevin, demon-descended — shapes the boundaries of the hard-won kingdom.. Warring for them and against them moved the mail-sheathed barons, proud and rebellious as the fallen host of Heaven. Now a grim border earl defied the island's Lord; now a mitred bishop plotted to make his temporal Master the thrall of Rome. Stern times were these; and in the bold barons lived again the eagle-plumed jarls of forgotten Thule, little softened by an age in which the prospering gilds brought the world to the fair harbours of Anglelonde. Yet the God more beautiful than Balder still spake to men, not only through an ecstasy of carven stone, but in the lives of His unearthly warriors. Wulfstan of Worcester, the last Saxon saint, fighting for the oppressed, Truth his flaming spear, Faith his bright shield of beaten gold, destroyed the battle-front of a Northern army with these ghostly weapons. Anselm of Aosta, counsellor of kings, braving the wrath of Rufus and the wiles of Henry, conquered through Right alone. And, as in the lusty May Fire Odin once sped the

Norsemen over unknown seas to plunder the rich outlands, now Urban called the champions of Christ to high adventure. Far in the heathen countries the most simple wight could win Paradise, as his barbarous forefather had won Valhalla, by a noble fall beside the Holy Sepulchre. Thus Love raised from the ranks of shaggy hus-carls, the dauntless fyrd unconquered at Senlac, leal until death to the Chieftain, a new knighthood aflame with the spirit of Chivalry.

In these years, when the Sacred Orders also awoke to fresh remembrance of the Dream that gave them birth, Hugh, son of the Sieur of Avallon, dwelt near the woody borders of Savoy. The mild cloisters of the plain could not long cage the tameless spirit of an eagle. Only in mountain solitudes, immense and lone, where a white-robed brotherhood — the hardest of them all — followed a life of savage purity at the foot of the great glistening peaks, could he encompass his desire for God. The gigantic bastions of the pass, bearing ancient forests on their huge flanks; the turrets bannered with wild light; the hollowed domes filled with clanging thunder, haunted the young monk, until the Vision of a mighty Cathedral rose ever before him, a Fabric that mortal workmen were powerless to devise. And as Anselm had beheld the Courts of Heaven beyond the snowy summits, Hugh often saw glowing shapes pass like mist around the rocky towers, or heard a Voice peal as a trumpet-call from the starry ramparts. Now whiles the Burgundian toiled in the wind-swept fastness of the erne, leagues away in the tranquil valley of the Somer-soettas, Guthlac, born of an aetheling, pondered the divine origin of Glaston, thinking in his heart that here in this green isle, as in far Syria, stood a Shrine hallowed by the Death Deeds done on Jerusalem's swart Hill.

III

Although Canterbury voiced the hests of Rome, and Winchester oft crowned the island's kings, neither could exceed the mysterious antiquity of outlying Glaston. Therefore went out much boasting from the monks over the vast processional of pilgrims that sought the massive nave of the Abbey Church on holy days. Ye who look upon the dim ghosts of the olden monasteries would marvel to have seen such flaming colour where is now gray stone. Here were the folk of the countryside in faded stuffs of green and blue and red; the burgesses wrapped by richer mantles; the baron and his followers, home from Palestine, fierce in bright armour and fiery-plumed helm; the perfumed courtier, a seven-day wonder because of the silken baldric and curiously woven webs of the East. Smoking torch and flaming cresset drew a blaze from broidered cope and jewelled pall. And in the flow of waxen tapers, numberless as the stars, burned an Altar of gold and ivory. The alleluias of the black-cowled Brethren thundered down the cloistered aisles, soaring above the shrill treble of the pipes.

Clouds of incense, shaken from silver thuribles, hid the old saints who stared out of the vivid tapestries, and the fair paintings wrought upon the walls. The Mass sung, the throng surged from the Galilee. A crowd of awe-struck cottars gathered around a churl healed by divine miracle at the shrine of Dunstan, to retell in harsh tongues the mysteries of the venerable place. The retinue of the crusader roared by with a squealing of stallions and the heavy tramp of marching men. The burghers loitered reverently beneath the flower-laden Thorn. Then, while the strange band slowly disappeared beyond the savage hills, a feast was spread by the cellarer, and wine-casks opened that the Chapter might make merry together.

This found little favour with the silent Guthlac, feared by the others because of what he had seen on the dark fen. Nor did the proud Fortress, surrounded with broad fiefs, please him who yearned for the time when holy men worshipped God in wattled cells, close to His green cloisters. This was the strange thing that befell him one Lammas agone, as he lay in the wildwood on a night of bright stars. All that day, above the sharp clang of steel on quarried stone, he had heard the unseen harpers of Avallon, until vain seemed man's toil on arch and spandrel. Though weariness dimmed his senses, still haunted by the old tales, the monk became aware that he was alone in a deserted waste from which every trace of the Abbey had vanished. Yet on a hill hard by blossomed a great white thorn-tree, and under its wide boughs rested an outlandish company clothed in shaggy bull-hides. One who seemed the leader sate apart, unheeded by the sleepers. His robe was such as the Magi wear upon a page of finest vellum, and his face, beautiful with the dark beauty of the South, was turned toward the swampy reaches. Following that awed gaze, Guthlac trembled to behold a clear shining flood the solemn wilderness, while a Chieftain, on whose Head gleamed a crest of light, entered the wild valley. No nobler Prince ever moved in the golden haze of a king's Hall, nor Heroes more wondrous than the Host that followed — such Beings as the Druid dreams of when the old Gods trouble him. Swiftly these passed between ferny wood and willowy water, gathering and braiding the slim rushes, until a forest Chapel, a winsome bower for the Queen of Heaven, who made of this sad earth a fragrant close, hid them within its thick-leaved living walls. Then Guthlac saw no more, and the radiance faded from the dewy bracken. Some said this came about through the wizardry of Avalloc, a magic rising from the mists of hell; others believed that the mad monk, crazed by much study, had dreamed of Joseph of Arimathea. None knew whether the vision came of God or devil.

Now not far away, on the border of Saxon Selwood, dwelt a new Order of an austerity so severe that the Angevin thought surely it would atone for all the sins of Anglelonde. Thus, from the lonely peaks of Chartreuse, men had journeyed at his bidding to the gentle meadows of the Somer-soettas. At first naught prospered. The countryfolk, indignant over the loss of their farmsteads, raged so furiously at the Carthusians that the haughty Brothers made ready to depart. Then there came to them in their distress a man of lofty stature, chiefest among the Brotherhood, Hugh of Burgundy, favoured of Henry. He, by reason of sense and humanity, saved what had been lost through pure holiness; and the contended peasants, justly dealt with, began to laud the Monk of the Mountains. Moreover, these praises spread to the monastery in the vale, where Guthlac heard them and longed to rest in the strengthening presence of this Saint. And it fell even as he desired. Partly from curiosity, partly through good will, the monk was made free to seek the strange community across the wolds. It was near the close of day when he passed the huts of wattle beyond the scanty pastures, and reached the Chapel on the edge of the forest. Wild doves cooed in the green twilight of the windless trees; a doe and her fawn stole from the underbrush to drink at a pool aflare with the sun. There was no sound of bell or chanting as Guthlac entered the little Minster. But before the altar, stately as the great Archangel limned on the Cathedral glass, stood a white-robed monk, from whose uplifted hands issued a mystical Flame.

IV

In those days when Hugh set out from the woods of Witham, on the road that led to the island valley encircled by marsh and mere, there was much unrest in Glaston. Not since the time of Turstine had such confusion overwhelmed the Chapter as now under the wild monk of Cluny; and the Brothers, remembering the nobility of Herlewin, the lavish generosity of Henri, and the mild fatherliness of Robert, paid little heed to this false monk sent by the betrayer of Becket, but looked to the Prior alone for guidance. Guthlac, who had sought sage counsel from the Eagle of the Mountain Eyrie, made clear how it was with them in the vale. Hugh heard that the venerable Abbey stood in the midst of vast possessions, a fair body without a head. Moreover, the memory of the ways whereby the last Abbats strove to enrich the ancient House from crypt to turret with wonders of carven stone, failed to prosper the building: for there was no leader with the vision to finish what had been so proudly begun. And Hugh, mindful of the castle on the broad plains of Burgundy where he once dwelt with his father, the Lord of a distant Avallon, hearing the sorry tale had been moved to visit this Cloister in distress. As he rode on his mule through the great Abbey lands and saw the number of men at toil in the mill, at the smithy, in quarry, vineyard and meadow, he bethought him also of the stern grandeur of the wind-swept Monastery of the Snows.

The monks welcomed the Carthusian, already known as the friend
and counsellor of the King, and soon told him the divine legend of the
mysterious founding: how Joseph of Arimathea, who wandered across
the world with the Relics of the Passion, at last found peace on the
Druid isle of Arviragus; and here, as Guthlac dreamed it, he had seen
Christ in the greenwood, even as in that lonely Garden of the South,
and worshipped in a Chapel sweet with ferny bracken, builded by
more than mortal arts. The stranger learned how in after years, when
the heathen host threatened the proud cities of the earth, here,
beneath the Hill of the Archangel, Truth still burned a starry flame in
that sad twilight, ever drawing the tameless hearts of the sea-rovers
captive to the Rood. Hither, too, had come the Cowherd of dark
Fochlad with the Scholars of Eiré, and David of high-gabled Camelot
to find a tomb for the Chieftain of the Dragon Crest. And a greater
thing had shed radiance upon them for a season, a glory surpassing
the shrines of the saints and the princely gifts of the heptarchic kings:
a mystery sung by the harpers, sought in the white deeds of heroes —
the vanished Cup, brought to the Forestland from the deserts of
Palestine. Though miracles found scant favour with Hugh, yet as he
left the halls of the Minster, the holy power of the past stirred within
him. Long time he stood apart to ponder the first little cluster of cells
that braved the wrath of the old Gods in their gloomy solitudes, and
the wooden walls of the war-like thanes that replaced them, stout as
the black galleys, the terror of the coasts. He thought of Ine, who
seized the huge blocks of stone left by the forgotten conquerors, to
raise the round triumphal arch, the barbaric arcades and squat
unbuttressed tower, to mark Christ's Triumph over the wilderness.
Thus the Brethren were to rejoice in one on whom they could rely in
this day of disorder, for the Prior of Witham often rode to them
through the cleft in the hills; and wherever he passed, from cellar to
guest-house, much waste was saved by his firm counsel. But it was
among the masons that he loved to tarry most, winning even Guthlac
to the simple beauty of a design for a Chapel that should hallow and
enshrine the Vision of the Founder.

In the mighty Church of Herlewin, hewn with rude axes, a pile of
massive piers, huge square buttresses, supporting a lengthy nave and
wooden roof unribbed by stone, Hugh saw the flaws that weakened
the masonry of those thick walls builded for eternity. Beside it stood
the stronger fabric of Henri, with new windows formed by the
interlacing of round arcades; and the work of Robert, who completing
the long line of the cloister, added deep-recessed door-ways, raised
the bell-tower, and embellished window, door, and capital with such
a profusion of chiseled ornament, that the whole seemed to the
Burgundian the fanciful creation of the Southland, strange as a
broidered baldric on a brawny Norman warrior. Now while the

workmen began to labour under his direction, either through the
jealousy of Peter or carelessness with the altar lights, flames fiercer
than any kindled from a Danish battle-brand swept the Monastery on
a night of high winds. For miles across the fen blazed the Fortress, a
monstrous torch in the darkness before it fell a blackened ruin. And
none would have known where to turn, save that Hugh heartened the
Chapter, and by his power with the Angevin obtained the services of
Ralph Fitz Stephen to carry on the work begun. Then the Chapel of
Mary rose from a base of rock-like strength, lightened with lofty
pillars. Naught could exceed the grave, austere and delicate, or
pointed arch, narrow rounded window, clustered shaft, and slender
turret, soaring as the soul doth from the earth-born foundation; nor
the splendour of the ceiling, wrought of such living fire as bathes the
thunder-shapen pinnacles. And in a latter time, when Hugh stood at
the altar, a Voice vast as that which echoes down a mountain gorge
sounded through the shadowy aisles, and through the Chalice in his
hand burned an unearthly light. Therefore, many believed with
Guthlac that the Grail, lost centuries ago by selfishness and sin,
appeared once more among the monks of Glastonbury.

With sorrow the countryfolk saw the departure of the Prior of
Witham, at Henry's command to take his seat beside the haughty
bishops of the realm. In forest town and fenland Abbey they listened
eagerly to the traveler's tale of the rugged acts of him to whom the kiss
of a leper was sweeter than the embrace of a king. And the ruler of the
powerful See of Lincoln yearned after these rustic people, ending his
deepest peace in the humble cell on the border of the wood. Through
the years that followed, he remained tameless and free of spirit, frank
yet tactful in speech, instant in kindness, savage against oppression.
And the Angevin found this plain monk in the hair shirt more proud
than any mail-clad prince of mortal kind. Because of the noble deeds
that shone as beacon lights in the troubled world, and because of the
majestic beauty of the Cathedral at which he laboured, often
spreading the mortar with his own hands, his fame went throughout
the kingdom. Here, too, as at Glaston, were miracles. A clerk had seen
an unearthly Shape hover about the lifted Cup, while a Voice like unto
an archangel's rang from the vaulted roof. Concerning this Hugh was
always silent. Yet those close to him, who remembered how he held
the Sacraments above the relics of all the tortured Saints, knew that
for him the Holy Grail was the Heart of Christ.

Ruined arch and broken tower mark in Avallon the close of that
mighty age when conquerors and their fierce men-of-war bowed
reverently to the simple goodness of the Saint through whom God
spake. But Hugh's great Minster still rises from the hill of Lincoln, the
first perfection of pointed art, the first expression of the soul of

Angleland. And as long as the wondrous fabric endures on earth, so long will live the memory of the stalwart Bishop-Builder, whose passing made a stir among the stars.

Some Parallels Between the Script Concerning Hugh of Lincoln and the Records of his Life in Documents

1. SCRIPT. Now, not far away, on the border of Saxon Selwood, dwelt a new Order of an austerity so severe that the Angevin thought surely it would atone for all the sins of Anglelonde. Thus, from the lonely peaks of Chartreuse men had journeyed at his bidding to the gentle meadows of the Somersoattas. At first, naught prospered.

1. HISTORY. Henry II carried out a vow of his to found three abbeys, the third of which he attempted to found at a wild spot at Witham, not far from Selwood Forest on the east side of Somerset, by granting the place to a few Carthusian monks and sending them there to establish their house as best they could. They failed, and Hugh was sent for.

The country folk, indignant over the loss of their farmsteads, raged so furiously at the Carthusians that the haughty Brothers made ready to depart.

The first prior, scared by the threatening aspect of the country people, who looked upon the monks as so many robbers come to spoil them of their goods, fled away in terror. The second, overwhelmed by difficulties, died at his post, and Henry's grand foundation was on the point of collapsing when a certain nobleman of Maurienne suggested to the King that Hugh of Avalon should be sent for.

Then there came to them in their distress a man of lofty stature, chiefest among the Brotherhood, Hugh of Burgundy, favoured of Henry.

He, by reason of sense and humanity, saved what had been lost through pure holiness, and the contented peasants, justly dealt with, began to laud the Monk of the Mountains.

The inhabitants of the place still held the houses and lands which had been granted to the monastery, no provision having been made for them elsewhere. It was Hugh's first care to procure their removal with full compensation for that which they were obliged to give up.

(*Visit of Guthlac*). It was near the close of day when he passed the huts of wattle beyond the scanty pastures, and reached the chapel on the edge of the forest.

When Hugh came to Witham, all was a wretched state. The monks were dwelling in huts of twigs, and that this was not due to their asceticism, but to their sad circumstances is suggested by a passage in the metrical life of Hugh (pp. 436-444).

(*Extract from another script of P. L. referring to Hugh of Lincoln.*)
He was most practical. Ye know he did bite into the bone of Mary Magdalene. Now know that the monks of Fecamp did present him with a sacred relic, a bone of this Saint, and Hugh to the horror of those present, while examining the bone, did take and bite theron. Ye can answer better than we why he did this, but it was from no disrespect.

(*From Perry's 'Hugh of Avalon'*, p. 301, ref. note.) Hugh's biographer Adam gives us many stories of his hunting for relics and eagerness to possess them. As, for instance, when at Fescamp, a bone of St Mary Magdalene. This relic was encased reverentially in silk coverings, and none of the monks had ever seen it bare, but Hugh, getting it into his hands, cut the covering. While the monks were in amazement at this proceeding they were still further horrified at seeing the bishop put the bone into his mouth and bite off a piece of it which he slipped into the hand of his attendant chaplain bidding him carefully preserve it. . . . At Peterborough also he contrived to cut off and secure for himself a tendon of the arm of St Oswald.

(*Note on 'The Augevin'*. Henry II inherited Anjou on the death of his father Geoffrey Plantagenet, son of Fulk of Anjou. His mother, the Empress Matilda, being heiress of Henry I.)

SCRIPT OF PHILIP LLOYD.
March 26 1923.
In the mighty Church of Herlewin, hewn with rude axes, a pile of massive piers, huge square buttresses supporting a lengthy nave, and wooden roof unribbed by stone. Hugh saw the flaws that weakened the masonry of those thick walls builded for eternity. Beside it stood the stronger fabric of Henri, with new windows formed by the interlacing of round arcades; and the

SCRIPT OF SYMON
See Script of December 9 1921
August 30 1921
Abbas Henricus beganne bell towre for to buyld, but more of lodgings for Abbat and Scriptorium: and alle buylded hee — fine buylding and strong. But little of chirche didde hee. Then Abbat Robert, hee some didde, and finished bell towre.
Ditto, October 5 1921
Ecclesia Regis Ini — Turstin hadde it brocan ad occidentem only — and

work of Robert, who, completing the long line of the cloister added deeply recessed doorways, raised the bell tower, and embellished window, door and capital with such a profusion of chiselled ornament that the whole seemed to be Burgundian, the fanciful creation of the Southland, strange as a broidered baldric on a shaggy Norman warrior.

Navis. . . . Herluin Abbas buylded apse ronde, but left Sanctuarium Regis Ini, and walle so holie. Herliun Abbas buylded navis et choro — larger ailes to Ecclesia Regis Ini, et transeptorii, et Sanct Maudelyn, et Capella Mortuarium ad occidentem. [He] bell towre begun, and tourelles ad occidentum. After [came] Henricus Abbas. He too buylded much in monasterio, Robertus Abbas finished muche of Herluin Abbat.

Ditto, January 7 1923

Winfrith speaks:

'I visualize Ina's church as having narrow aisles, but I cannot see anything like a triforium. The Roman influence must have been strong even in Ina's day. . . . Then I see Herlewin's church, real Norman, or Saxon built under Norman influence.'

Data known: parts of very massive round piers have been discovered. They belong to the first Norman period. Many choice, finely-chiselled fragments of sculpture in blue stone, from pier caps or arcades to doorways, windows or recesses, suggesting Burgundian influence, have been found underground about the position of the apse of Herlewin's Church. These are probably later than Herlewin, and are most likely of Robert's date.

21

Jerusalem

And did those feet in ancient time
Walk upon England's mountains green
And was the Holy Lamb of God
On England's pleasant pastures seen

And did the Countenance Divine
Shine forth upon these clouded hills
And was Jerusalem builded here
Among these dark Satanic mills?

Bring me my bow of burning gold
Bring me my arrows of desire
Bring me my Spear! O clouds unfold!
Bring me my Chariot of Fire!

I will not cease from mental fight
Nor shall my sword sleep in my hand
Till we have built Jerusalem
In England's green and pleasant land.

WILLIAM BLAKE

Further Reading

Ashe, G., *Avalonian Quest* (Methuen, 1971).
_____, *Camelot and the Vision of Albion* (Heinemann, 1971).
_____, *The Glastonbury Tor Maze* (At the Foot of the Tree, 1979).
_____, *King Arthur's Avalon* (Collins, 1957).
Bond, F. B., *The Company of Avalon* (Blackwell, 1924).
_____, *The Gate of Remembrance* (The Aquarian Press, 1978).
_____, *The Gospel of Philip the Deacon* (Macoy, 1932).
_____, *The Secret of Immortality* (Marshall Jones, 1934).
Bradley, M. Z., *The Mists of Avalon* (Michael Joseph, 1987).
Caine, M. *The Glastonbury Zodiac* (Grael Communications, 1978).
Campbell, A. Le Strange, *The Glories of Glastonbury* (Sheed & Ward, 1926).
Capt, E. R., *The Traditions of Glastonbury* (Artisan Sales, 1983).
Carley, J. P., *Glastonbury Abbey: The Holy House at the Head of the Moors Adventurous* (Boydell & Brewer, 1989).
Chant, A. G., *The Legend of Glastonbury* (The Epworth Press, 1948).
Coon, R., *Voyage to Avalon: An Immortalist's Introduction to the Magick of Glastonbury* (Griffin Gold Publications, 1986).
Crump, B., *The Round Table of the Gods* (privately printed, 1979).
Ditmas, E. M. R., *Glastonbury Tor: Fact and Legend* (Toucan Press, 1981).
Dobson, C. C., *Did Our Lord Visit Britain?* (The Avalon Press, 1936).
Fortune, D., *Avalon of the Heart* (The Aquarian Press, 1971).
Gasquet, F. A., *The Last Abbot of Glastonbury* (Sheed and Ward, 1895).
Gennaro, G., *The Phenomenon of Avalon* (Cronos Publications, 1979).
Gibbs, R., *The Legendary XII Hides of Glastonbury* (Llanerch Enterprises, 1988).
Greed, J. A., *Glastonbury Tales* (St Trillo Publications, 1975).
Hovey, C. H., *The Somerset Sanctuary* (Merlin Books, 1985).
Kenawell, W. W., *The Quest at Glastonbury: A Biographical Study of Frederick Bligh Bond* (Helix Press, 1965).
Lewis, L. S., *Glastonbury: Her Saints* (RILKO, 1985).
_____, *St Joseph of Arimathea at Glastonbury* (James Clarke, 1955).
Maltwood, K. E., *The Enchantments of Britain* (Victoria Printing & Publishing Co., 1944).
_____, *Glastonbury's Temple of the Stars* (James Clarke, 1935).
Mann, N., *The Cauldron and the Grail* (Annenterprise, 1985).
Mathias, M., *Glastonbury* (David & Charles, 1979).
Matthews, C., *Arthur and the Sovereignty of Britain* (Arkana, 1990).
_____, *Mabon and the Mysteries of Britain* (Arkana, 1988).

Matthews, J., *A Celtic Reader* (The Aquarian Press, 1991).

____, *An Arthurian Reader* (The Aquarian Press, 1989).

____, *At the Table of the Grail* (Arkana, 1983).

____, *Elements of the Arthurian Tradition* (Element Books, 1989).

____, *Elements of the Grail Tradition* (Element Books, 1990).

____, *Gawain, Knight of the Goddess* (The Aquarian Press, 1990).

____, *The Household of the Grail* (The Aquarian Press, 1990).

Matthews, J. & C., *The Arthurian Tarot* (The Aquarian Press, 1990).

____, *Hallowquest* (the Aquarian Press, 1990).

____, *The Western Way* (Arkana, 1985–7).

Moon, A., *The First Ground of God: A History of Glastonbury Abbey Estates* (Gothic Image, 1978).

Powys, J. C., *A Glastonbury Romance* (Macdonald, 1978).

Rahtz, P., *Beckery Chapel, Glastonbury, 1967–8* (Glastonbury Antiquarian Society, 1974).

____, 'Excavations on Glastonbury Tor, Somerset 1964–6', *Archaeological Journal*, vol. 127 (1970), 1–81.

____, 'Excavations at Chalice Well, Glastonbury', *Proceedings of the Somerset Archaeological Journal*, vol. 108 (1964), 143–63.

Reiser, O.L., *This Holyest Earthe* (Perennial Books, 1974).

Roberts, A., *Glastonbury: Ancient Avalon, New Jerusalem* (Rider, 1978).

Robinson, J. A., *Two Glastonbury Legends* (Cambridge University Press, 1926).

Target, G., *Holy Ground: A Guide to the Holy Places of Great Britain* (Bishopsgate Press, 1986).

Traherne, R. F., *The Glastonbury Legends* (The Cresset Press, 1967).

Vickery, A. R., *Holy Thorn of Glastonbury* (Toucan Press, 1979).

Williams, M. (ed.), *Glastonbury: A Study in Patterns* (RILKO, 1968).

Williamson, H. R., *The Flowering Hawthorn* (Peter Davies, 1962).

Of further interest . . .

AN ARTHURIAN READER

Selections from Arthurian Legend, Scholarship and Story

Selected and Edited by John Matthews

The Arthurian mythos is intricate and daunting — with current bibliographies listing over 12,000 titles. In this collection some unchallenged, long-neglected theories have been dusted off for examination and discussion by new generations of Arthurian scholars. From a medieval translation of a thirteenth-century text to essays by twentieth-century writers, *The Arthurian Reader* presents a cross-section of speculation both scholarly and esoteric, some well-supported by cross references, others containing some astonishing undocumented flights of fancy. All is part of the total spectrum of the mythos.

John Matthews' selection captures the essence of what has become known as the Matter of Britain and includes archetypal tales such as 'Sir Gawain and the Green Knight', 'Merlin and Grisandole', 'Arthur's Vision of the Grail', and 'Morte Arthure', an alliterative poem which is remarkably similar to Malory's 'Morte d'Arthur' yet pre-dates it by over a hundred years. Interspersed within such tales are definitive essays on Arthurian subjects by authors as renowned as A.E. Waite, Jessie Weston, Arthur Machen and Sir Thomas Malory.

Through this carefully-selected collection of writings, complemented with some stunning drawings and etchings from the original texts which are as much a treat as the rare prose, the reader will be drawn into the Arthurian world by a variety of approaches which lead to the Inner History of the islands.

A CELTIC READER

Selections from Celtic Legend, Scholarship and Story

Compiled and Edited by John Matthews

This scintillating, colourful anthology of Celtic myth, history and story is designed to give the reader an impression of the entire rich heritage of a remarkable culture. Ranging from accounts of mysterious Druids to sparkling stories and gravely beautiful poems, this collection represents every aspect of the Celtic world and brings it alive in all its drama.

This collection of lore, life and literature sets forth the Celtic world, from the Druidic priesthood and rites to the bardic heritage, from the distant origins of the Celtic peoples to the colour and drama of their culture. Tales of adventure, magic, mystery and wonder from pre-Christian Ireland and Arthurian Britain interweave with ancient fables, Taliesin's poetry, excerpts from *The Mabinogion*, historical investigations into the ancient past and modern adaptations of ancient themes. Combining the talents of authors like Iolo Morgannwg, Thomas Samuel Jones, Ross Nichols and 'A. E.', the result is a glowing tapestry of Celtic life.

Through this carefully-selected anthology, the reader is taken back to the ages of myth and legend and drawn into the remarkable and mysterious Celtic culture which gave rise to unforgettable art, intricate jewel-like myth and stories of gods, heroes and monsters. Fine drawings and engravings from a variety of artists are interspersed throughout, illustrating every aspect of the Celtic heritage.